Secularism, Women & The State:

The Mediterranean World in the 21st Century

Edited by Barry A. Kosmin and Ariela Keysar

ISSSC

**Institute for the Study of Secularism
in Society and Culture**

Barry A. Kosmin and Ariela Keysar
SECULARISM, WOMEN & THE STATE:
THE MEDITERRANEAN WORLD IN THE 21ST CENTURY

Copyright © 2009 Barry A. Kosmin and Ariela Keysar

This book may be downloaded free of charge at
www.trincoll.edu/secularisminstitute

ISBN: 978-0-692-00328-2

Published by

ISSSC

Institute for the Study of Secularism in Society and Culture
Trinity College, Hartford, CT

Cover and book design by Jo Lynn Alcorn

TABLE OF CONTENTS

II: WOMEN & SOCIETY

TABLE OF FIGURES

ACKNOWLEDGMENTS

The editors and contributing authors would like to thank the following individuals for their help and advice in reviewing and producing this volume and for their efforts in making the Rome Conference such a success.

John Alcorn
Peter Coy
Kay Davidson
Jay Demareth
Hugo Estrella
Emilio Gentile
Sara Howe
Carmela LaRosa
Kara Ledger
Chris Nadon
Juhem Navarro-Rivera
Frank Pasquale
Livio Pestilli
Rafael Gallego Sevilla
Mark Silk
Jesse Tisch
Suora Vicenza

Special thanks to the Posen Foundation for its continuing support.

Secularism, Women & the State:
The Mediterranean World in the 21st Century

Barry A. Kosmin & Ariela Keysar

T his volume grew out of a *salon* or *conversazione* on the theme of "The Prospects for the Secular State in the Mediterranean World in the 21st Century" hosted by ISSSC—the Institute for the Study of Secularism in Society and Culture. The event took place during June 2007 at Trinity College's campus located on the historic and beautiful Aventine Hill in Rome, Italy. The purpose of this gathering was to assemble a diverse group of people from different Mediterranean nations, academic disciplines and professions for a relaxed, multi-cultural exchange of information and opinion on one of the key political and intellectual questions of the moment, one which is on the agenda today in one way or another in every country in the Mediterranean region. How should the state and government respond to diversity of beliefs and worldviews in today's society?

Given the range of nationalities and world views—Muslim, Catholic, Orthodox Christian, Jewish, secular—represented among the participants, we did not expect a consensus to emerge. We had no wish to craft a conference declaration or statement but instead we succeeded in having some respectful and interesting discussions that enhanced our mutual knowledge and understanding. The intellectual focus of ISSSC is on studying the prevalence and impact of secular ideas, values and traditions in the contemporary world. Our 2006 international research conference in Hartford, Connecticut, which had the title "Who's secular in the world today?" focused on sociological research and cultural issues. Those proceedings were published in the volume *Secularism & Secularity: Contemporary International Perspectives*. In 2007 in Rome, the agenda was more on politics and the role of the state—and so on political science and government—combined with a clearer geographical focus. What was particularly unique about the conference was the large proportion of women scholars. One of the outcomes of our discussions was a consensus that gender relations and the status of women were key variables for understanding the prospects for secularism and secularity in all the Mediterranean countries; hence the title of this volume, *Secularism, Women & the State*.

The relationship and place of secularism and religion in government and public life have been major political issues since the time of the French Revolution and the Italian *Risorgimento*. This constitutional debate remains at the heart of many contemporary national disputes about democracy, pluralism, the role of women in society and educational policies. During the 20th century, the tensions and divisions surrounding the "church/mosque-state" question led to brutal civil wars in Spain, Greece, Lebanon and Algeria. In European states where this issue was thought to have been settled, the question has returned as a result of the migration of Muslim populations from the south to the north of the Mediterranean basin.

To what extent can we speak in the early 21st century of a "Mediterranean World"? Obviously it is not as tightly bound politically, culturally or economically as it was during the height of the Roman Empire, but even then there was a division between a Latin-speaking West and a Greek-speaking East. Yet Imperial Rome created a very similar interconnected world to our own, especially in terms of conflicts and fast moving international events around *Mare Nostrum* (our sea). We are not the first generation of people, as ancient historians such as Tacitus, Pliny or Josephus would tell us, to have to deal with complex and interlocking political problems affecting the interplay of military, economic, migratory and cultural forces. Moreover, well-educated citizens of the Roman Empire could probably follow much of the discussion and arguments that are presented here about constitutional arrangements, the problem of sovereignty, the role of the state in public and economic affairs, the function of the law, the role and status of women in society, republican versus monarchical or theocratic political systems, and the debates among faith and reason and religion and skepticism.

Today, the idea of an integrated Mediterranean region is a focus of French foreign policy and in 2008 President Sarkozy launched a Union of the Mediterranean. This concept has intellectual roots and reflects the influence of the great French historian of the *Annales* school, Fernand Braudel (1902-85).[1] Within the context of human history Braudel emphasized two themes —Technology and Exchange. His thesis was that it is imbalance that creates exchange and therefore leads to progress. This is very much the underlying theme of this volume.

The analyses in the chapters of this volume, given the social science background of the authors, tend to lay stress on transformations over recent decades. Certainly the European section of the Mediterranean world has seen remarkable and unpredicted changes as open and free societies have flourished alongside quite unexpected transformation of the economy. As recently as the 1970s, Franco's Spain and the Colonels' Greece were not conducive to democratic and especially secularist ideas. The speed of economic improvement in these countries since the downfall of the last of the fascist regimes has been impressive as has the accompanying social change. In Italy, too, there has been a political and social revolution with the surprising collapse of both the Christian Democrat Party and the national birth rate.

The regional migration of people northwards from poor to rich countries is much discussed now in political and economic circles. However, one often neglected and overlooked historical trend with important political consequences is that as the countries to the north of the Mediterranean have become more pluralistic or multicultural, those to the south and east have gone in the opposite direction and become culturally more homogeneous. Since the end of World War I, beginning in the 1920s, the Muslim majority countries have lost or expelled their minorities—their native Christians, their ancient Jewish communities, as well as their French, Italian, Greek and Armenian populations. Istanbul, Alexandria, Algiers, Tangiers, even Beirut are not the polyglot, cosmopolitan cities they once were. One consequence is that there is less pressure on these southern Mediterranean states to organize society and the polity in order to cope with diversity while on the contrary that need has increased in the European states. This bifurcation or polarization of the historical experience of the Mediterranean world during the late 20th century underlies much of the discussion here.

Yet the picture is complicated by the historical legacies of European colonial and Ottoman imperial rule. Greek Christians were ruled by Muslims but Turks never had European rule whereas Israel and Egypt had both sets of rulers. Political secularism has much deeper roots in Turkey than in Spain or Greece. In Europe, the traditional process of separating religion from politics has sought to limit the powers of a dominant religion or religious authority in the public, personal and political life of Europeans. Two models emerged. The first, which predominated in mainly Catholic countries (France, Spain, and Italy), is based on a process of formally limiting religious authority through a series of laws, decrees and international treaties. A second model evolved in countries where the decision-making center of the predominant religion was closer to home and where there was not an overall religious authority for all members of a given faith, such as in predominantly Orthodox countries (Greece) and Israel. This involved a gradual co-option of the religious institutions into the purview of the state. This was possible in many of these countries because of the strong identification that the

Orthodox and Jewish religions have with a particular nation.

Today, the fast pace of modernization including urbanization is affecting every Mediterranean country. Nevertheless, one cannot enter this arena without confronting the current debate about the relationship of Islam to secularism and democracy. The Arabic word for 'secular' ('*almaniyya*') is new in Arab political literature. It is derived from the word for "world" ('*alam*') and not from the word for "science" ('*ilm*') so it refers to the world we live in. Many of the chapters suggest that the separation of religion from the state in the Sunni school, where religion is incorporated entirely into the state, has become nearly impossible, as a result of the merger of religion with politics and politics with religion, and the disappearance of the boundaries between the two.

At stake in Europe's search for a secular balance with Islam are three pivotal issues: 1) freedom of expression as practiced in a pluralist secular democracy, which is absent in most predominantly Muslim countries; 2) the status of women in Islam, and, equally important, the West's perception of the way women are treated in Islam; and 3) the prevailing European views regarding sexual rights, identity and orientation and those expressed by spokespersons of Muslim communities in Europe.

The focal point for concern about women in Islam centers on the veil, as our authors on France and Turkey demonstrate. Is the veil simply an outward expression of one's faith or a beacon for the oppression of women? Both points of view have a basis of truth. The strict dress code enforced by the Iranian morality police and the *burqa* demanded by the Taliban are very real examples of oppression and hardly an example of Muslim women choosing freely to express their faith. However, for many European Muslims choosing to wear the veil is a matter of personal freedom and an important outward symbol of their faith and, in some case, ethnic provenance. The question of the veil has been discussed most decisively in France, where the French National Assembly overwhelmingly voted to ban the wearing of the veil in the public sphere (meaning that employees of the state or wards of the state, such as students in public schools, may not wear the veil during work or school). It should be noted that banning the veil from the public sphere is not a French invention; such bans have existed for decades in Turkey and Tunisia, where generally they are seen as significant advances in women's rights and secularism.

The chapters in Part 1, Secularism & the State, feature the experiences of nine Mediterranean countries with an assortment of constitutional arrangements and models such as strict separation of church and state, e.g., France and Turkey; religious concordats, e.g., Spain and Italy; confessionalism, e.g., Lebanon; and various forms of state religious establishment, e.g., Greece, Israel, Algeria and

Egypt. This focus on political secularism is augmented by data on the power of public opinion and cultural norms expressed through "national narratives," historical references and traditions. This approach leads to the chapters in Part 2, Women & Society, which involves looking at societal, demographic, economic and legal changes in various states. The insights and trends these chapters reveal are of crucial importance for understanding the future prospects of the region.

One conclusion that emerges from the majority of these contributions is a realization that though perhaps there can be secularism without democracy there can be no democracy without some commitment by the state to political secularism as well as freedom of conscience and the need for the modern state to respect it. In a secular democracy, the state does not promote values that came from one religious tradition in particular. The state also begins to protect individual rights to dissent not only from particular religious doctrines, but also from the norms and values that were imposed based on that doctrine. The general consensus is that women are the primary beneficiaries of such changes.

We believe the ideas and opinions expressed in this unique volume are worthy of a wide readership, especially at this time when international understanding is so vital and other parts of the world are experiencing similar challenges. Detailed information on many of the issues covered here has not been previously available in English. So we appreciate particularly the efforts of most of the authors for whom English is their second or third language, to help educate and inform English-speaking readers about their particular country and its people.

ENDNOTES

1. Particularly his famous three volume work published in 1949, *La Méditerranée et le Monde Méditerranéen a l'époque de Philippe II* (*The Mediterranean and the Mediter-ranean World in the Age of Philip II*).

Secularism & The State

1. Italy:
The Contemporary Condition of Italian *Laicità*

Giulio Ercolessi

Religion matters in Italian public life today. Yet some of the problems arising from Italy's new religious diversity—a result of a) recent immigration waves and b) secularization—are significant. To understand their scope, a short excursion into the historical roots of the present situation is probably necessary. The issue of state-church relations played a crucial role in the formation of the Italian state in the 19th century. It was important, for instance, in the formation of Italy's national liberal heritage. After the destruction of the French-established Napoleonic regional republics,[1] the divide between the Catholic Church and liberal-minded milieus widened. The heritage of the Enlightenment combined with the Romantic movement's mainstream assessment of Italy's religious history.[2] As a result, that history was recast in a negative light: the increasingly liberal public saw the Counter-Reformation as one of the main causes of the civic and political backwardness of Italian society after the end of the Renaissance in the 16th century.

If it had a starting point, the Italian *Risorgimento* (i.e., the process of unification and political and civil modernization of Italy) likely began in February 1848 with the recognition of equal civil and political rights of Jews and Waldensians (Protestants). The event that concluded the process was the taking of Rome in September 1870, which put an end to the temporal power of the Papal State.

To varying degrees, all liberals, both moderate[3] and more radical,[4] favored a strict separation of state and religion as a defining condition of Italy's political and economic modernization.

Italian *Laicità* and French *Laïcité*

In Italy—unlike France—these "secularist" views were more centered on the principle of individual freedom than on the ideological supremacy of the state and its sovereignty. The state, in other words, was not seen as competing with the church for cultural ascendancy. In fact, many of the political leaders of the Italian *Risorgimento* were, in their private lives, believers, often Catholics. Many others were, of course, ideological foes of Catholicism,[5] and the contribution of Jews and Protestants to the liberal cause was overwhelmingly disproportionate to their tiny demographic weight.

French *laïcité*—a basic and established principle of French political culture and constitutional law—is marked by its emphasis on national sovereignty above any sort of personal affiliation (whether it be religious, cultural, or political). France's Jacobin revolutionary tradition also recognizes the prominent cultural role of the state. To an extent, it includes not just separation, but also the predominance of the state even in some religious affairs:[6] for example, French clergy were not allowed to preach in the Breton language, and even today celebrating a religious marriage prior to the civil ceremony is forbidden under the French penal code.

Italian *laicismo*—in its more demanding interpretation[7]—is marked by Italy's *Risorgimento* and liberal tradition. Given its historical emphasis on protection of religious freedom,[8] neutrality is required of institutions, not necessarily of individuals; whereas in France, individuals themselves are expected to mute their personal beliefs as they enter the "sacred" public space, even as private citizens. The neutrality of public institutions has always been seen by Italian *laicisti* as crucial to safeguarding religious freedom from (basically Catholic) claims for religious and cultural uniformity; French *laïcité* is often seen (also by French courts) as a limit to the exercise of religious freedom.[9]

Obviously, this does not mean that the Italian idea of *laicità* and French *laïcité* have little in common. Italian liberals, like their French counterparts, sometimes had to be harsh in their fight against clericalism, especially in the 19th century. And both political traditions were instrumental in the emancipation of religious minorities and in the enhancement of individual freedom. To an extent, both had substantial links to the cultural heritage of the Enlightenment, and both endorsed scientific knowledge as a way to counterbalance Catholic influence. It should not be forgotten that Italian liberals of the 19th century were as indebted to the French as to the British (and later to the American) political philosophy; the latter had greater experience in dealing with different religious faiths and denominations. These differences between *laicità* and *laïcité* should not be overestimated, and yet they imply slightly different interpretations of what religious neutrality of public institutions should mean, even though these differences are often ignored or underestimated in current political and cultural debates.

Defining *Laicità* and *Laicismo*

Among nations, different political traditions in the field of state-church relations have shaped their political vocabularies. In Italy, France, and Spain—three countries with a common Catholic (and a common secularist) tradition, and a common Romance linguistic heritage—there are slightly different meanings for apparently the same word. However, in a globalized world, and especially in a part of the world with similar democratic traditions and institutions and problems, a common vocabulary is needed to avoid possible misunderstandings.

I propose to define *laicità*, *laïcité*, *laicidad* as "religious neutrality of public institutions," even though this is not the interpretation of those who have a negative or hostile attitude towards religious beliefs. *Laicità* is necessary to assure equal religious freedom and equal social dignity to all citizens: believers and non-believers, believers in the religion of their ancestors and believers in other faiths—or in no faith. *Laicismo* (same spelling in Italian and Spanish) or *laïcisme* should be interpreted here as the political position of those who want public institutions to be, remain, or become religiously neutral. In Italian contemporary history, Waldensians, Jews, and dissident Catholics usually were among the staunchest advocates of *Laicismo*. Hopefully, they will be joined soon by some liberal-minded Muslims.

There is no precise English (nor indeed German) translation for *laicità*, *laïcité*, *laicidad*, nor for *laicismo* and *laïcisme*. Even though the fight for religious freedom and separation of church and state was as significant to the history of English-speaking Western countries as it was to Southern Europeans, *laicità*, *laïcité*, *laicidad*, *laicismo*, and *laïcisme* are words that are typical of the national histories of countries where that fight was engaged against the power of the Catholic Church. Yet, they have assumed a much broader meaning over the years. So much so that Catholics themselves, even the most traditionalist ones, have come to describe their political position not as clerical, but as supporting an "upright" brand of *laicità*. In this paper I will favor the above-mentioned words in their original versions.

An Overview of Historical Developments in Italy

After Rome was taken by the newborn Italian state in 1870 and established as the new capital, a liberal law was passed[10] to grant the inviolability, the independence, and the diplomatic status of the Holy See and its officials. However, this law was never accepted by the Pope, who declared himself a "prisoner" in the Vatican and ordered committed Catholics to abstain from participation in Italian political life (*Non expedit* policy).

Although Catholicism was considered the "official religion of the state" by the 1848 Piedmont constitution,[11] a regime of separation and equality before the law was enforced.[12] The increase in the number of citizens entitled to take part in general elections led to a much looser application of the *non expedit* policy by the Vatican. It led, as well, to local electoral agreements between the Catholics and politicians sympathetic to the Catholic agenda, especially in the areas of religious schools, religious teaching in public primary schools, and the field of family law.[13] A Catholic party (*Partito Popolare*) took part in the general elections of 1919, the first to be held with universal male suffrage.

Following the revolutionary unrest of 1920, two members of *Partito Popolare* became members of the first Mussolini cabinet in 1922 but after the assassination of social-democrat leader Giacomo Matteotti in 1924 and the establishment of the dictatorship in January 1925, the party leader Luigi Sturzo became a standard-bearer for the antifascist opposition.

The Mussolini government[14] reversed decades of liberal policy in state-church relations. It sought the support of the Catholic Church; it reintroduced religious symbols in public schools and offices; and in February 1929, it signed a territorial treaty, a concordat and a financial settlement[15] with the Holy See. This concordat had huge consequences: it established the State of the Vatican City on a small part of the territory of the city of Rome; it gave the Catholic Church an important role, especially in public schools and in family law;[16] and it provided huge public funds for its activities. In exchange, the Vatican accepted the disbandment of the *Partito Popolare* and forced Sturzo into exile. Despite some controversies on the status of Catholic youth organizations in the following years, and protests against the discriminations introduced in 1938 against Catholics converted from Judaism,[17] the Catholic Church became a critical pillar of the fascist regime.

At the end of World War II, the *Partito Popolare* was re-established as *Democrazia Cristiana*. It became the largest party after the 1946 election of the Constituent Assembly. The Christian Democrats and the Communists jointly voted for Article 7 of the new republican Constitution. The text of Article 7 states that "The state and the Catholic church are, each within its own order, independent and sovereign. Their relations are regulated by *Patti lateranensi (Lateran Treaty)*. Amendments to these pacts which are accepted by both parties do not require the procedure of constitutional amendment." It was unclear whether or not this wording implied that *Patti lateranensi* were thus given constitutional standing. At first, Article 7 was commonly interpreted as stating the constitutionalization of *Patti lateranensi*, thus implying a number of exceptions to many basic constitutional principles.

A strong opposition was led by the socialist parties, together with the small center-left liberal parties (*Partito Repubblicano* and *Partito d'Azione*) and some of the deputies of the small and more moderate *Partito Liberale*,[18] but they were defeated.

The secularization of the Italian society that followed the restoration of democracy and the "economic miracle" of the 1950s and 1960s had important consequences for legislation. Contraception propaganda, previously forbidden under fascist law, became permissible in 1970.[19] Discrimination against smaller evangelical denominations, which was still carried out (albeit illegally) by local police authorities, was finally outlawed. Divorce and abortion laws were passed and confirmed in two general referenda held in 1974 and 1981, which resulted in two historical defeats of the Catholic Church (which had indirectly organized and strongly supported both referenda). Family law was reformed in 1975 to allow equality for married men and women (after years of Catholic resistance). Witnesses in courts were no longer forced to take an oath that included a reference to God.[20] Courts established some minimal protection for unmarried couples and other kinds of de facto families.

In the 1970s, the Constitutional Court came to the conclusion that the Constitution as a whole had established a general rule of *laicità* as a "supreme principle"—meaning that it could not even be modified by an amendment to the Constitution, because, like the modification of other basic "supreme principles" (democracy, the republican character of the state, human rights), the result would be a substitution, rather than a modification, of the Constitution itself.

In 1984, a new concordat was signed between the Catholic Church and the government of Socialist Prime Minister Bettino Craxi. This abolished the embarrassing references to the monarchy and the fascist regime still included in the 1929 concordat; it regulated only the basic principles of state-church relations, leaving much of the controversial (or financially relevant) issues for successive, more detailed agreements.

Religious Privileges

Today, the state provides public schools with church-appointed teachers of Catholic religion, and pays the teachers' salaries (students or parents have to declare at the beginning of the school year whether they want to attend religion courses or not). Catholic religious symbols continue to be (controversially) displayed in schools, courts, and public offices. Catholic schools have in recent years been granted public funds for the first time (in open violation of a specific prohibition stated in Article 33 of the Constitution: "Private bodies and individuals have the right to establish schools and educational institutes without financial burden to the state"). In some cases, Catholic ecclesiastical tribunals can still legally nullify religiously celebrated marriages.[21]

A large number of Catholic television and radio programs are broadcast daily, or weekly, by all the channels of the Italian state television and radio service (*Rai*), and also by the private television networks—at no cost to the church. Protestants and Jews have just a fortnightly TV program each, broadcast at about 2:00 a.m., and Protestants have a Sunday radio service at 7:30 a.m. There is no "secularist" TV program of any kind, and the non-theistic point of view on controversial ethical issues has been steadily reduced. Instead, debates between Catholic and Muslim clergies are common.

State Funding of Religion

More than five billion euros are probably allocated[22] each year to the Catholic Church and its organizations by the state and regional and local administrations. That amount of money is far greater than the sum that was formally agreed upon in the 1984 concordat, which stated that the public financial support to the Catholic Church, including priests' salaries, would be decided by taxpayers themselves through their personal choices. According to the concordat provision, every taxpayer can indicate whether 0.8% of the entire national revenue collected through the personal general income tax known as *Irpef (imposta sul reddito delle persone fisiche)* should go to the Catholic Church or to the state, or to the smaller denominations that have stipulated a similar agreement with the state. About 40% of taxpayers actually make a choice; typically, about 80% of them favor the Catholic Church. Unlike churches, the state never campaigns in favor of the Treasury, nor does it explain in advance what kind of social or charitable projects would benefit from such a choice. Most taxpayers think that, if no choice is made, the money does not go to any church. As a consequence, only 10% of taxpayers make an explicit choice for the state. But almost everybody in Italy ignores the fact that the total amount of the 0.8% of the national revenue of the *Irpef* tax is not allocated to churches on the basis of the number of preferences they receive, but rather on the basis of the percentage of the choices that were actually expressed. Therefore, if 80% of the 40% of taxpayers who expressed their choice choose for the Catholic Church, it will receive 80% of the total even though it had actually been chosen by only 32% of taxpayers.

Moreover, this mechanism is only a minor part of the total amount of taxpayers' money that is given annually to the Catholic Church by the state, the regions, the local administrations, and other public or publicly owned bodies for an astonishingly diverse number of reasons. As already mentioned, only since the mid-1980s have smaller scale agreements been signed with religious minorities, as provided for by the Constitution. Although these agreements have been given the name of *intese* (literally: "understandings") by Article 8 of the Constitution, in order to stress that their rank is lower than the concordat, they are in fact formal agreements between the government and a religious minority that have to be ratified by Parliament with a formal law. Unlike the concordat, they were never recognized as having the power of subverting constitutional principles. So far, *intese* have been stipulated and ratified with some Protestant and evangelical denominations and with the Jews; a financial arrangement identical to that provided with the 1984 concordat was offered to all of them, but some rejected a percentage of the total *Irpef* revenue higher than the actual number of preferences they get. Baptists, in the name of separation of church and state, volunteered to waive this entitlement, but no other minority did the same. Two *intese*, with Buddhists and Jehovah's Witnesses, already signed by the center-left governments of the years 1996-2001, were not ratified by the subsequent Berlusconi parliamentary majority. They were reintroduced as government bills in 2006, but failed to be passed before the early dissolution of Parliament in February 2008. Following the controversies on the status of Muslims after 9/11, a general law on religious freedom has not yet been approved. An *intesa* with them has not even been proposed, due to the absence of any unitary body representing Muslims living in Italy (most of them, by the way, still foreign citizens—see below).

Culture Wars

In 2005, a proposal to amend a very restrictive law approved by the former Berlusconi parliamentary majority on stem cell research and artificial insemination was defeated, despite very favorable polls. Since the participation of 50% of the electors is required for the validity of a referendum, the Catholic Church very strongly urged Catholics (and Catholic politicians) to abstain rather than vote against the proposal, thus "enlisting" 40% of usual referenda non-voters in the ranks of those opposed to the modification of the law.

This open intervention by the Catholic hierarchy in Italian politics was the most determined, forceful, and direct in decades, its previous interventions having always been performed through formally independent Catholic citizens' political or social organizations. This new attitude was a consequence of the dissolution of the Christian Democrat Party following the anti-corruption investigations, rallies, and trials of the early 1990s and the reshaping of the Italian political system. This is now composed of two coalitions, each competing to win the

Catholic vote (a vote that is largely overestimated by politicians as a consequence of its incorrect but recurrent identification with centrist or undecided electors). However, the result of the stem cell research referendum seems to have been much more the consequence of a growing anti-scientific and anti-technological attitude, rather than a reversal or a slowing down of the secularization process. A very comprehensive study of the actual behavior of Italians revealed that Italian society is still becoming more, not less, secular. However, the Catholic hierarchy was rather successful at portraying that result as evidence of a new power balance in the society: possibly a first step in the direction of a reform of the abortion law.

An attempt to make consensual divorce easier and less expensive was defeated in Parliament in 2006. With the exception of a few very minor regional laws, no general statute for the protection of *de facto* families (unmarried couples) exists. Nor are gay families legally recognized. Even succession laws limit quite severely the testator's freedom to dispose of his/her estate at the expense of the legal family. A very moderate government bill on the legal recognition of gay couples, which was the result of an exhaustive negotiation between the two competent ministers,[23] was abandoned, due to controversies inside the "center-left" parliamentary majority that supported the Prodi government. Together with Ireland and Austria, Italy is at present the only remaining Western European country that does not recognize gay couples or accord them any rights.

Euthanasia is strictly forbidden, despite the fact that the public has long supported it (according to opinion polls), and the courts are largely lenient towards the issue. Living wills, too, are not yet recognized, at least in principle, and the Catholic Church strongly opposes any recognition, which, they claim, could "open the gate" to undeclared euthanasia.

In recent years, many municipalities, especially in Central and Northwestern Italy, have provided more decent, dignified premises for civil marriage ceremonies and funerals. Others have stubbornly refused to do so: civil marriages often still take place in municipal registry offices. In some Northeastern municipalities in the Veneto region and in much of the South, civil funerals have to take place in the open air—even in winter and with bad weather. The number of religious and civilian marriages and funerals appears to depend largely on practical arrangements made or omitted by municipalities.

The New Multi-religious Society

The entire issue of the state-church relations debate has been profoundly transformed in recent years due to the increasingly diverse religious composition of the Italian society, itself a consequence of immigration from non-Catholic countries. Internal religious pluralism has also been growing in the last fifteen years, due to active proselytism by "popular" Evangelicals, especially Pentecostals, and Jehovah's Witnesses, not to mention minor groups. Although both movements are nowadays far more numerous than the historical Protestant churches, with membership in both groups probably about 350,000, this phenomenon does not appear to pose any major political problem so far, and these movements do not appear to have any claim of a political nature nor a relevant presence in any kind of public debate.

However, immigration is a recent phenomenon because Italy had been, for a century, a land of emigration (both internally and to other countries). Like other countries in the same situation (e.g., Ireland and Portugal), Italians considered themselves "naturally" non-racist. The memory of the fascist racist laws against the Jews had been rapidly erased, and responsibility was exclusively attributed to the dictator. Throughout the years of the civil rights struggles in the U.S., and during the years of apartheid in South Africa, the Italian media in particular often showed a sense of superiority and considered their Catholic and/or humanistic heritage a sort of insurance against every possible racist virus within their own ranks. The illusion faded once Italian society became more diverse.

A general census is carried out in Italy every ten years; the latest one occurred in 2001. According to the Istituto Geografico De Agostini, there were about 3,000,000 foreign citizens legally residing in Italy in 2007.[24] Together with an estimated 800,000 illegal immigrants, that amounts to about 6% of the population. This is one of the lowest percentages in Western Europe but it was about twice the number in 2001, and then newcomers have a much higher birth rate than the native population. (Italy has one of the lowest birthrates in the world.)

Muslims are—arbitrarily, for the reasons given below—often estimated to number around one million, with only 3% of them Italian citizens. Italian converts are estimated to be fewer than 10,000, mostly women who converted in order to marry a Muslim man. Moreover, a considerable percentage of immigrants from traditionally Muslim areas are from Albania and Bosnia, two Balkan countries that were largely secularized until a few years ago. The other main region of origin of immigrants from traditionally Muslim territories in Italy is the Maghreb, especially Morocco.

So far, obtaining Italian citizenship has been extremely difficult for immigrants, except through marriage (hence, the obvious temptation of sham marriages). A bill was introduced by the center-left Prodi government elected in spring 2006; it was aimed at tackling for the first time the subject of individual integration, on the basis of a voluntary acceptance of basic civic and constitutional principles. It was not clear, however, whether dual citizenship would have been indiscriminately allowed. The bill, however, failed to be passed before the early dissolution of Parliament in February 2008. In Italy, the new situation has led to a broad but superficial consensus among politicians for the need "to get beyond" the traditional conception of *laicità* in public institutions and to give the Catholic Church and other denominations a more emphatic "public role" (whatever that might mean). There is nothing really new in this idea. Italian liberal supporters of separation and "secularism" have been hearing this argument for decades: since 1929, fascists, Christian Democrats, and Communists have all claimed that our idea of *laicità* was a thing of the past.

"Religious Dialogue" as a Substitute for an Italian Integration Strategy

Although there is not much reason for hope, the Italian social situation at the moment seems less compromised than in France, Netherlands, and Great Britain, paradoxically, thanks in part to the past inertia and inefficiency of Italian politics and government. This inertia at least partly spared the country some urban development disasters that held sway in previous decades. In Italy, French-style *banlieues* were hardly built to provide housing for the previous internal immigration, so they could not become mass ghettoes for foreign immigrants when upward mobility seemed blocked everywhere. Thus, at least for the moment, Italy enjoys a greater degree of *mixité* (integration) than France, although the main reason for this is the markedly lesser diversity—for the moment—of Italian society in comparison with European countries that experienced decolonization in the postwar period and immigration from poorer countries several decades earlier.

What might bring disaster unless Italy learns from others' experience is the political establishment's inability to understand that only strict separation of church and state can make integration possible without creating rival, conflicting communitarianisms. Socio-economic problems might be worsened by political incompetence.

Dreaming that religions—all religions, despite occasional deviation— always naturally promote peace, tolerance, and human rights, the Italian political establishment seems to be putting its hopes for integration essentially into "inter-religious dialogue." While only a tiny minority of immigrants in Italy from Muslim countries attend mosque, it is precisely to the mosques, and to the dialogue between their representatives and the Catholic clergy, that much of the Italian political establishment seems willing to entrust the task of integration. The other side of this is the considerable part of the political establishment that instead aims to gain votes by racist and xenophobic demagogy, or that promises to stem new waves of migration without any change in the economic gap between the two shores of the Mediterranean and between global North and South.

And it is precisely by means of a body—the "Advisory Council for Italian Islam" of the Ministry of the Interior—created on the bases of religious affiliation and expertise in the sociology of religion, that the Italian state has started to tackle the issue of integration, broadly, and not simply the specific issues related to the needs deriving from mere religious observances (as already is done in the *intesa* with the Jews).

Hence the priority given by the (relatively) better part of the political establishment to reaching an *intesa* with the present Italian Islam, by applying to that religion, too, the possibility of the regulation provided for by Article 8 of the Constitution: an *intesa* that (unlike those reached with the various Protestant denominations) must be reached, they insist, with a "unitary" delegation, not with the smaller and more liberal groups. In the eyes of most of the political establishment, regulations introduced by an *intesa*, and based upon (alleged) religious affiliation, should be the real vehicle for integrating into Italian society immigrants from countries of the Islamic tradition. Better said, this will be the substitute for any policy of integration.

As a matter of principle, concordats and agreements with other denominations have always been seen by the Italian *laicisti* as violations of the principles of religious neutrality, equality before the law, and equal dignity of citizens. However, given the regime of the concordat, the *intese* that have been reached with religious minorities have seemed to many a lesser evil, a way to at least lessen inequalities; so far, the already stipulated *intese* have generally not granted unjustifiable privileges.

However, we do not even know how many immigrants from Muslim countries moved to Italy not only to better their economic lot but also, primarily, to fulfill their aspiration to live in a less authoritarian society. In societies that nominally recognize full freedom of religion and freedom of conscience, making assumptions about religious affiliation on ethnic or racial grounds is intolerable. It is as if an Italian, upon moving to Sweden, could or should be automatically labeled, treated, and considered a Catholic by that country's authorities. Even worse would be if s/he were given Catholic priests as representatives. This is a crime that, although involuntary, is particularly execrable, because it is directed against individuals who are not free to openly express their own apostasy, given that they may reside in areas where Muslim fundamentalists believe that apostasy should be punished by death.

The fact is that a fundamentalist organization related to the "Muslim Brotherhood" (*Ucoii, Unione delle comunità islamiche in Italia*) operates the majority of Italian mosques. It is essentially with them that any "unitary" *intesa* would be signed. Such *intesa*, obviously, would have to include the possibility of granting to the signatories the revenue from the 0.8% *Irpef* tax, as is already the case for the religious minorities that have signed the existing *intese*. Obviously, the signatories would also benefit by the perverse multiplier mechanism previously described. It is also quite predictable that many Italian citizens who are not Muslim but who are generically anti-Western or pro-Third World, would indicate the Muslim religion as beneficiary of the 0.8% *Irpef* tax share as a sympathy measure. The most likely outcome of such an *intesa* with a "unitary" delegation of current Italian Islam would be the definitive foreclosure of any possibility of success by a future progressive or liberal Islam in Italy.

Dangerous Public Policies

If "unitary" *intesa* is reached with current Italian Islam, it would very likely exclude Italian Islam from these possible reformist developments and would assure that a quite fundamentalist brand of Islam, which is currently the large majority of organized Italian Islam, would have all the means necessary to block progressive developments, if only by directly occupying every available public space.

The strategy of a constitutional *intesa* with the "unitary" delegation is a decisive step by Italy towards integration on the communitarian model. In the Netherlands, a traditionally tolerant and liberal society, this model has fostered the birth of completely separate societies, within which have developed the most obscurantist, illiberal, and totalitarian tendencies, on the one hand, and the most xenophobic and racist tendencies, on the other. The communitarian model of integration entails inevitable discrimination against the weakest minorities. Where will we stop in the politics of "recognition"? Who will establish the difference between a religion and a "sect"? It also entails discrimination to the detriment of the already largely secularized majority. Why must those who are not believers subsidize or give hypocritical deference to every sort of religious faith, even if they oppose a faith's political demands or deem religion to be little more than superstition?

Moreover, a strategy of integration based on "inter-religious dialogue" could easily lead to new limitations on individual freedom and to renewed forms of discrimination. The Catholic Church (which is at the moment uncertain on what is the best strategy in dealing with Islam) and other minorities with a traditionalist political agenda could be tempted to try to re-establish old prohibitions and discriminations with the help of the less secularized newcomers and with the excuse of mutual security and religious or multiethnic correctness. The plight of individuals who belong to communities that do not recognize some fundamental human rights (that is the situation of apostates, minors, women, homosexuals) will worsen. The communitarian way to integration dramatically weakens the protection of the rights of these individuals.

Basing every attempt at integration upon inter-religious dialogue (in practice, among representatives of the two largest religions) is the first step towards future political settlements at the expense of the individual freedoms of those who are not represented. It might also lead to sinister developments of a Bosnian or Lebanese flavor. Those politicians who choose to subtract resources from secular public school and transfer them to the non-free school, i.e., to confessional (Catholic) school, will find it hard to deny the same treatment to Islamic religious schools—schools that the most fundamentalist families will not delay in demanding in order to block the integration of their children into the values of secular democracy.

Unfortunately, beyond the rhetoric, the Italian political class and system do not understand that the strict religious neutrality of institutions and the secularity of schools are—more than ever—the only possible guarantor of equal social dignity of all citizens, and therefore the best possible means for social integration. Neutrality does not harm anybody: the only limitation to cultural pluralism should be the full acceptance of individual human rights (with no discrimination based on religion, gender, sexual orientation, or age) and the full acceptance of liberal democracy. Those things, after all, constitute our common European constitutional heritage.

ENDNOTES

1. Especially after the bloody repression against a large part of the intellectual class of Southern Italy in 1799 in Naples, following the collapse of the Parthenopean Republic.

2. The Swiss Protestant historian Sismondi, was highly influential during this time. Jean-Charles-Léonard Sismonde de Sismondi, *Storia delle Repubbliche italiane* (Torino: Bollati Boringhieri, 1996) (this is a recent abridged edition; the first volume appeared in 1807; first complete or. ed. *Histoire de la renaissance de la liberté en Italie, de ses progrès, de sa décadence et de sa chute*, Paris, 1832).

3. Embodied by Piedmont statesman Camillo Benso, Count of Cavour.

4. Such as the Milan 1848 anti-Austrian revolt led by republican leader Carlo Cattaneo.

5. E.g., Freemasons, followers of the new positivist philosophical movement and immanentist idealists, etc.

6. This attitude dates back to the tradition of Gallicanism, long before the French Revolution.

7.   Politically, a rather minority point of view nowadays.

8.   In both the positive and negative sense (both of which, in any case, were tradition-ally opposed by the Catholic Church, and fiercely so).

9.   A typical example of this different approach was what happened when the Jew-ish observance of Yom Kippur happened to coincide with general elections. This coincidence of events occurred recently in two different years, both in France and in Italy. Orthodox and observant Jews believe they are not allowed to vote before sunset on Yom Kippur. In France, it was said that this was their own business: separation of state and religion compelled the state not to take into account the private problem of conscience of a minority of individuals. In Italy, it was intellectuals and politicians—who were known as staunch advocates of the Italian brand of *laicità*—who asked for a modification of the electoral law that would extend voting time for a few hours that year, in order to allow Orthodox Jews to vote after sunset. This more liberal and less state-centered idea of *laicità* introduces a notion of neutrality that does not align with indifference on issues concerning individual freedom of conscience.

10. The so-called *legge delle guarentigie*, i.e., "statute of the guaranties."

11. The basic constitutional law of the new state. The *Statuto Albertino* was named after King Charles Albert of Savoy, who conceded it.

12. Initially, it was enforced with limitations to minorities' freedom of proselytism. But a lot of foreign—especially British—Protestant missions had the opportunity to proselytize in many regions in the following decades, leading to the presence of small Protestant minorities also outside the centuries-old historical Waldensian territory, confined to some Alpine valleys of Piedmont.

13. Divorce was never introduced during the monarchic period.

14. Despite the dictator's strong anticlerical attitude as a (Socialist) youth.

15. The three agreements are known together as *Patti lateranensi*, as they were signed in the Lateran Palace in Rome.

16. Ecclesiastical annulments became the only possibility of achieving a *de facto* divorce for well-off couples until 1970.

17. Not against anti-Jewish discriminations in general, which they basically supported.

18. Including the prominent anti-fascist philosopher and historian Benedetto Croce, who, as a senator appointed in the pre-fascist period, made one of the very few opposition speeches of the fascist era against their ratification in the Senate in 1929 (throughout the period of the monarchy senators were appointed by the king).

19. Following not a Parliamentary decision but a Constitutional Court decision.

20. Again, only thanks to a Constitutional Court decision and not to a Parliamentary vote.

21. As a consequence, there were no post-divorce alimony duties; however, a small degree of control on those decisions, similar to that necessary to give legal effect in Italy to foreign decisions, was introduced in the 1970s by the Italian courts in order to limit previous abuses.

22. It is impossible to ascertain the exact amount.

23. A former Communist and a former Christian Democrat, both now members of the newly formed "Democratic Party" the largest mainstream party of the center-left coalition.

24. 3,690,000, according to another estimate by the Catholic charity Caritas Migrantes.

BIBLIOGRAPHY

Italian *Laicità* and French *Laïcité*, Defining *Laicità* and *Laicismo*:

Arturo Carlo Jemolo, *Chiesa e Stato in Italia negli ultimi cento anni*, Torino, Einaudi, 1963

Francesco Ruffini, *Relazioni tra Stato e Chiesa. Lineamenti storici e sistematici*, ed. by Francesco Margiotta Broglio, Bologna, Il Mulino, 1974

Walter Maturi, *Interpretazioni del Risorgimento. Lezioni di storia della storiografia*, Torino, Einaudi, 1962

Ignazio Silone et alii, *A trent'anni dal Concordato*, Firenze, Parenti, 1959

Gaetano Salvemini, *Clericali e laici*, Firenze, Parenti, 1957

Guido Calogero, *Quaderno laico*, Bari, Laterza, 1967

La laïcité, n.75 of the French quarterly review "Pouvoirs," Seuil, 1995

Henri Pena-Ruiz, *Qu'est-ce que la laïcité?*, Gallimard, 2003

Guy Coq, *Laïcité et République. Le lien nécessaire*, Paris, Félin, 1995

Guy Coq, *La laïcité. Principe universel*, Paris, Félin, 2005

Philippe Lazar, *Autrement dit laïque*, Liana Levi, 2003

Hubert Bost (ed.), *Genèse et enjeux de la laïcité. Christianismes et laïcité*, Genève, Labor et fides, 1990

Jean Baubérot, *La laïcité, quel héritage? De 1789 à nos jours*, Genève, Labor et fides, 1990

Jean Baubérot, Michel Wieviorka, *De la séparation des Églises et de l'État à l'avenir de la laïcité*, L'aube, 2005

Claude Dagens, Jean Baubérot, *L'avenir de la laïcité en France,* Parole et Silence, 2005

Nicolas Sarkozy, *La République, les religions, l'espérance*, Paris, Cerf, 2004

Paolo Cavana, *Interpretazioni della laicità. Esperienza francese ed esperienza italiana a confronto*, Roma, Ave, 1998

An Overview of Historical Developments in Italy:

Carlo Dionisotti, *Chierici e laici*, Novara, Interlinea, 1995

Guido Verucci, *L'Italia laica prima e dopo l'Unità 1848-1876*, Roma-Bari, Laterza 1996

Guido Verucci, *Cattolicesimo e laicismo nell'Italia contemporanea*, Milano, Angeli, 2001

Pietro Scoppola (ed.), *Chiesa e Stato nella storia d'Italia. Storia documentaria dall'Unità alla Repubblica*, Bari, Laterza, 1963

Rosario Romeo, *Cavour e il suo tempo*, 4 volumes, Roma-Bari, Laterza, 1969-1984 (the mainstream liberal position during the Italian Risorgimento)

Alessandro Galante Garrone, *I radicali in Italia (1949-1925)*, Milano, Garzanti, 1973 (the more radical secularist side)

Norberto Bobbio, *Una filosofia militante. Studi su Carlo Cattaneo*, Torino, Einaudi, 1972

Giorgio Spini, *Risorgimento e protestanti*, Milano, Il Saggiatore, 1989 (first ed. Napoli, Esi, 1956)

Giorgio Spini, *Italia liberale e protestanti*, Torino, Claudiana, 2002

Alberto Cavaglion (ed.), *Minoranze religiose e diritti. Percorsi in cento anni di storia degli ebrei e dei valdesi (1848-1948)*, Milano, Angeli, 2001

Giorgio Peyrot et alii, *La posizione delle chiese evangeliche di fronte allo stato*, Torino, Claudiana, 1970

Ruggero Taradel, Barbara Raggi, *La segregazione amichevole. "La civiltà cattolica" e la questione ebraica 1850-1945*, Roma, Editori riuniti, 2000

Angela Pellicciari, *Risorgimento da riscrivere. Liberali e massoni contro la Chiesa*, Milano, Ares, 1998 (the author is the leading figure in the present Catholic revisionist anti-Risorgimento movement)

Giorgio Rumi, *Gioberti*, Bologna, Il Mulino, 1999 (more moderate and mainstream Catholic view)

Giacomo Biffi, *Risorgimento, stato laico e identità nazionale*, Casale Monferrato, Piemme, 1999 (the author was the archbishop of Bologna)

Dina Bertoni Jovine, *Storia dell'educazione popolare in Italia*, Bari, Laterza, 1965 (the conflict over popular education and public schools)

Gaetano Salvemini, *Stato e Chiesa in Italia*, Milano, Feltrinelli, 1969

Ernesto Rossi, *Il manganello e l'aspersorio*, Bari, Laterza, 1968 (first ed. Firenze, Parenti, 1958)

Ernesto Rossi (ed.), *La conciliazione*, Firenze, Parenti, 1959 (the author was a prominent antifascist leader, and a co-author, together with Altiero Spinelli, of the "Ventotene Manifesto," that prompted European unification since 1943)

Benedetto Croce, *Storia d'Italia dal 1871 al 1915*, Bari, Laterza, 1967 (or. ed. 1927)

Benedetto Croce, *Storia d'Europa nel secolo decimonono*, Bari, Laterza, 1965 (or. ed. 1932: these two Croce books were instrumental in keeping alive a liberal presence in the Italian cultural scene of the 1930s)

Giovanni Miccoli, *In difesa della fede. La Chiesa di Giovanni Paolo II e Benedetto XVI*, Milano, Rizzoli, 2007

Susan Zuccotti, *Il Vaticano e l'Olocausto in Italia*, Milano, Bruno Mondadori, 2001 (or. ed. *Under His Very Windows. The Vatican and the Holocaust in Italy*, 2000)

Aldo Capitini, Piero Lacaita (ed.), *Gli atti della Costituente sull'art. 7*, Manduria-Perugia, Lacaita, 1959

Giambattista Scirè, *Il divorzio in Italia. Partiti, Chiesa, società civile dalla legge al referendum (1965-1974)*, Milano, Bruno Mondadori, 2007

Religious Privileges and State Funding of Religion:

www.italialaica.it: this web site contains the largest data base on *laicità* related issues in Italy

Critica liberale, monthly review, edited by Enzo Marzo

Micromega, monthly review, edited by Paolo Flores d'Arcais

Enzo Marzo, Corrado Ocone (ed.), *Manifesto laico*, Roma-Bari, Laterza, 1999

Raffaele Carcano (ed.), *Le voci della laicità*, Roma, Edup, 2006

Eugenio Scalfari (ed.), *Dibattito sul laicismo*, Roma, Biblioteca di Repubblica, 2005

Gustavo Zagrebelsky, *Lo Stato e la Chiesa*, Roma, Biblioteca di Repubblica, 2007 (the author is a former president of the Italian Constitutional Court)

Dora Bognandi, Martin Ibarra (ed.), *Laicità umiliata*, Torino, Claudiana, 2006 (a Protestant pleas for the preservation of *laicità*)

Roberto Bin et alii (ed.), *La laicità crocifissa? Il nodo costituzionale dei simboli religiosi nei luoghi pubblici*, Torino, Giappichelli, 2004

Roberto Beretta, *Chiesa padrona. Strapotere, monopolio e ingerenza nel cattolicesimo italiano*, Casale Monferrato, Piemme, 2006 (the very critical view of a Catholic journalist)

Culture Wars:

Gustavo Zagrebelsky, *Contro l'etica della verità*, Roma-Bari, Laterza, 2008

Piero Bellini, *Il diritto d'essere se stessi. Discorrendo dell'idea di laicità*, Torino, Giappichelli, 2007

Giulio Giorello, *Di nessuna chiesa, La libertà del laico*, Milano, Cortina, 2005

Gian Enrico Rusconi, *Come se Dio non ci fosse. I laici, i cattolici, la democrazia*, Torino, Einaudi, 2000

Vittorio Possenti (ed.) *Laici o laicisti? Un dibattito su religione e democrazia*, Firenze, Liberal, 2002 (a mainstream Catholic point of view)

Paolo Naso, *Laicità*, Bologna, Emi 2005 (the point of view of an ecumenical Protestant)

Sergio Aquilante et alii, *Chiese e Stato nell'Italia che cambia. Il ruolo del protestantesimo*, Torino, Claudiana, 1998

Marcello Vigli, *Contaminazioni. Un percorso di laicità fuori dai templi delle ideologie e delle religioni*, Bari, Dedalo, 2006 (the author was one of the leaders of the Catholic dissenters' movement in the 1970s)

Daniele Menozzi, *La Chiesa cattolica e la secolarizzazione*, Torino, Einaudi, 1993

Franco Garelli, *Forza della religione e debolezza della fede*, Bologna, Il Mulino, 1996 (the author is one of the sociologists whose advice is most valued by Italian bishops)

Valerio Pocar, Paola Ronfani, *La famiglia e il diritto*, Roma-Bari, Laterza, 2003

Bioetica. Rivista interdisciplinare, quarterly journal, edited by Maurizio Mori

Eugenio Lecaldano, *Dizionario di bioetica*, Roma-Bari, Laterza, 2007 (the author is a leading scholar in secular bioethical studies and related individual rights issues)

Eugenio Lecaldano, *Bioetica. Le scelte morali*, Roma-Bari, Laterza, 2005

Paolo Bonetti, *Discorrendo di etica e bioetica*, Lungro di Cosenza, Marco, 2005

Chiara Lalli, *Dilemmi della bioetica*, Napoli, Liguori, 2007

The New Multi-religious Society, "Religious Dialogue" as a Substitute for an Italian Integration Strategy:

Giovanni Sartori, *Pluralismo, multiculturalismo e estranei. Saggio sulla società multietnica*, Milano, Rizzoli, 2000

Elena Bein Ricco (ed.), *La sfida di Babele. Incontri e scontri nelle società multiculturali*, Torino, Claudiana, 2001

Guido Bolaffi, *I confini del patto. Il governo dell'immigrazione in Italia*, Torino, Einaudi, 2001

Giovanna Zincone, *Uno schermo contro il razzismo. Per una politica dei diritti utili*, Roma, Donzelli, 1994

Silvio Ferrari (ed.), *Musulmani in Italia. La condizione giuridica delle comunità islamiche*, Bologna, Il Mulino, 2000

Stefano Allievi, *Musulmani d'Occidente. Tendenze dell'islam europeo*, Roma, Carocci, 2002

Stefano Allievi, *Islam italiano. Viaggio nella seconda religione del paese*, Torino, Einaudi, 2003

Andrea Spreafico, Andrea Coppi, *La rappresentanza dei musulmani in Italia*, Roma, XL, 2006

Giuseppe Caputo (ed.), *Il pregiudizio antisemitico in Italia. La coscienza democratica di fronte al razzismo strisciante*, Roma, Newton Compton, 1984

Marco Martiniello, *Le società multietniche. Diritti e doveri uguali per tutti?* Bologna, Il Mulino, 2000 (or. ed. Sortir des ghettos culturels, Paris, Science Po, 1997)

Enzo Pace, *L'islam in Europa: modelli di integrazione*, Roma, Carocci, 2004

Gilles Kepel, *La revanche de Dieu. Chrétiens, juifs et musulmans à la reconquête du monde*, Seuil, 1991

Gilles Kepel, *Jihad. Expansion et déclin de l'islamisme*, Gallimard, 2000

Olivier Roy, *Global Muslim. Le radici occidentali del nuovo Islam*, Milano, Feltrinelli 2003 (or. ed. *L'islam mondialisé*, Seuil, 2002)

Khaled Fouad Allam, *L'Islam globale*, Milano, Rizzoli, 2002

Jocelyne Cesari, Andrea Pacini (ed.), *Giovani musulmani in Europa. Tipologie di appartenenza religiosa e dinamiche socio-culturali*, Torino, Fondazione Giovanni Agnelli, 2005

Antoine Sfeir, René Andrau, *Liberté égalité islam. La République face au communitarisme*, Paris, Tallandier, 2005

Jeanne-Hélène Kaltenbach, Michèle Tribalat, *La République et l'islam entre crainte et aveuglement*, Gallimard, 2002

Vincent Geisser, Aziz Zemouri, *Marianne et Allah. Les politiques français face à la "question musulmane,"* Paris, La Découverte, 2007

Oliver Roy, *La laïcité face à l'islam*, Stock, 2005

Jonathan Laurence, Justin Vaïsse, *Intégrer l'islam. La France et ses musulmans: enjeux et réussites*, Paris, Odile Jacob, 2007 (or. ed. *Integrating Islam*, Brookings Institution Press, Washington, D.C., 2006)

Malek Chebel, *Manifeste pour un islam des Lumières. 27 propositions pour réformer l'islam*, Hachette, 2004

Ghaleb Bencheikh, *La laïcité au regard du Coran*, Paris, Renaissance, 2005

Fethi Benslama, *Déclaration d'insoumission. À l'usage des musulmans et de ceux qui ne le sont pas*, Paris, Flammarion, 2005

Mostafa El Ayoubi (ed.), *Islam plurale*, Roma, Com Nuovi tempi, 2000

2. France, Italy and Spain: Political Secularism and Public Opinion

Barry A. Kosmin

Political Secularism

Secularism and its variants are terms much discussed today, paradoxically as a consequence of religion seeming to have become more pervasive and influential in public life and society worldwide. This situation poses a number of questions. First, a definitional one: What are the spheres of secularity and secularism? According to our understanding *secularity* refers to individuals and their social and psychological characteristics and behavior while *secularism* refers to the realm of social institutions.

Secularism is an approach or outlook towards society and the contemporary world. It involves no metaphysical claims. It is not a distinct or complete belief system and is not directly concerned about ultimate truth, matters of faith or spirituality. Thus secularism is not a personal attribute. Rather it involves collective behavior, organizations and legal constructs that reflect the institutional expressions of the secular or mundane, particularly in the political realm and the public life of a nation.

Forms of secularism can be expected to vary across societies in reaction to the local culture or religious environment in which they developed. This variation arises from the "historical baggage" that reflects the symbolic and cultural encoding of religious legacies in national public institutions and mentalities. Nevertheless, in ideological terms we can assert that secularism essentially involves the rejection of the primacy of religious authority in the affairs of this world. This process, which is usually referred to as *secularization,* is most evident in the West in the governmental or political realm, where the outcome has meant the "desacralization of the state."[1]

The idea of separating the institutions of the state, government and public life from the direct involvement and influence of organized religion arose during the Age of Enlightenment. This constitutional principle presupposes that the political world is a realm of human artifact, which means at a minimum that religion and politics belong to separate spheres, to independent and autonomous domains of human activity. It became a feasible proposition as a result of the two great revolutions of the 18th century.

In fact the American and French revolutions produced two intellectual and constitutional traditions of secularism and the secular state—a "soft secularism" and a "hard secularism." That associated with the French Jacobin tradition became dominant in Mediterranean Europe. It was suspicious of and antagonistic to religion and its influence on the state and society. This situation arose from the historical reality of the *ancien regime* and the revolutionary experience in France. The absolutist monarchy grounded its legitimacy in the Catholic religion so the Revolution involved a joint struggle against despotism and religion—the monarchy and the Roman Catholic Church. It produced a political construction that continues in France under the regime of *laicité* bound up with *La Loi de 1905*. This same historic dynamic and process involving a two-front struggle for liberty also applied in Italy during the *Risorgimento* (1848-1870) and in Spain against the Franco regime (1939-75).

The battle between the Revolution and the Church, between secular democracy and conservative tradition, dominated French, Italian and Spanish politics and history for nearly 200 years. A key charge against the Church by local patriots was that it constituted a foreign body that owed its allegiance elsewhere. The political compromise was the Concordat, first established by Napoleon I, and later adopted by most majority Catholic nations. This system did not really separate church and state but sought to regulate the relations between them.[2]

It is theoretically possible for a state to be religious and its population to be secularized and so exhibit high levels of secularity, or conversely for the state to be secular and the population largely religious.[3] However, over the long haul in a democracy there is a logical tendency for the superstructure and the substructure to align. Thus in the complex world of modern Western democracies, we can observe the process of secularization in nations on at least two major levels.[4] One is the secularization of national institutions and structures, such as the organs of the state and government. The other level is the secularization of society—the secularization of human consciousness that leads to increased levels of secularity in belief, behavior and belonging among the populace. In a polity where popular sovereignty is acknowledged, change (or reform) at the institutional level happens as a result of political forces emanating from developments in society that are reflected in public opinion and attitudes. Thus, over time we would expect the level of secularism of the state to become aligned with the level of secularity of the population.

This chapter reports on contemporary, national public opinion as regards a key aspect of political secularism in the three major Western European Mediterranean states, France, Italy and Spain. In order to fully appreciate and understand the true political significance and social importance of this data it is necessary at the outset to distinguish not only the work of the three traditional functions of government—the legislature, executive and judiciary—but also three levels in public life and political action. The first level is the state and its permanent structures and constitutional arrangements including its historic legacies and fictions such as its symbols. It needs to be considered separately from the apparatus of government and the daily administration of public services by temporary office-holders. In turn, government needs to be differentiated from the realm of political parties, campaigns and episodic elections. Of course, there are overlaps and conflations of personnel and activities but in a functioning democracy the various levels of public life are not a single playing field. This realization is crucial for a proper understanding and appreciation of the opinion poll and social survey data presented here.

The key question we will be analyzing is: "*Do you think that religious leaders should or should not try to influence government decisions?*" This question could be interpreted or understood in a number of ways. However, it is clearly about the governmental decision making process and presumably it relates to everyday public policy issues. The question goes deep into the realm of political secularism, far beyond questions of constitutional forms and niceties or of religious establishment *per se*. It essentially measures anticlericalism—the public's response to the call in "vernacular thinking," "to keep religion out of politics."

The data are drawn from an AP/IPSOS international poll in 2005. They cover representative national samples of Spain, France and Italy. All are Mediterranean states with strong cultural ties in the form of Romance languages and a common Catholic religious tradition and cultural legacy.

At first glance the results in Figure 2-1 seem to validate the thesis that religion has lost much of its social significance as well as its authority.[5] The overall pattern of response shows that a clear majority in each country clearly rejects the interference of religious leaders in the decisions of democratically elected governments and so adopts what can be considered to be a "hard" secularist position. France is clearly the extreme in terms of this "political secularization index." The legacy of its early revolutionary tradition of "hard" secularism which was referred to earlier seems to have endured. Two and a half times as many Italians as French provide positive pro-religious responses towards religious intrusion or involvement in government policies. In contrast, the level of antagonism to clerical intrusion into public life and so towards the power and authority of organized religion is significantly higher in France than Italy (22 percentage points). The findings suggest that public opinion in the major states of EU is not yet homogeneous with regard to the process of political secularization.

The Religious Identification Factor

There is another possible explanation of these results. Rather than reflecting differences in secular-religious outlooks the data could well reflect variations in political culture. Perhaps in Italy "lobbying" the administration and especially legislatures is a legitimate part of the political system. Of course the Italian answers may reflect negativity about the current system of government. It is commonly assumed that the political system in Italy is more dysfunctional than is that in France or Spain and its political elite is more distrusted so Church influence is not seen as detrimental. The idea of "lobbying" and factionalism is much less formalized and acceptable in France with its *dirigiste* approach. In fact it could be argued that the negative response to this question is essentially an anti-democratic one. Why should religious leaders be denied the right of advocacy on questions of the day and be more restricted than leaders of other institutions from participating in politics? Separation of formal ties between religion and the state and constraints on religious hegemony need not be extended to legitimate democratic interventions. Historical experience is important here. Religion is associated with clerical power and authority. In Spain it is particularly feared and distrusted more than most other elements in civil society because of the record of its past interventions. The common historical judgment on clerical power and authority when it had political dominance over the state is negative. Moreover, the historical memory of religious authoritarianism is much stronger and more recent in Spain than Italy. In Spain it only disappeared with the end of the Franco dictatorship in 1975.

One could look in another direction to explain the patterns in Figure 2-1, towards national differences in current levels of religiosity and secularity. This argument assumes that national differences in the extent or pace of secularization in the public/civic realm merely reflect those at the personal/individual level across the populations of the various countries. The problem here is that measuring "religion" is not as simple as it might appear at first sight. The phenomenon has a variety of aspects to it—belonging, belief, behavior—on both the individual and societal levels. No single question fully covers this complexity of social reality and meaning. However, one obvious place to start to look for an explanation of

Figure 2-1

Do you think that religious leaders should or should not try to influence government decisions?

	Italy	Spain	France
Should	30	17	12
Should Not	63	76	85
Unsure	7	7	3
Total	100	100	100

Source: IPSOS: The AP/IPSOS survey was conducted in May 2005. In each country approximately 1,000 people were surveyed and there was a margin of error of ±3%.

Figure 2-2

National Religious Composition

	Italy	Spain	France
Catholics	92	80	71
Other Religions	2	2	10
No Religion	5	17	19
Refused / Unsure	1	1	-
Total	100	100	100

the results in Figure 2-1 is the religious profile of these countries.

Figure 2-2 provides the overall religious profile of each country using the AP/IPSOS survey data for 2005. The figure shows that at the superficial level of nominal religious identification the various societies show the commonalities of a common heritage of Roman Catholic Christianity whose main challenger is No Religion rather than any other form of religion. Italy is clearly the most Christian nation. On the obverse indicator, the "secularization of loyalties and ties," Italy again seems to be the exception.

The Roman Catholic Church is a hierarchical body of believers with a strong tradition of centralized leadership and direction by an "infallible" Pope. Though the Pope lost temporal power in 1870 with the demise of the theocracy of the Papal States, through concordats with national governments or via support for Christian Democrat political parties with a clear Catholic social agenda, the

Church has a continuing involvement in national politics in Europe. This makes an assessment of Catholic public opinion very salient to the issue of mass popular support for political secularism. Thus one immediate reaction to the data in Figure 2-2 is to ask whether the 21 percentage point higher rate of identification with Catholicism in Italy compared to France, accounts for the 18 percentage point gap on the first row of Figure 2-1. If so, what we are really observing is the socio-political outcome of theological beliefs. To refute or confirm this argument and to prove the salience or otherwise of national culture we need some sort of control group. Fortunately the survey data provide this. One way to test whether the pattern of responses in Figure 2-1 reflects the legacy of religious difference independent of national political traditions is to focus analysis just on the Catholic respondents across these nations.

The self-identifying Catholic proportion of the three national samples varies considerably, as Figure 2-1 demonstrates. Nevertheless, even after isolating Catholic respondents the answers to the question in row 1 of Figure 2-3 are almost a direct replica of row 1 in Figure 2-1, varying only by one or two percentage points. This remarkable result shows that there is no difference between Catholic opinion and national opinion overall today in these countries. Support for theocracy, along with ideas such as "the divine right of kings," has long ago evaporated in the West. The data suggest that French Catholics subscribe to the national political culture and *laicité* as much as other Frenchmen.

The Salience of Religion Factor

Nevertheless there are national differences on the key question that have to be explained. Figure 2-4, which asks about the importance of religion in the life of the individual respondent, can be considered a religious intensity or "salience of faith" scale. The question deals with a more personal aspect which may be seen as having a behavioral outcome or perhaps as being more meaningful to the respondent than "identification." The responses in the top row of Figure 2-4 are a much better predictor of the results in the top row of Figure 2-1 than are the religious identification data in Figure 2-2. The rank ordering and alignment of the countries show again Italy is one extreme and France is the other. When the results are presented in a binary fashion contrasting the scores for "important" and "not important" by country then really sharp differences can easily be observed. There is much more of an even division of opinion on this question in Spain whereas in Italy and France there are clear national majorities of opinion for or against religion's importance.

Figure 2-3
**Opinions of Catholic Respondents:
Do you think that religious leaders should or should not
try to influence government decisions?**

	Italy	Spain	France
Should	32	19	13
Should Not	62	73	84
Unsure	6	8	3
Total	100	100	100

Figure 2-4
How important would you say religion is in your own life?

	Italy	Spain	France
Very important	38	19	14
Somewhat important	41	27	23
Not too important	14	28	31
Not at all important	6	24	32
Not sure	1	2	-
Total	100	100	100

Total important	80	46	37
Total not important	19	52	63

The Gender Factor

One possible factor that could be an influence on national patterns of response to political secularism could be gender. Females are generally found to be more religious in outlook than males and Catholicism in particular has long had a stronger hold over European women than men. Secularization is also thought to have a "co-ed" effect in that it reduces male-female differentials across a range of social and psychological variables.

The pattern of responses to the key question in Figure 2-5 shows that neither thesis seems to operate in this arena. The gender gap across the top row ranges from only one to three points. "Secular" France does seem to demonstrate the smallest gender differentials overall but in Italy and Spain the male-female gaps are hardly noteworthy.

The Age Factor

The secularization of Europe advanced very rapidly in the years after World War II and it quickened even further in the period of prosperity ushered in by the "economic miracle" associated with the Treaty of Rome and European Economic Community (1957), which became the European Union (1993). France and Italy were founding members of the EU and Spain joined in 1986. Spain especially underwent very fast modernization after it emerged from the authoritarian/clerical dictatorship of Franco (1939-75). Nevertheless Italy and France also have a history of anti-democratic regimes, fascist regimes (Mussolini and Vichy) that are in the life experience of the oldest generation. Given the socio-economic and political changes that these three societies have undergone over recent decades we might expect to find considerable generational differences in opinions about political secularism.

Figure 2-6 shows the pattern that history might suggest. France, with its longer established and more deeply rooted system of *laicité*, shows a high level of consensus across the generations. With each younger age group, "political secularism" in France (row 2) gets slightly more support.

The Spanish data reflect what history might have predicted. The oldest age group, which was raised and educated under the Franco dictatorship, holds very different opinions to the rest of the population. In fact, once the break was made with fascism the pattern seems to have quickly adopted a remarkable resemblance to that of France. Interestingly, the oldest Spaniards are less secular than the oldest Italians; they are also less willing to venture an opinion (18%).

The age data even more perhaps than the religious variables explain why Italy is the odd man out on this issue. The pattern of opinion by age suggests that the level of support for "clericalism" and "secularism" does not appear to have changed much over time. In fact there is even a trend among the youngest Italian adults to reject secularism so that they are beginning to resemble older Spaniards even though a majority still reject clerical interference in government.

Conclusions

The analysis of these survey results demonstrates the complexities involved in theorizing about the sociology of religion and secularization and political

Figure 2-5
National Opinion by Gender:
Do you think that religious leaders should or should not try to influence government decisions?

	Italy		Spain		France	
	M	F	M	F	M	F
Should	29	31	15	18	11	12
Should not	65	61	81	72	86	84
Not sure	6	8	4	10	3	4
Total	100	100	100	100	100	100

Figure 2-6
National Opinion by Age Group:
Do you think that religious leaders should or should not try to influence government decisions?

	Italy				Spain				France			
	18-34	35-49	50-64	65+	18-34	35-49	50-64	65+	18-34	35-49	50-64	65+
Should	38	28	24	25	12	12	13	31	9	10	13	16
Should Not	57	66	71	63	85	84	79	51	88	86	82	80
Not Sure	5	6	5	12	3	4	8	18	3	4	5	4
Total	100	100	100	100	100	100	100	100	100	100	100	100

sociology especially with regard to international comparisons of secularity and secularism. What we can observe across all three nations is indeed secularization in both realms, the social and the institutional, but the pace varies. Secularization at the macro-level of national structures advances more in some societies and is more unidirectional than is the micro-level of personal belief. This outcome is possible because there is a general public acceptance in Western European democratic states of the need for pluralism and of the privatization of religion. Nevertheless this privatization of religion can take different forms both at the macro- and micro-levels as is most clearly illustrated by the cases of Italy and France. In addition, it is necessary to recognize that support for political secularism, particularly, is not an indicator of anti-religious sentiment in other areas of life. Nor does it necessarily correlate with disbelief in the transcendent on the personal level.

It is possible to argue that neither separation of religion from the state nor the privatization and state supervision of religion necessarily leads to the undermining of the public acceptance or legitimacy of religious intrusions into politics. Nevertheless, the survey findings in Figure 2-1 suggest that in the three countries analyzed here, the field of governance is largely treated as a single system so its various levels are often conflated in the minds of the public and in the commentary offered by the media on social surveys and polling trends. However, despite these reservations, the data presented in the tables are robust enough to support some important conclusions. Although some variations in national cultures resulting from the different religious and political histories persist, a common ('secular') trend towards public acceptance of political secularism and a marked preference for the concept of the "secular state" can be observed. The Enlightenment belief that religion should be divorced as much as possible from government activity has now spread well beyond the U.S. and France and is now the overwhelming consensus among public opinion in Spain and to a lesser extent in Italy too. That this consensus now extends to self-identifying Catholic public opinion is also remarkable.

In terms of public support for political secularism Spain is now more similar to France than it is to Italy. From a historical perspective such evidence of a trend towards convergence in Western public opinion across Mediterranean Europe, as shown in Figure 2-1, would have been considered truly amazing seventy years ago during the Spanish Civil War and on the eve of World War II. Political secularism seems a user friendly political construction. It is adaptable and can come in both harder and softer forms. These attributes probably help to enhance its public appeal and acceptability today in the West. The result is a majority Western consensus for "popular sovereignty" and a distrust of political interference by the clergy of any religion. This "anticlericalism" suggests the tendency is to favor "assertive" rather than "passive secularism,"[6] the French rather than American revolutionary tradition and form of political secularism. It aims to constrain organized religion and remove it from the public square. It tolerates religion only as a matter of private conscience and divorced from the day to day affairs of the polity.

Endnotes

1. Rodney Stark and Laurence R. Iannaccone, "A Supply Side Reinterpretation of the 'Secularization' of Europe," *Journal for the Scientific Study of Religion,* 33 (1994): 230-252.

2. See Ercolessi and Sansonetti in this volume.

3. N.J. Demareth III, *Crossing the Gods: World Religions and World Politics* (New York: Rutgers University Press, 2002).

4. Barry A. Kosmin, "Contemporary Secularity and Secularism," in *Secularism & Secularity: Contemporary International Perspectives,* eds. Barry A. Kosmin and Ariela Keysar (Hartford, CT: ISSSC, 2007).

5. Bryan Wilson, *Religion in Secular Society* (London: Penguin, 1966).

6. Ahmet T. Kuru, "Passive and Assertive Secularism: Historical Conditions, Ideological Struggles, and State Policies toward Religion," *World Politics* 59 (July 2007): 568-594.

3. Greece: Selective Secularization and the Deprivatization of Religion?

Lina Molokotos-Liederman

Introduction

This chapter addresses the question of how the secularization thesis applies to the case of Greece. This question is particularly relevant given the weight of Greek Orthodoxy on the country's religious and cultural landscape and on the historical circumstances that have shaped the nation's political and social life. First we shall look briefly at some of the definitions of and debates on secularization and then highlight specific aspects of Eastern Orthodoxy in relation to the process of secularization. Then we shall continue with an introduction to the larger context in which the Greek case should be viewed, including a brief description of the religious landscape. Finally the conflict over national Identity Cards is used as a case study in order to highlight the ambiguity of the secularization thesis with regard to Greece.

Bryan Wilson's original definition of secularization as a "process whereby religious thinking, institutions, and practice lose social significance" is an important starting point in defining the concept.[1] Secularization includes numerous social processes, such as:

- Secularization at a societal level (separation of church and state); the institutional level (the modernization of religion itself); and individual level (decrease of formal religious practice).[2]

- The relative decline of some religious indices (measuring concrete, but also subjective aspects of religiosity, such as church attendance, religious belief, etc.).[3]

41

- Re-organization of the nature and form of religion, including an individualization of religious practices ("do-it-yourself" religiosity).[4]

- The privatization of religion, becoming a personal matter relating to the individual, and, thus, its marginalization from public life.[5]

The notion of secularization is currently viewed more as "a theory with relatively limited application, particularly suited to the European case, but very much less helpful elsewhere."[6] Increasingly, scholars are questioning the validity of the secularization argument, especially outside the Western European context. A related criticism that concerns the specific topic of this chapter is the extension of the secularization thesis beyond the Protestant and Catholic cases, from which sociologists of religion originally developed the concept. Furthermore, Jose Casanova's argument on the "deprivatization of religion in the modern world,"[7] with religious traditions exiting the private sphere and entering public life is particularly relevant to the Greek case, as this chapter will illustrate.

Over the last five decades of Greece's post-war history—decades marked by a civil war, the fall of the dictatorship in 1974 and EU membership in 1981—the country has gradually shed its traditional image and developed into a modern European state. Greek society has evolved into a semi-industrial and service-oriented economy where a discrepancy between economic and social development has also left its mark. Economic prosperity and consumerism have been accompanied by large socio-economic gaps and an unevenly paced social development (visible in the spheres of education, employment, and social policy). Throughout this process, Greece has progressively experienced social and structural differentiation, rationalization, and increasing social and cultural diversity. But it has done so in its own way, and at its own pace, given its particular historical circumstances and political and social development. In this respect, Greece is a country that is undergoing a selective process of secularization, as there are points where the Greek case can give "pause for thought." The next sections illustrate this point and highlight the weight of Greek Orthodoxy on the country's religious and cultural landscape, and the particular historical circumstances that have shaped Greece's political and social life.

The Secularization Thesis and Eastern Orthodoxy

Orthodox Christianity is marked by the absence of a strong centralized and hierarchical administrative structure, such as we find in the Catholic Church.[8] Orthodox churches are autocephalous entities headed by autonomous Patriarchates that have the right to elect bishops in each administrative jurisdiction. Local churches are decentralized, but united in spirit through the Ecumenical Patriarchate (in Istanbul/Constantinople, Turkey) and the other Orthodox Patriarchates. "Unity of the Church is a unity in faith, not an administrative unity," wrote Jean Meyendorff.[9] This type of organization affects how the Orthodox faith is practiced and lived today.

The decentralized structure of Eastern Orthodox Churches allows fairly flexible religious practices, associated with an absence of strictly applied religious regulations and prohibitions. The lack of rigid application of religious rules, accompanied by some degree of elasticity when necessary, is the result of the concept of *oikonomia* in Greek Orthodoxy. This permits various possible ways of practically implementing Orthodox law, thus implying a certain degree of flexibility, conciliation, discussion and openness. One example is the relatively mild language against divorce, abortion or contraception by higher Orthodox clergy that we often find in speeches by the Catholic Church and the Pope (for example, during his 2007 visit in Brazil). The non-centralized organization of Orthodox Christianity also relates to the close link between the Orthodox faith and the nation. Eastern Orthodox Churches tend to identify themselves with specific national and ethnic characteristics. The Church is usually thought to reflect—even embody—the national character; and religious belonging is considered equivalent to national or ethnic affiliation. This is evident in: (a) the effects of nationalism on the Orthodox Church in the 19th century, (b) the "re-territorialization"[10] and revitalization of many Orthodox national churches after the fall of communism, and (c) the strong public links that are still visible between church and nation in many Balkan countries, such as Greece and Serbia. In this sense, Orthodoxy acts as a marker of collective and individual identities, a "genre of identity,"[11] whereby religion is used symbolically, thus diluting or losing its religious content.

When thinking about the relationship between secularization and Eastern Orthodoxy, one emerging research question is whether (a) the decentralized structure of the Orthodox Churches, (b) the flexibility and adaptability of the Orthodox faith (the principle of *oikonomia*), and (c) the links between church and nation are factors that can collectively determine the extent to which countries with Orthodox majorities are more or less compatible with (or prone to) the process of secularization.

The relationships between secularization and Eastern Orthodoxy have to be examined in depth through different case studies. But there are indicators suggesting some secularizing tendencies in countries with Orthodox majorities. First, the flexibility of religious practices and lack of strict religious rules (*oikonomia*) in Orthodox Christianity both point to loose or diffused forms of religiosity (see the Greek case below, for example). This can often mean lower expectations of observing religious norms and practices (regular church attendance, praying, belief in God, etc.). It also points to somewhat open attitudes towards some social issues—for example, divorce, contraception or abortion—thus suggesting a secularizing thread in Eastern Orthodox countries. Second, Eastern Orthodoxy acts as a collective "genre of identity"[12] and an all-encompassing force, "a religious tradition that has been absorbed into different national identities."[13] This may suggest a propensity towards a certain degree of secularization.

However, there are also indicators suggesting the contrary, thus not in alignment with the secularization thesis. The intertwining of religion and politics in countries with Orthodox majorities and close relations between religious and state institutions also suggest a more visible and public role of religion. These factors point to a weaker institutional and structural differentiation between the sacred and secular spheres in such societies and, thus, a more diluted secularization process. Furthermore, the strength of church-nation links in many countries with Orthodox majorities points to close relations between religion and citizenship and, thus, a tendency to possibly exclude (or include) individuals or groups based on the correlation among their religion, ethnicity, and nationality.

Collectively, these contrasting hypotheses suggest, at best, an uneasy relationship between Orthodoxy and the processes of globalization, secularization, and rationalization. They also indicate a *partial* accommodation of and adaptation to the values of modernity. Looking more closely at data on religiosity in Eastern European countries (Romania, Serbia, Bulgaria, Russia, Ukraine, etc.) would be useful in verifying and testing these hypotheses. Further examination, using case studies, would also help highlight the complexities and contradictions in applying the secularization thesis to Eastern Orthodoxy. Greece is taken here as an indicative example illustrating these processes, among others.

The Greek Religious Landscape

Greece has a special place in the European religious landscape. It can be viewed as the daughter of a mixed marriage: it looks towards and espouses elements from both the West and the East. Most Greeks have a dual outlook; they relate both to the West and East on account of Greece's mixed religious, cultural, and historical profile. Greece has been strongly shaped and influenced by both its ancient heritage, which was the historic originator of what became Western democracy and rationalism, and its Byzantine legacy. Yet, it did not *directly* experience the Renaissance, the Reformation or the Enlightenment, and it is also the only predominantly Orthodox country not to have lived under Communism. Having joined the European Community in 1981, it is one of the older European Union member-states. At least until Bulgaria and Romania joined in 2007, it was at the most eastern edge of the Union. It also marks the border between Europe and the Muslim world. Because of this, Greece has a somewhat specific socio-religious profile compared to the Western European religious model of secularization and religious modernity/post-modernity.

Orthodoxy constitutes Greece's cultural and religious heritage, dating to before the creation of the modern Greek state in the 19th century. It goes back to the Byzantine Empire, when Emperor Constantine made Christianity the official religion of the State and transferred the capital from Rome to Constantinople. Orthodox Christianity became the glue uniting the Byzantine Empire. Subsequently, during the era of the Ottoman Empire, the Eastern Orthodox Church was the guardian of Greek language and culture under Ottoman rule. These important factors have cemented the historic link that developed between Orthodoxy and Hellenism. This "Helleno-Christian"[14] heritage gradually led to an overlap between national/ethnic and religious identity and a tendency to identify Greek citizenship with the Orthodox faith.

How does the legacy of the Eastern Orthodox Church translate into today's Greek political and social life? The independence of the Church in 1833 from the Ecumenical Patriarchate, and its re-creation into the Autocephalous Orthodox Church of Greece (OCG), took place just after the founding of the modern Greek state in 1827. Relations between the Greek Church and State were formalized under Article 3 of the Greek Constitution, which stated that the "prevailing" religion of the Greek population is Eastern Orthodoxy under the authority of the autocephalous Church of Greece, united spiritually with the Ecumenical Patriarchy.[15] But the independence of the OCG from the Ecumenical Patriarchy also meant its subordination to the authority of the Greek State. The close relationship that developed between Church and State and between religious and political leaders entangled the OCG in Greece's turbulent political history. However, if this situation limited the OCG's independence by placing it under the authority of the Greek State, it did offer the Church special privileges, especially financial support by the Ministry of National Education and Religious Affairs (which pays the salaries of all clergy). The OCG is a legal person or entity in Public Law and enjoys both legal and financial benefits (such as tax and military service exemptions for Orthodox clergy) and ownership of real estate and land (Article 18).

Beyond the formal relationship between Church and State, the OCG and the Greek State are also interconnected symbolically today. The Church is generally considered to be a homogenizing and unifying force that can be solicited by the State. The power of the OCG, both as a religious institution with a political weight and a cultural and spiritual force, is still taken into consideration in Greek political life, as evidenced by the presence of the Archbishop and other members of clergy during several national holidays and political occasions, for example during the swearing in ceremony of the President or of a new government. The OCG does not have a *direct* influence on State affairs, but it can exercise a rather implicit and diffused influence on government. Inevitably, given such close Church and State relations, there have been many tensions. Throughout modern Greek history, Church and State have confronted each other in a variety of conflicts, including over the establishment of civil marriage (1982) and divorce (1983) by Greece's first socialist government; the proposed expropriation of Church properties; and the removal of religious affiliation from Greek ID cards (2000). The eventual separation of Church and State remains under occasional discussion but it is unlikely that any constitutional change will be approved by Parliament in the foreseeable future.

The strong visibility of the OCG in Greece's political life extends to Greek society, where it still enjoys a deeply rooted social and cultural influence: Greek Orthodoxy defines itself (through the Church), and is viewed by others (the State, Greek population, etc.) as the defender of national identity. It is an important component of national identity and acts as a main reference point, a chain of national memory, linking the country's historical past and cultural heritage. It is also regarded as a symbolic safety net protecting against a globalizing world that might threaten to erase the national, ethnic, cultural and religious characteristics of Greece.

The OCG has responded to the process of European integration by developing various European initiatives. These have included opening a representation office in Brussels; addressing European issues in the Church's discourse; establishing some links and a basic dialogue with other European Churches and religious actors. But between 1998 and 2007, this process was also concomitant with strong ideologically based discourses by the late Archbishop Christodoulos, who used anti-European and anti-Western rhetoric in many of his public statements. Following the death of Archbishop Christodoulos, Archbishop Ieronymos II was elected in his place in February 2008; compared to his predecessor, Ieronymos II is viewed as a moderate religious leader. It remains to be seen how his leadership will influence the Church's position in Greek society, its outlook towards the rest of Europe, and the process of European integration.

In religious and ethnic terms, Greece is considered one of Europe's most homogeneous countries: according to 2002-2003 European Social Survey (ESS) data, approximately 93% of the Greek population of 11 million is Orthodox Christian.[16] However, since the 1990s Greece has been receiving an increasing number of immigrants from different religious and ethnic backgrounds, so its demographic composition is diversifying. There are historic religious and ethnic minorities that have lived in Greece for many decades and generations. Judged by size, the most important non-Orthodox religious minorities include Muslims (Greek citizens of Turkish origin living primarily in Northern Greece) and foreign-born Muslims living in Greece; Catholics (both Greek citizens and foreign-born Catholics living in Greece); Jehovah's Witnesses, Protestants and Jews.[17]

Churchgoing is oriented mostly to rites of passage (baptisms, weddings, and funerals) and various religious/national holidays. This is evident in the high rates of church attendance during Easter and popular religious and national holidays. According to the ESS[18] and other surveys on Greek religiosity (e.g., the 2004 European Values Survey and Georgiadou and Nikolakopoulos 2001), most (63%) of Greeks go to Church, either only on special occasions (33%) or only once a month (30%).[19] However, if Greeks go to Church only occasionally, they pray more often. Up to 44% of Greek respondents say they pray every day.[20] Greeks also have one of the highest self-definitions of religiosity in Europe. On a scale of 1 (not religious) to 10 (very religious), more than half of Greek respondents (54%) state that they are an 8 (20%), 9 (17%) or 10 (17%).[21] Furthermore, 46% of Greek respondents indicate that religion is extremely important in their lives.[22] Therefore, the level of religiosity seems uneven. On the one hand, some religious behavior is relatively weak. On the other hand, religion plays a significant role, as more than half the population defines itself in religious terms. According to the above statistics, what distinguishes Greece from most European countries are "subjective indicators of religiosity" (self-definition), rather than the objective/hard data, such as Church attendance and prayer.[23]

Religious freedom in Greece varies according to legal status among main groups: (a) "known" religions[24] (OCG, Old Calendarists, Catholic Church, Islam, Judaism, Protestant Churches and Jehovah's Witnesses) and all "other" (i.e., not-known or unrecognized) religions (according to Article 13.2 of the Greek Constitution); and (b) "Legal Persons in Public Law" (Judaism, Islam, and the OCG) and "Legal Persons in Private Law" (the Catholic Church, Old Calendarists, Jehovah's Witnesses and Evangelical Churches and some Pentecostal Churches). This distinction creates legal obstacles for some minority religions. Article 13 of the Greek Constitution protects the freedom of conscience and religious worship for "known" religions.[25] Most "known" religious groups are organized and have their own places of worship and associations (including schools for Catholic, Jewish and certain Muslim communities). However, licensing for the construction or operation of places of worship by "other" (i.e., unknown) religious minority groups is subject to a rather long administrative procedure and approval by the local bishop and the Ministry of Education and Religious Affairs. Article 13 also prohibits proselytism against, or for, any religion, including Orthodoxy. In practice, this rule has almost exclusively been used against religious minorities. Since the mere distribution of literature by certain minority religious groups has often been interpreted (and prosecuted) as an act of proselytism (for example, in the case of Jehovah's Witnesses), the definition of proselytism in Greece seems problematic.

Women's Issues

The position of women both in the Church and in society has been viewed statically by the Greek Orthodox Church, as not requiring any substantive revisions or changes. Greek Orthodoxy has been rather skeptical or critical towards feminist concerns and issues, viewing them as Western ideological products threatening the authentic character and unbroken continuity and tradition of the Church and of what it means to be Greek. In both theological and social terms, women are considered equal to but different from men in terms of their unique social functions in the family, in the Church and in society at large. [26]

The OCG has rejected the ordination of women as priests, considering it a non-issue because of a variety of theological and other reasons, collectively amounting more to traditional Church practice, rather than substantive theological reasons. However, due to the extensive and growing supporting roles of women in the Church in a variety of educational, administrative and philanthropic functions within the OCG, there have been some attempts to address, discuss and re-evaluate women's issues in Greek Orthodoxy. The OCG has created a special Synodical committee for women's issues and reinstituted the female diaconate. Ordained ministry is not viewed by Orthodoxy as the only meaningful way to provide service to the Church so the re-introduction of deaconesses by the Church can be viewed as one step in strengthening the position of women in the OCG. But its restriction to the monastic order so far, limiting the work of female deacons from the wider society,[27] suggests that there is plenty of room for further action and reform.

Feminism in Greece has had a rather reformist character aiming to re-evaluate gender roles, but not to drastically overturn the overall balance.[28] Women in Greek society are viewed as equal to but different from men, following a prevailing socially accepted model of women as homemakers, spouses, mothers and the primary caregivers for the whole family. This paradigm may be progressively evolving as more Greek women are gradually entering the work force, thus potentially altering established gender roles and the traditional model of the Greek family. Nonetheless, in this respect, compared to other European countries, the pace of social change in Greece may take some time, partly because Greek women still remain below the European average of female participation in the labor force.[29] Within this context, the position of Greek women and their sense of self as individuals, mothers, spouses, workers and citizens suggests a dynamic tension in trying to reconcile cultural tradition and the family (in which the influence of the Greek Orthodox Church must not be overlooked) with economic independence and social autonomy.

How Far Does the Secularization Thesis Apply to Greece?

How does the brief overview of Eastern Orthodoxy and the Greek religious landscape help us address more specifically the question of secularization in Greece? The answer seems ambiguous. At a political/institutional level, the lack of Church-State separation and, thus, the close relations between the OCG and the Greek State, indicate that religion still benefits from a strong public visibility in Greece's political life. The current situation in Greece seems to contradict the secularization thesis. During the leadership of the late Archbishop Christodoulos, the OCG activated its public role both in Greek society and politics, and it deployed its symbolic power when it saw fit. Some argue that Greek Orthodoxy is still so all-encompassing that it does not permit a true differentiation between the secular and sacred spheres.[30] However, the new Archbishop Ieronymos II is a moderate religious leader, known for being open-minded and non-confrontational. But Church-State relations do not solely set Greece apart from other European states: Greece is somewhat similar to a number of countries, where there is no separation of Church and State and/or where religion and national identity are closely linked. Many European and non-European nations fit this category (for example, Poland, Ireland and Israel)—nations where religion and national identity often overlap.

Another element that seems to contradict the secularization argument in Greece is the "de-privatization of religion."[31] Orthodoxy still benefits from a strong visibility in the Greek State and the public consciousness. Archbishop Christodoulos aimed for the "de-privatization of Greek Orthodoxy" by rejecting the marginal public role of religious institutions in Europe[32] and by trying to breathe new life into public religion in Greece. This situation originated well before Archbishop Christodoulos assumed the public role of head of the OCG and promoted his vision of the Greek Orthodox Church. It remains to be seen if and how the leadership of Archbishop Ieronymos II, who is known to keep a low public profile, will reinforce the de-privatization of Greek Orthodoxy in social and political terms. Whether the secularization of social and political life in Greece will also eventually mean the privatization of religion is another question that remains to be answered in the future.

The National Identity Cards Issue

To illustrate these observations, it is useful to look at a case study, which allows us to observe more concretely the specific ambiguities in the process of secularization in Greece. The national Identity Cards conflict that erupted in 2000 divided Greek society over whether ID cards should continue to list the card holder's religious affiliation below his/her name. It was a debate that touched a sensitive issue between the Greek population and the Church of Greece and shook Church-State relations.[33]

On the one hand, the fact that the ID cards conflict even took place, and the strong role of the Church in the controversy, refutes the secularization arguments in the Greek case. On the other hand, the resolution of the conflict (the decision to finally drop religion from ID cards, see below) is evidence for the secularization thesis, as it suggests a step towards the privatization of religion. Both the mapping of public opinion in Greece, and an analysis of the arguments that shaped the ID cards debate, suggest that the applicability of the secularization thesis in the Greek situation remains ambiguous at best. The ID cards is not the only example of the challenges of applying the secularization thesis in Greece; but it illustrates this point quite well.

Most Greeks favored citing religious affiliation on ID cards. According to Greek public opinion polls conducted in 2000 and 2001 on average approximately three-quarters of those surveyed were in favor of including religion on ID cards and only one-quarter were against it.[34] This trend is also consistent with a sample of letters to the editor, drawn from seven Greek mainstream newspapers between 1993 and 2004 as part of an in-depth study of the ID cards crisis in Greece.[35] This seems to confirm a widely held perception of ID cards as highly symbolic and synonymous with Greek identity as a whole. It also confirms the de-privatization of religion thesis as it indicates a desire to keep religious affiliation public on a state document. It also suggests a refusal to confine religious identity to the private sphere.

Yet the positive views of the general public are in contrast to the critical stance of Greek mainstream news media, as indicated by two content analyses of the ID cards debate in the Greek daily press.[36] The discrepancy indicates a divergence between elites and opinion leaders (including journalists, academics, intellectuals and political figures in the elite press) and the majority of the general public in Greece (as expressed in public opinion polls and letters to the editor).

Three identifiable opinion groups emerged: the negative, the neutral and the positive. Their positions mirrored those on other broad issues, such as Church-State relations, Greek identity, globalization and European integration,[37] and are somewhat representative of the diversity of perspectives and views on what it means to be Greek.

Those groups that supported the inclusion of religious affiliation on ID cards chose their position for cultural and historical reasons, namely the existence of an inseparable link between Orthodoxy and Hellenism and, thus, between nation and religion. They argued that Orthodoxy is one of the few elements— and a distinctive one—holding Greek identity together, and they endorsed an all-embracing view of Helleno-Orthodoxy. Accordingly, they viewed the close Church/State relations in Greece as reflective of the historic links between nation and religion, and they supported an active public role for the Greek Church. Because of this, they consider the removal of religious affiliation from ID cards as an attempt to dilute national cohesion, and a first step towards a separation of Church and State, which they view as incompatible with the Greek social and political situation.[38] For this opinion group, the ID cards became an important symbol for preserving Orthodoxy as an integral part of Greek identity, and a contribution to Europe's overall spiritual void. They viewed Orthodox faith as a spiritual shield against the threat of homogenization, cultural absorption by the EU, and globalization.

The critics of religion on ID cards acknowledged the historic connection between Orthodoxy and Hellenism but restricted its scope to Greece's historic heritage, and, thus to the cultural and spiritual sphere. They distinguished between Hellenism and Orthodoxy, which they regarded as separate entities forming modern Greek identity, and they rejected the exclusivity of Orthodoxy in defining Greekness. Accordingly, they argued that mixing political and religious power eroded the State and the Church and democracy itself. Thus, they viewed the removal of religion from ID cards positively, as a first step towards the liberalization of Church/State relations. For this opinion group, Greece's Orthodox heritage should not become a defensive mechanism preventing European integration. They wanted Greece to be an active partner in Europe and viewed the European Union as multicultural and diverse, rather than a threat to national identities and cultures.

Groups with a neutral stance acknowledged the link between nation and religion as a strong element of national identity. However, they underlined the failure of Greek's political parties to address socio-economic issues, and criticized the Greek left's habit of dismissing the attachment of large segments of Greek society to Orthodoxy, thus underestimating the role of faith and tradition in an era of increased insecurity and accelerated change. They argued that because of the political parties' failure to address key problems, the Church's advancement of Orthodoxy has become a safety net against a variety of insecurities. For this opinion group, the ID cards controversy represented a wider confrontation between secular and religious ideologies. The OCG's position on the ID cards issue reflected its weakness and its fear that the EU might accelerate the secularization process in Greece and erode the importance of Orthodoxy in Greek society and public life.

The dividing lines on issues ranging from the ID cards, to Church-State relations, to Greek identity, to European integration, by no means reflect binary oppositions between religious anti-European traditionalists and secular pro-European modernizers. They are representative of the complex social, political, and ideological rifts within Greek society. There are rifts between various types of elites and segments of Greek society along degrees of secular and Orthodox orientation. They are indicative of contrasting dynamics in a society that is going through a concomitant process of selective secularization and de-privatization of religion collectively leading to an "identity crisis."

Concluding Remarks

A brief overview of structural characteristics of Orthodoxy—namely its decentralized structure, its flexibility and adaptability and its strong links between Church-Nation and Church-State—provides a general context in which to place the Greek case. It also offers the opportunity for some initial reflections on the relationship between Orthodoxy and the process of secularization, which needs further investigation. Greece has provided a specific case study that illustrates the complexities of the secularization thesis, particularly given the country's unique history and geopolitical location (situated between East and West). Greece is a modern European society with secularizing elements, but is also a society that maintains distinctive and, sometimes traditionalist, aspects. Greece is undergoing a process of secularization at its own pace and according to its own religious, political, social and historical profile. The OCG has clearly not been marginalized or excluded from public life in Greece. At a political level, the Greek state is not a secular state *per se*, as there is no separation of Church and State and the OCG is technically a department of the State. The OCG has political clout but the Greek case is not in any way an example of a theocracy, as the OCG has no *direct* influence on state affairs.

At a societal level, Greece cannot be considered as strictly secular, since religion is not confined to the private sphere. But it is also unclear whether Greece can be considered a profoundly religious society (as can other religiously homogeneous countries, such as Poland and Ireland, where individual religiosity, church attendance and membership are high). There is a somewhat superficial level of church attendance and religious practices in Greece, but a relatively deeper attachment to Orthodoxy, as a cultural, spiritual and historical point of reference in defining Greek identity. This is even the case among Greeks who have a minimal connection with the Church.

The concept of secularization is multifaceted and multi-dimensional. If we can speak about secularization in Greece, then we must distinguish among different or even contradictory processes of secularization occurring in different phases and spheres. In this, the Greek case is an example of "selective secularization." Orthodoxy is salient as a marker of self and collective definition. Moreover, the continued deployment of the Church as a defender of national identity suggests a diffused, but also very public, form of religion. Therefore, if there is "diffused" religion, according to which Orthodoxy is dispersed into a broad "cultural melting pot of Greekness losing its religious specificity,"[39] there is also "de-privatized" religion, putting into question a common assumption that religious institutions and actors in a secular 21st-century Europe are to be confined to the private sphere.

ENDNOTES

1.   Bryan Wilson, *Religion in Secular Society* (London: C.A Watts and Co., 1966): 14.

2.   Karel Dobbelaere, "Secularization: A Multi-Dimensional Concept," *Current Sociology* 29/2 (1981).

3.   Steve Bruce, "The Social Process of Secularization" in *Sociology of Religion*, edited by Richard Fenn (London: Blackwell Publishing, 2003): 248-263.

4.   Danièle Hervieu-Léger, *La Religion pour Mémoire* (Paris: Cerf., 1993); Grace Davie, *Religion in Modern Europe: A Memory Mutates* (Oxford: Oxford University Press, 2000).

5.   Jose Casanova, *Public Religions in the Modern World* (Chicago: University of Chicago Press, 1994).

6.   Grace Davie, *The Sociology of Religion* (London: Sage Publications, 2007): 65.

7.   Ibid., 211.

8.   Victor Roudometof, "Orthodoxy As Public Religion in Post 1989 Greece," in *Eastern Orthodoxy in a Global Age*, eds., V. Roudometof, A. Agadjanian and J. Pankhurstv (Walnut Creek, USA: Altamira Press, 2005): 84-108, 10.

9.   Jean Meyendorff, *The Orthodox Church: Its Past and Its Role in the World Today* (Crestwood, NY, USA: St. Vladimir's Seminary Press, 1981): 214.

10. Victor Roudometof, "Greek Orthodoxy, Territoriality and Globality: Religious Responses and Institutional Disputes," *Sociology of Religion* 69/1 (2008).

11. Roudometof, 2005: 7-8.

12. Ibid., 7-8.

13. Agadjanian and Roudometof, 2005: 18.

14. The intertwining of Greek identity with Orthodoxy was coined in the term "Helleno-Christianity" (*ellino-christianismos*), which was first used by Spiridon Zambelios in the 1850s.

15. *Constitution of Greece, Fifth Revisionary Parliament of the Hellenes, Basic Provisions:* http://www.hri.org/MFA/syntagma/ (accessed on May 23, 2007).

16. Theoni Stathopoulou, "Religiosity and Trust in Institutions: Emerging Trends in Greece and Europe," in *Politics and Religions*, edited by K. Zorbas (Athens: Papazisis Publishers, 2007): 161-187, 170-171 [in Greek]. (See below data on religiosity in Greece).

17. Since 1951 the Greek National Statistical Service has not included questions based on religious criteria in its national census and surveys. Additionally, estimates are difficult given the change in immigrant populations since the 1990s. Some useful sources include a 2002 report by Greek Helsinki Monitor-Minority Rights Group; the sources listed in the 2002 volume by Richard Clogg on Minorities in Greece; the 2004 U.S. State Department's International Religious Freedom Report; a 2004 article by M. Baldwin Edwards; and interviews with religious minority group representatives conducted in 2004 as part of a Leverhulme funded project on "The Religious Factor in the Construction of Europe: Greece, Orthodoxy and the EU" (Molokotos-Liederman, 2007a).

18. ESS (2002-03, 2004-05 and 2006-07).

19. ESS data, as quoted in Theoni Stathopoulou, "Religiosity and Trust in Institutions. Emerging Trends in Greece and Europe," in: *Politics and Religions*, edited by K. Zorbas (Athens: Papazisis Publishers, 2007):161-187 [in Greek].

20. Ibid.

21. Ibid.

22. Ibid.

23. Stathopoulou, 2007.

24. Known religions include Orthodoxy, Old Calendarists, Roman Catholicism, Islam, Judaism, Jehovah's Witnesses, and Adventists. There is no formal mechanism or process for a religious group to become recognized as a "known" religion in Greece; this status can usually be achieved after approval of a permit to operate a place of worship.

25. http://www.hri.org/MFA/syntagma/.

26. For an overview of the role of women in Greek Orthodoxy see Eleni Sotiriu, (forth-coming 2009) "The Traditional Modern: Rethinking the Position of Contemporary Greek Women to Orthodoxy," in *Orthodox Christianity in 21st Century Greece: The Role of Religion in Politics, Ethnicity and Culture*, eds. Makrides and Roudometof (Aldershot: Ashgate).

27. Ibid.

28. Ibid.

29. Effie Fokas and Nikos Kokosalakis, (2008) "Greece: Overview of the National Situation," unpublished report part of the "*Welfare and Values in Europe: Transitions related to Religion, Minorities and Gender*" (WaVE) project, 11.

30. Mappa, 1997, as cited in Roudometof, 2005: 92.

31. Roudometof, 2005: 95.

32. Ibid.

33. For more details and analyses on the ID cards conflict, see Vasilios Makrides "Between Normality and Tension: Assessing Church-State Relations in Greece in the Light of the Identity Cards Crisis," in *Religion, Staat und Konfliktkonstellationen im Orthodoxen Ost-und Sudosteuropa*, edited by Makrides, Peter Lang, (2005):137-178; Lina Molokotos-Liederman, "Looking at Religion and Greek National Identity from the Outside: The National Identity Cards Conflict through the Eyes of Greek Minorities," *Religion, State and Society* 35/2 (2007a); Lina Molokotos-Liederman, "The Greek ID Cards Controversy: A Case Study on Religion and National Identity in a Changing European Union," *Journal of Contemporary Religion* 22/2 (2007b); and Roudometof, 2005.

34. See Molokotos-Liederman, 2007b.

35. Ibid.

36. See Molokotos-Liederman, 2007b; and Nikos Demertzis, "Politics and Communication: Facets of the Secularisation of Orthodoxy," eds. T. Lipowats, N. Demertzis, and V. Georgiadou, *Religions and Politics in Modernity* (Athens: Kritiki, 2002): 142–82. [in Greek].

37. For a more detailed analysis, see Molokotos-Liederman, 2007b.

38. However, there were some individuals in this group that supported a separation of Church and State. For example, Father G. Metallinos (who was in favor of including religion on ID cards, and in 2000 brought the ID cards case to the European Court of Human Rights) had indicated his support of a strict separation of Church and State in order to stop political parties from using the Church for their own political interests.

39. Vasilios Makrides and Lina Molokotos-Liederman, "Orthodoxy in Greece today: an introduction," *Social Compass* 51/4 (December 2004): 468.

4. Turkey:
The Islamist-Secularist Divide

Binnaz Toprak

Party Politics

In April 2007 and the months that followed, there were several demonstrations, organized by NGOs, against what the demonstrators perceived as a serious threat to the secular foundations of the Turkish Republic. Directed against the policies of the ruling AKP government, and in particular its stand on the election of a new President, these demonstrations were a few weeks apart, the first held in the capital city of Ankara, the second held in Turkey's largest city, Istanbul, followed by others in various Anatolian towns. Although estimates differ over the number of demonstrators—between 300,000 and one million people attended the Istanbul meeting—everyone agreed that these demonstrations, with their endless rows of crowds, were the largest in the history of the Republic. In the aftermath of events, the foreign press reported that the demonstrations revealed the division of the country into "two Turkeys."

The issue at stake—the presidential election—indeed turned into a tug-of-war between two sides: those who are sensitive on the question of secularism, and the supporters or sympathizers of the AKP, a party whose leadership has roots in the Islamist politics of the 1980s and the 1990s. The AKP came to power following the 2002 elections, after Erbakan's Refah Party split and a new party was founded under the leadership of what was called the "reformists." Although the AKP leadership tried to distance itself from the old-style Islamist party of Erbakan and campaigned around a new program of consolidating democratic reforms and EU membership, and although it pursued policies that proved those commitments in the five years since its rule began, it was nevertheless unable to convince the secular public that its leadership and cadres had radically changed the position they had taken prior to 2002.

Much of this doubt stemmed from the lifestyle of its leadership and followers. In particular, the overwhelming presence of "veiled" or covered women among the wives of its leadership and ranks, and the conservative position of the party concerning moral issues such as adultery (which the party attempted to criminalize in 2005) was troubling. Additionally, there was a more recent concern that the party was gradually "Islamizing" the country by appointing its own sympathizers, who share similar lifestyles, to important positions of power. This debate started with the appointment of the new chairman of the Central Bank whose wife is covered, followed by the appointment of others with covered wives to major posts within the government bureaucracy. The last straw in this debate was the candidacy of the Foreign Minister, Abdullah Gul, for the office of the President of the Republic. Although Gul is a respected politician both within the country and among European Union circles, he had one drawback: a covered wife who, furthermore, had sued the Turkish state at the European Court of Human Rights over the headscarf issue, a lawsuit that she withdrew, however, when Gul became the Foreign Minister.

The events following his candidacy have clearly shown the division within the country. The first round of elections for the Presidency in the National Assembly was contested by the staunchly secular opposition party, the Republican People's Party, which took the case to the Constitutional Court; while the court was considering the objection, the military issued a "warning" through its internet site that the army was concerned about the "rising tide of Islamic fundamentalism" in the country and would not stand by; civilian demonstrations and protests spread from one city to another; the Constitutional Court finally agreed with the opposition's objections; and the electoral rounds for the Presidency ended, followed by the decision to hold early elections. At the root of this controversy lies a century-and-a-half-old debate about the role of Islam in Turkish society, a debate that has deeply divided the country in recent years. The beginning of this debate can be traced back to the mid-19th century, when the Ottoman Empire began to modernize. Much like other great empires that had fallen behind in the race for industrialization, the Ottomans too found the panacea in modeling their institutions on Western examples. While the late 19th century witnessed the acceleration of this debate between the Islamist and the Westernist camps, it came to a conclusion in 1923 with the establishment of the Republic by revolutionary cadres who were committed to a program of total Westernization. Repressing the Islamist opposition during the one-party years, the original founders of the Republic succeeded at both removing Islam from the public sphere and marginalizing people who wanted Islam to have a more visible role both socially and politically in Turkey. This, however, proved to be short-lived.

After the transition to democracy in 1946, the Islamist "underground" chose to play by the rules and advance its agenda through political party competition. From 1950 on, this started an intense political debate about the role of religion, which has continued to this day.

On the one side of this division are the "secularists." Traditionally, the "secularist camp" consisted of the judiciary, the bureaucracy, academia, the intelligentsia, mainstream business circles and the press, the army, and the urban educated middle- and upper-middle classes. Over time, however, positions have changed. In each of the categories cited above, there are those who are increasingly sympathetic to the rights claims of the Islamists, and who now see that the real problem lies in the radical, repressive understanding of the Republic towards questions of identity. On the other side are the "Islamists." These were, traditionally, mostly people of rural, small town, or lower middle class backgrounds who represented the Muslim periphery and who were not, or could not, be part of the "Westernized elite" of the center. They were excluded from the political power circles, social status groups, and (prestigious) intellectual circles of the Republic. At the same time, they benefited the least from an economic system that followed import-substitution policies until 1980, as a result of which connections with the government was the key for success in economic entrepreneurship. Like the "secularist" camp, their status has also changed over the years: they now occupy important positions of power within the state bureaucracy, the government, and the economy. Thanks to political Islam and its electoral successes, they now constitute what might be called a "counter-elite" of politicians, entrepreneurs, intelligentsia, journalists, university students, and middle- and upper-middle classes. What now divides these two groups are questions of lifestyle, and especially gender relations.[1]

The Status of Women

At the root of both the Republican and Islamist projects lies the issue of the status of women in society. For the Republican aim of being a part of what its founders considered to be the "civilized" West, the position of women in a Muslim society had to be radically altered. The restructuring of gender relations during the early Republican years was one of the most important achievements of Kemalism. Many of the legal and educational reforms during the early years of the Republic were designed to empower women so that they would have equal status in the public sphere. In this transformation, the Republic was indeed radical in its abolition of Islamic law and its creation of educational and career opportunities for women. As early as the 1930s, there were large numbers of women in hitherto male professions such as the judiciary, medicine, and academia. To this day, Turkey is the only country in the Muslim world whose legal system is progressive and gender blind in terms of women's rights. Consider, for example, a recent amendment to the Criminal Code that recognizes marital rape as a crime, a provision that exists in only few countries in the world, let alone in a Muslim-majority society. Although not all women benefited from these changes, more and more women do, as Turkey becomes economically more advanced and women are given greater opportunities for higher education and employment. The lifestyle that goes with this Republican project is one that includes mixed-gender public places, whether these are schools, restaurants, bars, discotheques, or beaches.

The Islamist project throughout the world, on the other hand, is largely based on the segregation of sexes. Although political Islam in Turkey should be distinguished from radical Islamist movements elsewhere, and although it does not argue for same-sex public life, its understanding of how the genders should be placed in the public sphere differs from the Republican understanding. This difference is most strikingly apparent in the covering of young girls and women, and in the segregation of sexes in, for example, separate swimming areas in resorts, private all-girls' or all-boys' high schools, as well as different codes of conduct (such as liquor bans on restaurants or hotels owned and frequented by the Islamist community). Although this system has not been imposed upon anyone, there have been several attempts to do so by Islamist municipalities or governments, although fierce opposition by the secularist groups has thus far prevented such policies from being implemented. Examples of attempts to impose such rules by various Islamist parties in government or in municipal administration abound: fining individuals who eat in public during Ramadan; separating city buses along gender lines; including pedagogically objectionable Islamist texts in primary and secondary school curricula; relocating restaurants and bars to the outskirts of cities; criminalizing adultery; categorizing punishment for rape on normative distinctions of the raped woman's status as married, divorced, or virginal; banning alcohol in municipal-owned recreational or art centers; and even to changing the internationally yellow city pavements to the Islamic green.

This controversy amounts to a "culture war" over morality and a debate over what constitutes moral behavior. Traditionally, the Islamic understanding of moral behavior is closely linked with an Islamic theology that considers the community life of believers to be under the control of religious law and religious principles. Historically, this Islamic insistence on social control has given the men of Islamic theology and jurisprudence the authority to decide the limits of moral life. Accordingly, both in historical examples of the Islamic state as well as its contemporary versions, the Islamic way of life has meant the ordering of gender relations on the basis of sex segregation. This has often led to the exclusion of women from the public sphere and their seclusion behind veiled bodies and/or gender-mixed public space, as in Afghanistan under the Taliban regime.

This Islamic idea that morality must be regulated by the state, through control of public and private lives, is in sharp contrast to the secular understanding, which sees morality as a matter of individual conscience and choice. It is here that the "culture war" between the Islamists and secularists in Turkey is most fiercely fought. At the center of both the Islamist and the secularist universe is the question of women's covering. This question needs to be addressed within the context of Turkey's history during the Ottoman period, when Muslim women were secluded from the public sphere and imperial decrees forbade colorful veils from thin material. We must be mindful, as well, of the collective memory of the secular public of both this past and the Republic's radical alteration of gender relations. For both women and men who have internalized the Republican understanding of gender equality, covered women are symbols of repressed sexuality and the gender-biased conception of public life. For the Islamists, on the other hand, it is a symbol of a Muslim way of life that the Republic destroyed. For both sides, the issue of women's covering is an issue of individual freedom of belief and democratic rights of choice. For the Islamists, women who cover do so because of their belief, a point that is repeatedly voiced by the covered women themselves (as reflected in academic studies based on surveys or interviews), who cite the individual's civil right to dress as she pleases. For the secularists, on the other hand, covering of women cannot be taken as a free choice since most young girls are forced to cover by families at an age when they cannot decide for themselves; nor can it be taken as a civil right when demands of covering are extended to the public sphere, such as in the case of university students or civil servants (universities and civil bodies being two places that must be organized on secular principles of religious impartiality, according to this view).

At issue, as well, is a certain resentment of established elites by people who were marginalized by the Republic and left out of political power circles and high status groups. These people now constitute what might be called a counter-elite. There were, of course, always large numbers of women who covered despite the Republic's discouragement of it. In a recent study based on survey research, Carkoglu and Toprak found that 64% of women in Turkey cover.[2] Unlike the fez, which was banned in the 1920s, the veil was never outlawed except for civil service women. Nevertheless, the elite strata of the Republic were quick to adopt Western style clothing; for women, this meant getting rid of the veil.

It was largely peasant women, women of traditional families in towns, or rural migrants in cities, who covered. Hence, among the social establishment in Turkey, the head cover has long been associated with rural or lower-class origins. However, with the growing success of Islamist parties since the mid-1970s—and especially in the last few decades—a new entrepreneurial class has emerged in Anatolian cities that come from conservative, religious families, and benefits from connections with government. Also emergent are new groups of people in major metropolitan cities who now occupy important positions of power within politics and the state bureaucracy. Thus, for the first time in the history of the Republic, there is a growing number of women who are economically well off, who no longer live in the margins of Turkish society, and who want to be educated. Although the head cover of peasant or lower-middle class women has never been seen as a major threat by the secularists, the fact that the new middle-class women in conservative milieus are wearing what in Turkey is called the "turban" has suddenly become a major concern. For example, the secularists often say that while they do not object to the covering of women per se (since they admit that traditional or peasant women always covered), nevertheless the "turban" is a new style that signifies a political statement by Islamist groups. Although the survey mentioned above found that women who said that they wear the "turban" were only 11% of the 64% who cover, and although there has been a drop of 10%—from 74% seven years ago—in the overall percentage of covered women, perceptions suggest otherwise. Many secularists will argue that "turbaned" women are "everywhere" and are increasing in numbers. Hence, the visibility of covered women in public spaces—spaces that were previously occupied only by the secular elite, or even in the international arena as wives of politicians—seems to be a major reason behind the resentment.

The old status groups, therefore, feel threatened by, and resent the emergence of, a new middle class that has adopted a lifestyle different from their own. They feel threatened because, as Turkey becomes more economically advanced, this new class (which has both economic means and access to political power circles) will eventually "Islamize" the country. And they feel resentful because the lifestyle of this new class resembles the lifestyle of the countryside that they always disparaged, a lifestyle that had previously been isolated in rural areas, small conservative towns, and the outskirts of cities. Psychologically, one can liken the change to the resentment of the old aristocracy in Europe as the new bourgeoisie, thanks to its economic wealth, began impinging on the same public space as the titled aristocracy. The Islamists, too, are aware that no matter how successful they are economically, politically, or intellectually, they will be excluded from the social circles of the old establishment. In fact, the Islamists will often remark that "they are the Blacks of Turkey" and that status groups are caste-like—reserved only for "White Turks."

Conflicting National Images

Also at issue in this conflict is what one might call an image problem. For the secularists who have internalized the Republic's vision of placing Turkey among the "civilized" nations of the West (what Turkish leftists in the 1960s and the 1970s derided as "a revolution of the wardrobe"), Turks who resemble, either in dress or lifestyle, the "backward, reactionary Muslims" of the *ancien regime*—or the rest of the Muslim world—are an embarrassment, and will mar Turkey's image in the international arena. The gaze here is outward: what Western *foreigners* will think of Turkey when, for example, Prime Minister Erdogan's covered wife stands side by side with Jordan's queen or with the wives of officials from the EU countries, or when Western journals print pictures of covered women or demonstrations by Islamist crowds, or when foreign tourists take pictures of poor neighborhoods. One often hears complaints that "this is not representative of Turkey." There is a certain self-conscious and at times defensive attitude towards Western foreigners, as if their judgment of Turks and Turkey automatically involves scrutiny. In short, in the collective psyche of the secular Turks, there is a certain schizophrenia towards the Western world involving both admiration and suspicion. This schizophrenic attitude operates in several arenas: secularists' historical consciousness; the fact that the Republic called on them to forget the past (it even changed the national alphabet and vocabulary so that new generations would have no access to that past); the fact that Turkey's official historiography equated the Islamic civilization of the Ottomans with obscurantism; the idea that the Republic represents an enlightened world based on progress; and, finally, the notion that Western civilization offers the only model for a modern, enlightened society.

The debate goes back to the late 19th and early 20th centuries, and pits two schools of thought against one another: the Islamists' and the Westernists'. Whereas the Westernists favored adopting Western institutions and civilization along with technology and industry, the Islamists preferred only the latter and argued that Islamic civilization and culture were superior to that of the West. The Republic was established by the Westernists, and the reforms undertaken during its formative years were designed to replace Islamic civilization with Western civilization. Hence, although the distinction between Islam and the West is no longer valid, and fails to describe Turkish culture today, public visibility of an Islamic way of life, most apparent in forms of dress, triggers fears among secularists of a return to the Islamic past. On the other hand, from the perspective of the Islamists, the

Republic symbolizes the defeat of their 19th-century stand *vis-a-vis* civilization versus technology and industry. Although the various Islamist parties have, since the 1970s, been keen on industrial development and technological transfer, and have acquiesced to the idea of working within a democratic system, their vision of a Muslim society remains essentially unchanged. The ruling AKP, for example, subscribes to political and economic liberalism. It has committed itself to Turkey's entry into the European Union, has undertaken important reforms to consolidate democracy, and has followed a growth-oriented-free-market economic policy. When it comes to social issues, however, it is conservative, and both its leaders and followers adhere to a lifestyle that conforms to Islamic conceptions of social life. Hence, whereas secularists see the project of development as including cultural change, the Islamists see it as mostly confined to the economic and political spheres. This has meant two different interpretations of how Turkey should situate itself in the international arena. The secularists want to see Turkey transformed so that it resembles any other country in the West. In this conception, Islam is not necessarily unimportant in people's lives; it is just kept private. The Islamists, on the other hand, would like to see Turkey transformed economically and politically, but they want it to remain socially Islamic, and—more encompassingly—Islamic in its worldview.

Public Opinion

In the study by Carkoglu and Toprak mentioned above, this division of the country into two different publics was clearly an important indicator of differences of opinion on social and political issues. There is one-third of the population which is urban, better educated, has higher income and wealth, is less religious, has a self-perception of someone on the Left, sees Islamic fundamentalism to be on the rise and is concerned about it—versus two-thirds of the nation which is predominantly urban or small town, is less educated, has less income and wealth, is more religious, and has the self-perception of someone on the Right. On every single question, cross tabulations of the data showed that the one-third subscribes to more liberal-democratic views, whereas the two-thirds is more conservative and is less concerned with minority rights.

However, it also seems that this "culture war" is taking place at the level of elites, whether they be the political or intellectual elites of each "camp." That is, unlike the impression one gets by following public intellectual debates, ordinary citizens do not seem very concerned with issues of culture. Perhaps, like publics everywhere, especially publics in less developed countries that do not have large groups of "post-industrial" citizens, they are more interested in questions related to the economy and their own well-being. Many studies, based on surveys, have shown that when asked to point out the major problem in Turkey, a very high percentage of the population picks economic issues such as inflation, high standard of living, etc. Although the headscarf ban for university students has occupied the public agenda for over two decades, and although 75% of the public favors lifting the ban, various surveys show that only 1%-2% of the Turkish population says the headscarf issue is among the most important problems that Turkey faces. In general, the survey by Carkoglu and Toprak in 2006,[3] along with their earlier survey in 1999, revealed that the majority of Turkish citizens believes that the Republican reforms have led to progress; that support for an Islamic state based on Islamic law is extremely low; that Islamic terrorism is condemned; that believers in Islam do not necessarily have to be practicing Muslims; that tolerant views towards people with different life styles are commonly held; and that there is a shared social life between secularists and Islamists. However, the surveys also revealed that this seeming toleration is limited, and that it does not extend to groups who are in the minority, whether these be minority Muslim sects, non-Muslims, different ethnic groups, or people with different sexual preferences. Within this context, the surveys also showed that the understanding of a rights-based public life finds little support in Turkey and that there is a clear division between the "us" and "them," the "us" signifying Muslim-Sunni-Turk, the "them" pointing to Alevi-non-Muslim-Kurd.

In conclusion, it can be argued that after over eighty years of Republican secularism and over half a century of democratic rule, both the secularists and the Islamists are learning how to share the same public space—although this learning process is still characterized by a lack of consensus caused by political exploitation of fear, on the one side, and politicization of moral issues, on the other. Yet, compared to the early years of the Republic, when secularism was enforced by the state elite on the rest of the rural population, and when those who followed an Islamic way of life were completely marginalized, the Islamists today have more freedom to integrate into the power and status groups of Turkish society. Moreover, the political struggle between the two sides within a secular-democratic framework has resulted in greater tolerance towards each other. Nevertheless, the cultural divisions continue to occupy a primary place in Turkish politics, and a meaningful *modus vivendi* likely depends on Turkey's further democratization and economic growth.

ENDNOTES

1.   Binnaz Toprak, *Islam and Political Development in Turkey* (Leiden: E.J. Brill, 1981) and Binnaz Toprak, "Islam and Democracy in Turkey," *Turkish Studies* 2 (June 2005): 167-186.

2.   Ali Çarkoğlu and Binnaz Toprak, *Türkiye'de Din, Toplum ve Siyaset (Religion, Society and Politics in Turkey)* (Istanbul: TESEV Yayınları, 2000).

3.   Ali Çarkoğlu and Binnaz Toprak, *Religion, Society and Politics in a Changing Turkey*, (Istanbul: TESEV, 2007).

5. Lebanon: Confessionalism and the Crisis of Democracy

Hassan Krayem

This paper addresses the questions of why and how the process of state building in Lebanon failed, and to what extent this failure can be attributed to its confessional, consociational model of democracy, the role of the ruling elite, or external factors. It also addresses the prospects for an alternative constitutional model and for the creation of a secular democratic state.

The Formation of the Lebanese Political System

The political system in Lebanon has always been characterized by a high degree of freedom of expression. This freedom first justified Lebanon's existence as a state and later its continuing independence. However, the multi-confessional social structure on which it is based produced an unstable system of governance and a deficient democracy. In fact, Lebanon's confessional state is characterized by the absence of equal opportunity, a lack of political and administrative accountability, and rigid political institutions, which, periodically, generate disagreements. In addition, the Lebanese political system suffers from a lack of cohesion, due to a weak national identity and poor social integration, whether in terms of its citizens, regions, confessional communities, or social classes.

Lebanon has a confessional political system based on a formula which allocates political and administrative functions to the major sects. Consequently, the Lebanese case is interesting and distinct, as well as conflicted. France created present-day Lebanon on September 1, 1920. The establishment by the League of Nations of a French Mandate over the territories of Lebanon and Syria followed the collapse of the Ottoman Empire in the First World War. Since 1920, modern Lebanon has been characterized continuously by domestic confessional conflict.

Lebanon's Muslims and Syria opposed the establishment of Greater Lebanon from the very start. At the same time, others in the region have laid claim to part or all of its territory. Both factors have added to the country's political instability.

The newly formed Lebanon continued the Ottoman's confessional Millet tradition. According to the 1932 census—the last taken in Lebanon—Christians constituted a slight majority (51%) over Muslims (49%). France recognized the diversity of the confessional communities from the start and structured political representation accordingly.

In 1943, the National Pact led to Lebanon's independence, but it also rigidly institutionalized the confessional system. The pact was an unwritten agreement between the president, Bishara al-Khuri, and the prime minister, Riad al-Sulh. Khuri and Sulh agreed to several general principles: First, they agreed to view Lebanon as a neutral, independent, and sovereign entity having an Arab character. Second, they pledged that Lebanon would not seek unity with Syria and the Arab world, nor special ties with France in particular or the West in general. In effect, the latter aspect led many observers to label the pact as the "double negation agreement." Third, the pact established a confessional quota providing for representation of Christians and Muslims in a six-to-five ratio throughout government and public posts. Furthermore, the offices of President, Prime Minister, and Speaker of Parliament were assigned to the Maronite, Sunni, and Shia communities respectively.[1] This confessional ratio, based on the 1932 census, assigned the dominant role to the Maronite sect.

Shehabism

This particular distribution of power faced challenges in subsequent years because of changes in the internal and regional balance of forces. In 1958, a short civil war broke out, lasted for six months, and caused the death of several thousand people.[2] On July 15, 1958, American Marines intervened to end the crisis, though initially the conflict escalated. On July 31, after a compromise deal between the U.S. and the United Arab Republic, the army commander, General Fouad Shehab, was elected president. Shehab had kept the army neutral in the crisis and thus gained the approval of most parties. Politically, Lebanon's power-balancing approach was reaffirmed after the 1958 crisis.

President Shehab introduced a number of administrative and political reforms based on his conviction that Lebanon's problems were caused by regional, confessional, communal, and socio-economic inequalities. He began reforming the civil service as well as social policy. Lebanon's monetary laws were also introduced during Shehab's mandate, as was the Central Bank. During the period of Shehabism (between 1958-1970) primary education, primary health care, and essential social services expanded. The Shehabist statist policies sought to build a modern state, capable of managing development and providing equitable distribution. This, it was hoped, would lead to national and social integration. This attempt to reform the Lebanese system from within ultimately failed. The regime not only mobilized many enemies against its efforts, but also failed to build a strong social base in support of its policies. Shehabism depended heavily on an expanded state bureaucracy and the army, in particular the military intelligence services (the Deuxieme Bureau).

Shehabism was further weakened when regional conditions began changing in the late 1960s. The 1967 Arab-Israeli war engendered regional polarization and greater radicalization of the Palestinian resistance movement. The results of the parliamentary elections of 1968 and the presidential election of 1970 reflected this divide. Shehabist candidates lost ground in the parliamentary elections, while Sulayman Franjiyyah, supported by traditional, conservative forces, defeated Elias Sarkis, a Shehab ally, in the presidential election.

Descent into Civil War

In the 1970s, the tension inherent to the Lebanese system and multiple regional developments contributed to the breakdown of government authority and the outbreak of the civil war in 1975.[3] The cause of the war was neither exclusively internal nor exclusively external.[4]

Internally, socio-political polarization among the Lebanese population increased.[5] There was growing migration of the rural population to Beirut, particularly into poor neighborhoods around the capital, where they confronted rising inflation and a high cost of living. Socio-political tensions fueled rural uprisings and workers' strikes, and this helped provoke the emergence of a militant student protest movement.[6]

The polarization of the public into two broad camps, and around two different contending political programs, intensified the crisis in the political system. Kamal Junblatt formed and led a self-proclaimed "democratic, progressive, and non-sectarian" front, which later allied itself with the Palestinians. The conservative forces, led by the predominantly Christian Kata'ib (Phalange) Party, formed another block called the Lebanese Front. The presence of the Palestinian resistance movement and the support it enjoyed from wide segments of the Lebanese population complicated the conflict further. The vulnerable political system could not withstand the pressure, and internal compromise became harder to achieve. In the spring of 1975 street clashes developed into full-scale war, which lasted, in various manifestations, for 15 years.

Inter-Lebanese battles during the civil war years, in the Aley and Shouf mountain areas in 1983, in Beirut in 1976-1984, and in villages east of Sidon in 1985—increased the sectarian character of the Lebanese conflict. Confessional segregation reached its peak, and confessionally based militias ruled their various regions in closed and semi-closed enclaves.

A state of political paralysis prevailed in Lebanon between 1986 and the end of President Gemayel's term on September 23, 1988. The inability to elect a successor at the end of the president's term created a political vacuum, which threatened to lead to partition. Gemayel appointed an interim cabinet headed by the Army commander, Michel Aoun, but the cabinet's authority was only accepted in predominantly Christian areas. Executive power was thus split between Aoun's military and Hoss's civilian government. The two governments stood against each other, both claiming exclusive legitimacy. On March 14, 1989, Aoun and army troops under his command began a self-declared "War of Liberation," ostensibly against all foreign forces. In reality, the effort was directed exclusively against the Syrians. This war had devastating consequences. Instead of curtailing the Syrian presence in Lebanon, it provoked an increase in Syrian forces to some 40,000 troops. On January 30, 1990, another war broke out, this time between Aoun's troops and the Lebanese Forces militia led by Samir Geagea. This intra-Maronite war was militarily inconclusive yet politically decisive because it eroded the capacities of both forces to reject or alter the Ta'if Agreement that had been reached in Saudi Arabia and was in the process of implementation.[7]

The 1990 Ta'if Agreement

In 1989, 62 Lebanese deputies—those still alive from the 99 originally elected in 1972—met in the city of Ta'if in Saudi Arabia to discuss national reconciliation. The National Accord Document, or the Ta'if Agreement as it came to be known, was the outcome of a process of reconciliation between the Lebanese, with the effective participation of the Syrians, other Arab states, and the international community.[8]

The Ta'if Agreement, which was a compromise between Lebanese deputies, and leaders of political parties, tackled many essential issues pertaining to the structure of the political system and to the sovereignty of the Lebanese state. Indeed, the two issues were interrelated. The mechanism for regaining sovereignty was preceded by an affirmation of the identity and unity of Lebanon. It was also preceded by domestic political, administrative, and other reforms. The essence of this compromise was acceptance of Ta'if as a package deal. It constituted the right formula to end the war internally. However, it also demanded acceptance of incomplete sovereignty for a considerable period of time.[9] This resulted from the inter-relationship between the Syrian presence in Lebanon and the Arab-Israeli negotiations that started in Madrid in 1991, which thus linked the Lebanese and Syrian tracks in the negotiations. However, this formula allowed Lebanon to regain a minimal degree of stability in order to rebuild its institutions, revive its economy, and reinforce its capacity to face changing regional and international conditions.

The 1990 Ta'if Agreement and the Reproduction of the Lebanese System

Any agreement or compromise is a synthesis of conflicting interests and ideas. As such, on one level Ta'if constituted an effective deal that provided the basic mechanism for ending the civil war. However, at another level, it was perhaps not the optimal arrangement for launching the process of rebuilding a more stable political system. Ta'if stated that the abolition of political sectarianism constituted a basic national goal to be achieved according to a gradual scheme. It introduced 31 constitutional amendments, which were approved by the Lebanese Parliament on August 21, 1990. The reforms did not fundamentally alter the political structure, which is still predicated on political sectarianism. The changes aimed at creating a new and more equitable confessional system. The agreement did state that the abolition of confessionalism was a national goal; however no specific deadline or timetable was set for its implementation. Indeed, a confessional equilibrium in representation was formalized in the post-Ta'if constitution. It is worth noting that since 1943 political confessionalism has been considered a temporary arrangement that should be expunged whenever possible.

The political reforms proposed by Ta'if were marked by a powerful contradiction. This was evident in the gap between the sectarianism the agreement perpetuated and the democratic aspirations it gave voice to for a modern, secular, non-confessional, and stable Lebanon. The new confessional formula offered up by Ta'if was based on reducing the prerogatives of the President of the Republic and transferring executive authority to the Council of Ministers, as a collegial body. According to Article 17 of the post-Ta'if constitution, "Executive power shall be entrusted in the Council of Ministers, and the Council shall exercise it in accordance with conditions laid down in this constitution." The original article stated "Executive power shall be entrusted to the President of the Republic who shall exercise it assisted by the Ministers in accordance with conditions laid down in this constitution."

Ta'if also allowed for equitable participation of Christians and Muslims in the cabinet. This parity was also evident in the distribution of seats in Parliament and in appointments to Grade One civil service posts and other public positions. As mentioned earlier, this new distribution of power was an expression of a balanced confessional formula, and the elimination of confessionalism was relegated to an unspecified future. In a transitional phase, according to Article 95 of the Lebanese Constitution, confessional parity is to predominate.

This unstable formula, based on the impossible and unattainable condition of a confessional balance, leaves the door open to a renewal of conflict, just as the 1943 formula did, and does not allow for the revival of a stable political system, one that is urgently needed to fulfill such essential tasks as the reconstruction of the country's infrastructure, the revitalization of the economy, and the rebuilding and development of public and private institutions. Still, the Ta'if Agreement was implemented in a way different from what was originally intended. It led to an increase in Syrian influence and a lack of balanced domestic representation in Parliament and the Council of Ministers. The imbalance in confessional representation is political, however, since in proportional terms Christians and Muslims are represented in Parliament evenly. Politically, however, the Syrian management of Lebanese affairs had imposed artificial representation of some political forces.

In the first two years of the agreement's implementation, it was obvious that the Lebanese demanded reconstruction and the state's revival, but disagreed on which model should be adopted. Would Lebanon be rebuilt according to the traditional liberal economic model, which existed before the war? Or would it seek to revive the strong Shehabist state? Or would a new model that would provide for both a sharing and a concentration of power be adopted?[10]

A sectarian balance replaced the hegemony of one sect, and power became centralized, in contrast to the previous system that was characterized by a concentration of power in the hands of the President, but with a practical distribution of power between traditional leaders, often from peripheral areas, who formed a dominant class ruling the central government. However, the most alarming consequence of Ta'if's implementation was the intensification of confessional conflict and divisions leading to political and administrative paralysis.

After the election of General Emile Lahoud to the presidency in October 1998, a different system was applied with a clear separation of powers, but also an obvious increase in the power of the President and the military. The President's relations with the governments of Prime Minister Rafik Hariri were characterized by continuous conflicts indicating how delicate and difficult it was to produce a stable formula of governance. The post-Ta'if state has not yet been able to establish a clear and relatively stable formula to rule, govern, and exercise authority. One can also note the lack of new socio-political forces and leaderships fully committed to implementing the agreement and moving the nation towards a more democratic system.

The 2000-2007 Political Crisis

The 2000 parliamentary elections modified the political landscape by polarizing the political spectrum between those loyal to the President and an opposition gravitating around Hariri and Walid Junblatt. This opposition emerged the big winner from the election, allowing the return of Hariri as Prime Minister, only this time in a system that balanced off the President and Prime Minister. Early signs pointed to a conflicting, unstable and problematic arrangement.

Over the next four years, the political process remained deadlocked, held in stalemate by the ongoing power struggle between Lebanon's two leading political figures—the Prime Minister, Rafiq al-Hariri, and President Emile Lahoud. The political stalemate ended when the president's term came to an end in September of 2004. Constitutionally, Mr. Lahoud was required to stand down, since the president is limited to one six-year term. Mr. Lahoud, however, actively campaigned to have his period in office extended—a development that would mark a definitive victory for him over the Prime Minister, and that was therefore strongly opposed by Mr. Hariri and his allies. In 2004, the final decision on extending the presidential mandate beyond the constitutional maximum was made by Syria, by a rather sudden move in the last week of August. To initiate the necessary moves to extend the term of Lebanese President Emile Lahoud by another three years the Syrian President started a process of cosmetic consultations with some selected Lebanese politicians, which was ended by an order to the Speaker of the Parliament and to the Prime Minister to work for speedy implementation of the term extension. This decision came against a backdrop of strong international and internal opposition. International effort to de-legitimize the ongoing extension was headed by the United States, France and other European countries.

Mr. Lahoud's term was extended, and Mr. Hariri was removed from office as he decided not to accept the nomination and to wait for the general election due in the spring of 2005. The extension of Lahoud's term and, more important, the insensitive manner in which it was handled provoked considerable anger. It broadened and deepened support for the Christian-led, anti-Syrian opposition movement to include figures such as the Druze leader, Walid Jumblatt. He also joined other opposition figures in calling vigorously for a "rebalancing" of ties with Syria, pushing Mr. Lahoud on to the defensive. The loose opposition alliance promised to contest the May elections fiercely, seeking to turn the poll into a public referendum on the Syrian-backed order that governed from Beirut.

On February 14, 2005, a massive explosion killed Rafik Hariri and 16 others casting an instant, stunned silence across Lebanon. The mourning for the former Prime Minister quickly became as much a show of national protest and unity as of grief. A demonstration in Beirut on March 14, 2005, brought more than one million people into the streets, almost a third of the country's population. This was a national rejection of impunity for political assassinations, a significant development in a country whose history is scarred by unpunished assassinations. Street opinion in Beirut blamed Syria for his death. The popular anger against Syria and its stooges reinvigorated Lebanon's opposition. An emerging alliance of former foes from across the sectarian spectrum used the tragedy as an opportunity to push its agenda.

On top of the pressure from the Lebanese, outside pressure on Syria's President Bashar Al-Asad intensified. The United States imposed some mild sanctions—and threatened more—under its Syria Accountability and Lebanese Sovereignty Restoration Act. Ending the Syrian occupation is one of the few regional policies on which America and France were able to co-operate and they were the prime movers in September 2006 of U.N. Security Council Resolution 1559, which ordered Syrian forces to quit Lebanon.

The restoration of Lebanese sovereignty would be a wonderful thing. However, Resolution 1559 contains a second, less remarked-upon demand. This calls for the disarming of all Lebanon's private militias, only one of which—Hezbollah, "Party of God"—is in fact still under arms. This has created an internal problem for Lebanon, a problem that is connecting Lebanon to its contradictory future options: a free Lebanon from Syrian control with a united strong state and society or a free Lebanon but a divided society and a weak state.

In the spring of 2005, the Syrian troop withdrawal from Lebanon and the Lebanese parliamentary elections were presented abroad as a turning point for Lebanese democratic development. In reality, the change was more limited as the old problems of Lebanese politics persisted. What was impressive about the events in Lebanon during 2004-2006 was the cohesiveness and political polarization between two broad camps of loyalists and opposition forces. This is notable, especially in a society with a history of ethnic and religious strife. The so-called red and white revolution was marching under one banner: the Lebanese flag. But its challenge is to remain unified in its struggle and not collapse under parochial interests. The broad coalition of the opposition included important new social forces that were entering the political arena for the first time in great numbers and with a clear vision. These groups included the youth, women's organizations, middle class and professional associations, and the business community. They were not only determined to push for this immediate transition towards a free and independent political system but were also aware of the difficult agenda awaiting them after parliamentary elections. In reality the challenges at the forefront range from controlling budget deficit, managing national debt, and building an effective and efficient public administration and a more stable political system based on national reconciliation, greater participation and institutional development.

The parliamentary elections in June 2005 led to the triumph of the opposition and the forming of a new government led by the Coalition of 14 March and support of more than 71 deputies out of 128 in the Lebanese parliament. These elections were also characterized by a level of genuine competition that had not been seen in 30 years.

However, the momentum for change created by the Syrian withdrawal and parliamentary elections rapidly dissipated, and the old divides in Lebanese politics and society resurfaced. The July 2006 Israeli-Lebanon war and the intensive polarization it has created, led to yet another political confrontation between the government supported by the March 14 coalition, and the Hezbollah-led opposition. This confirmed that the political game continues to be played by the old sectarian rules. Lebanon today is suffering from an increasingly divided society and growing political crisis. In addition, its neighbors still tend to treat Lebanon as an arena for regional conflict. External powers promote and support the national and democratic aspirations of the Lebanese people partly because these are directed against another power: Syria.

Conclusion

The compound nature of politics in Lebanon has produced a long and well established legacy of freedom and open institutions. Syria ruled Lebanon in an autocratic way and so was rejected and resented by many Lebanese who were not used to authoritarianism. Fortunately, the Lebanese people have not embraced authoritarianism regardless of the tremendous pressure of the culture of war and three decades under the special style of Syrian hegemony.

However, the dilemma and continuing crises of the post-Taif Agreement state in Lebanon result from the fact that a national and non-sectarian form of representation cannot be carried out by sectarian forces, within a sectarian structure, and under a system which is based on a confessional power-sharing formula. Change requires new forces and a different political and civic culture. The deficient democracy in Lebanon needs to be addressed through a gradual program of transcending political confessionalism and the adoption of reforms that lead towards a secular state system.

ENDNOTES

1. For further details on the National Pact, see Farid El-Khazen, "The Communal Pact of National Identities: The Making and Politics of the National Pact," in *Papers on Lebanon # 12*. (Oxford: Center for Lebanese Studies, 1991), pp. 5-17; Tabitha Petran, *The Struggle Over Lebanon* (New York: Monthly Review Press, 1976), p. 33; and Roger Owen, "The Political Economy of Grand Liban, 1920-70," in *Essays on the Crisis in Lebanon*, edited by Roger Owen. (London: Ithaca Press, 1976), p. 27.

2. For 1958 crisis, see Fahim Qubain, *Crisis in Lebanon* (Washington, D.C.: The Middle East Institute, 1961).

3. See Walid Khalidi, *Conflict and Violence in Lebanon: Confrontation in the Middle East* (Cambridge: Harvard University, 1979).

4. See Tabitha Petran, *op. cit.,* ch. 5.

5. See Kamal Salibi, *Crossroads to Civil War: Lebanon 1958-1976,* (New York: Caravan Books, 1976).

6. Petran, 1987, *op. cit.*, pp. 130-33.

7. Annie Laurent, "A War Between Brothers: The Army-Lebanese Forces Showdown in East Beirut," *Beirut Review 1*, 1 (Spring 1991): pp. 88-101.

8. For a full text of the Tai'f Agreement, see *Beirut Review*, 1991, *op. cit.*, pp. 119-172.

9. Richard Norton, "Lebanon after Tai'f: Is the Civil War Over?" *Middle East Journal*, v. 45, #3, (1991): p. 466.

10. Michael Hudson, "The Problem of Authoritative Power in Lebanese Politics: Why Consociationalism Failed," in eds. Shehadi and Mills, 1998, *op. cit.*, p. 237.

6. Israel:
The Challenge of a Democratic and Jewish State

Asher Arian

Introduction

U pon his election as Israel's president in June 2007, Shimon Peres, twice prime minister of Israel, Nobel laureate for peace, former head of the Socialist International, and former head of Israel's Labor Party, did two things. First, he went to the Western Wall of the Temple in the Old City of Jerusalem, Judaism's holiest site, and second, he paid a call to Rabbi Ovadia Yosef, the spiritual head of Shas, one of Israel's non-Zionist, ultra-Orthodox parties. The contrasts in this story illuminate the anomalies of religion in Israeli public life. Where are the boundaries? What is Jewish? What is religious behavior? Can one survive politically without paying homage to religious leaders and espousing religious sentiments? What could the word secular mean in that type of context: Non-religious? Anti-religious? Impervious to religion? Without religion?

Israel is a Jewish and democratic state. Seventy-six percent of Israel's population of 7.2 million is Jewish, 20% is Arab (mostly Muslim, some Christians), and the rest are mostly non-Jewish immigrants from the former Soviet Union or those whose Jewish status is still undetermined by the authorities. These facts are enough to perplex an entire nation. The issue of religion—and its role and definition in Israel today—is complicated by the various meanings of Jewishness. Judaism may be considered a religion; a nationality; a culture; or all of these, and more. For Orthodox Jews, religion and nationality are one and the same. Religious observance and belief, while desirable, are, however, not essential for membership in the community.[1] In short: Who is a Jew? What is an Israeli? What is the role of religion? What is the basis of citizenship? These ambiguities represent only some of Israel's problems.

Israel is not a theocracy; it is a modern parliamentary regime that has granted decision-making power, on certain aspects of public and private life, to religious authorities. For the Jewish population, it is the Orthodox rabbinate whose interpretations are binding; for members of other religions in Israel[2]—Muslim, Druze, and almost a dozen Christian denominations—it is the respective religious authorities of those communities. Marriages performed by Conservative or Reform rabbis are not acceptable, nor are mixed marriages. However, couples married abroad can register their marriage.

Religion is a potent issue in Israeli politics: religious parties are willing to support policies of the non-religious in order to achieve cherished goals. This has led to a series of arrangements generally referred to as the status quo. It is hardly static, however, and both sides try to gain advantage whenever possible. The National Religious Party has succeeded, over the years, in winning support for legislation to institutionalize religious arrangements, but the Party lost its advantage when ultra-Orthodox, non-Zionist parties won control of many institutions. The result—a legalization of structures that supported the worldview of religious groups, enhancing their budgets, power, and patronage—came as a blow to secular parties in Israel.

Knesset legislation that addresses religious matters includes the following:

1. The Law of Return (1950) assuring that every Jew has a right to immigrate to Israel.
2. The law (1951) making the Jewish Sabbath an official day of rest for Jews and requiring a permit to employ a Jew on the Sabbath.
3. The Law of Citizenship (1952) granting citizenship to every Jewish immigrant, his or her spouse, and their children and grandchildren.
4. The 1953 law granting the Orthodox rabbinical courts sole jurisdiction over marriage and divorce among Jews.
5. The 1962 law prohibiting pig raising in Israel except in areas with a concentrated Christian population.
6. The law (1986) prohibiting Jews from displaying leavened food for sale during Passover.
7. The law (1990) allowing local authorities to regulate whether enterprises involved in entertainment (movies and theaters) should be allowed to operate on the Sabbath and holy days.

Collective Identity

Almost all Israeli Jews agree that Israel should be a Jewish state. When asked, in a 2003 survey,[3] what "a Jewish state" meant, half replied to the open-ended question with statements such as: a state with a Jewish majority; a Zionist state; a state with Jewish symbols; and a state that stresses Jewish history, culture, and values. A little more than a third of respondents gave a "religious" answer, such as religious observance or a Jewish theocracy; and 7% offered an anti-religious interpretation.[4] With a distribution like that, it is not surprising that the issue of separation of religion and state is contentious and emotional.

The call to separate religion and state has never had wide appeal, although it has been discussed. Before the 1992 elections, Avraham Burg won approval in the Labor Party central committee for a resolution calling for the separation of synagogue and state. Party leaders, however, were so concerned that the resolution would hinder future coalition-building plans with the religious parties that they called a special session to overturn the decision at the next meeting. In a 2007 survey,[5] 44% of Israelis supported separating religion from the state; 56% opposed it.

Questions regarding personal religious behavior, on the one hand, and the role of religion in public life, generate very different responses (see Figure 6-1). Despite enormous change in other spheres of Israeli life, the proportion of respondents who observe "all" or "most" of Jewish religious law is amazingly stable at 25-30%; the other responses provided were "some" and "none." These numbers are consistent with estimates that about a quarter of Israeli Jews are observant in an Orthodox sense or even beyond that (including 6-10% haredi, or ultra-Orthodox); that about 40% are determinedly secular; and that the rest are somewhere between those poles.

Figure 6-1
Self-Reported Religious Observance and Role of Religion in Public Life

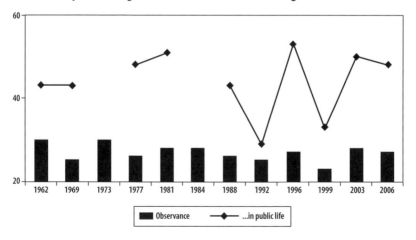

Religiosity and policy preferences aside, feelings of collective identity are important to Israelis. For most Jews in Israel there is no contradiction between being Israeli and being Jewish. Israel is "Jewish" in the sense that its language is Hebrew, its school curriculum is heavily laced with Jewish history and the Bible, and its holy days are Jewish in origin and set according to the Hebrew calendar (although important events such as summer vacation, payday, and even the date when winter uniforms are distributed in the army are determined by the Gregorian calendar). An overwhelming majority of Jews in Israel—93%, in the 2007 survey—selected either "Jewish" or "Israeli" as their prime identity when given four identities to rank: Jewish, Israeli, ethnic classification (Ashkenazi or Sephardi), and religion (observant or secular).

Almost 40% of respondents chose "Jewish" and "Israeli" as both first and second choices. Ethnic and religious observance identities were chosen far less often. While the notion of Israel as a Jewish state provides a common denominator for most Israeli Jews and secular nationalism is rife with religious symbolism, the meaning assigned to the Jewish state is unstable and varies greatly across groups. This lack of consensus provides the basis for a struggle between cultures, often defined in oppositional terms: religious vs. secular, primordial vs. civil, Jewishness vs. Israeli-ness, or *Eretz Israel* (Land of Israel) vs. the state of Israel. Religion has become intertwined with nationalism—especially since 1967, when religious authorities advocated keeping the territories taken in the 1967 war, thus establishing the link between the people, their history, God, and the land. Religion and nationalism have since become linked in the public consciousness and in coalition politics; for this, the settlement movement Gush Emunim and the National Religious Party deserve much of the credit. Fueled by the growing strength of the ultra-Orthodox, non-Zionist haredi camp, and especially the Shas party, the "internal" identity schisms only sharpened. Moreover, the overlap between internal identity dimension and external identity dimension became clearer and stronger over the years. The term *hardal* (literally "mustard"), an acronym for haredi and *dati leumi* (national religious), captures this process—whereby national religious Jews grew closer to the haredim in their religious observance, and the non-Zionist ultra-orthodox community became more nationalistic regarding the Arab-Israeli conflict—within the religious sector. This amalgamation was severely challenged in 2005 when Prime Minister Ariel Sharon led the unilateral disengagement from the Gaza Strip and the removal of settlements (many of them inhabited by religious Jews), thus sundering the intimate connection between nationalist religious Jews and the non-Zionist, ultra-Orthodox Jews.

Two additional surveys, conducted in 1996 and 2006, attempted to measure internal and external collective identity dimensions.[6] The two scales correlated strongly and similarly in both years (.60 in 1996 and .62 in 2006). The internal dimension included the value priority of democracy, the primary identity as Jewish or Israeli, the state-religion issue, and the primacy of democracy or Jewish religious law (α=.68 in 1996; .72 in 2006).[7] The external identity scale was defined by attitude toward the Israeli-Arab conflict and its sub-issues: the territories issue, peace talks, a Palestinian state, the Oslo agreements (support for unilateral disengagement in Gaza in 2006), and the value priority of Greater Israel (α=.81 in 1996; .77 in 2006). Since the focus here is on the meaning of "Jewish" and "Israeli," only the internal scale will be discussed here.

The distribution of the internal identity dimension is relayed in Figure 6-2. The scale's low score was "Israeli"; the high score was "Jewish." The structure of the distribution changed dramatically after 1996; the 2006 curve was much more polarized. In 2006, the scale's mean score was 46.8 (to the Israeli side of the scale)—compared to 49.6 in 1996 (see Figure 6-2). The correlation with religiosity remained strong. When the means of the internal identity scale were broken down by religious self-identification, the polarization seen above remained. Those who self-identified as religious scored 71.1 on the scale in 1996, compared to 74.3 in 2006. The parallel means for the secular were 29.0 and 25.9, respectively. The traditionalists moved from 47.1 in 1996 to 41.1 in 2006. Religiosity is a powerful factor when it comes to ordering people's views regarding what should go on within the state and what the country's foreign policy should be. In fact, the variables of religiosity and the plans for the future of the territories explain most of the variance in analyses of many political issues facing Israelis, and so not age, gender, class, status, education, nor income.

Some of the change between 1996 and 2006 can be attributed to the very large influx, beginning around 1990, of immigrants from the former Soviet Union, a group that was under-represented in the 1996 sample. Many of the immigrants were strong nationalists, but were unfamiliar with Jewish religious ritual. Because they are a very large voting bloc (more than a million came after the collapse of the Soviet Union), the shifts in their voting have determined the electoral results in a number of close contests, and their parties and politicians have played an important role in sustaining certain governing coalitions. The presence of this group (which was interviewed in Russian for the 2006 sample) is a factor in the shift away from the religious pole.

The enormous scale of Soviet immigration since the 1990s increased the presence of non-religious sentiments, since even former Soviet citizens who were indisputably Jewish were unlikely to have been exposed to much Jewish tradition during the 70 years of Soviet rule. Issues of religion and state became focused by their personal experiences. Many found that the Orthodox rabbinate's monopoly on matters of marriage and conversion prevented them from living normal lives. Children of mothers not deemed Jewish according to rabbinical law found themselves in ambiguous circumstances. Those who wanted to marry a non-Jewish partner were forbidden from doing so in a state-sanctioned ceremony. And if these non-Jews wanted to convert, they found long lines and stubborn authorities who were very reluctant to complete the conversion process. In 2004, there were about 350,000 non-Jewish immigrants, but in 2003, only 923 conversions were performed, a rate that has stayed constant for the last seven years.[8] Concomitantly, new churches opened and the sale of non-kosher meat flourished, since many of the non-Jews who arrived with these Jewish immigrants were Christian.

The waves of Russian immigration underscored the Orthodox rabbinate's monopoly over marriage and conversion. The Law of Return granted every Jew in the world the right to immigrate to Israel. Passed in 1950 in the shadow of the Holocaust, the question of "who is a Jew" seemed simple. Whoever the Nazis identified as a Jew and sent to the death camps was to be offered refuge in the newly established state. The anomaly of admitting non-Jews to the country as Israeli citizens did not occur to lawmakers in Israel's formative years. The 1952 Law of Citizenship granted citizenship to every Jew, his or her spouse, and their children and grandchildren. A single Jewish grandparent was sufficient to secure the right to citizenship upon immigration to Israel. Granting Israeli citizenship had no bearing on the Orthodox rabbinate's determination of whether the person was, or was not, a Jew. Stories abound of immigrants tracing their rights to Israeli citizenship to a grandparent who had no connection to Judaism other than an accident of birth. Imagine a young Bolshevik whose progeny, decades later, came to Israel. Or a Jewish woman in Kurdistan who married a Muslim man and bore him nine sons. Eventually, she was allowed to enter Israel along with her family of 170 people—children, grandchildren, and their spouses. Were Americans to contemplate immigrating to Israel under existing rules, perhaps as many as 20 million people would be eligible under the Law of Return.

Over the years, the debate over "Who is a Jew" has been heated. Should Israel adhere to the *halachic* (Jewish religious law) definition, which identifies a Jew as anyone born of a Jewish mother, or a convert? Should one's paternal legacy count? And what about one's own self-identification? The only legislation that resulted from this debate was the 1970 amendment defining a Jew as either a) one born to a Jewish mother or b) a convert to Judaism. But this did not settle the issue. The conversions performed by non-Orthodox rabbis (rabbis of the Reform and Conservative Jewish movements, for example) were challenged; attempts to add

Figure 6-2
Internal Identity Scale Distributions, 2006 and 1996

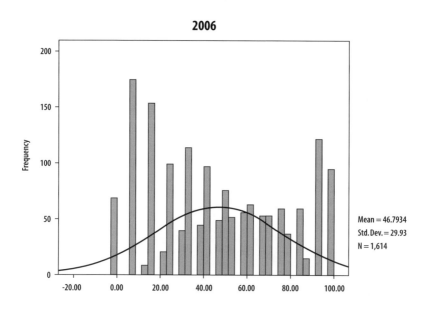

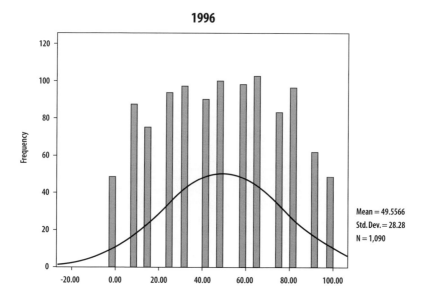

the words "according to *halacha*" in characterizing legal conversion also failed.

The Orthodox rabbinate will not sanction a marriage between a Jew and a non-Jew, for example, so if the rabbinate questions one partner's Jewishness, no religious ceremony can be held. Since no other branch (such as Conservative or Reform) of Judaism is recognized, and civil marriage does not exist, many couples find that there is no state-sanctioned institution through which they can marry. Many Jews who might qualify nevertheless choose not to be married by the Orthodox rabbinate; as many as half the marriages registered by the Ministry of the Interior are not performed by Orthodox rabbis. The number of marriages recorded by the rabbinate actually decreased between 1998 and 2002 despite the large growth in population of the marrying-age cohort.[9] This drop is explained by the large number of couples marrying outside the country—in Cyprus, for example. A marriage performed elsewhere is recorded by the appropriate clerk in the Ministry of the Interior, but the Jewish nature of the marriage is not certified by the rabbinate, and this may emerge as a problem later on, should a divorce occur.

The secular, or non-religious, behavior of Israelis is undeniable. Still, the perception persists that the power of the Orthodox religious parties is increasing. In 2006, these parties won 27 seats of the 120-member Knesset. The Shinui Party, which ran on a platform of decreasing the power of the haredim, won 15 seats. The Orthodox parties can tolerate the seculars and try to educate them, but they abhor the Conservatives and Reform, who they believe have usurped the titles, prayers, and ceremonies of Judaism. Orthodoxy becomes more influential in Israel as the power of the other Jewish denominations increases in other Jewish communities around the world.

Political Parties

The debate over Jewish religious law in public life has been a one-sided affair: religious law has been promoted by all the religious parties, partially acquiesced to by non-religious coalition partners, and rarely opposed. The one exception—an example of a group successfully opposing the role of religious law—was Shinui in 2003. Its platform was antireligious—strenuously against the special privileges that had been granted over the years to religious individuals and institutions in areas such as army service and government budgets. Shinui opposed what it saw as the pilfering of the public treasury for the benefit of one group in the name of religion. Having declared that it would refuse to join a coalition in which the ultra-Orthodox Shas also participated, Shinui, having won 15 of the 120 seats in the 2003 elections, got its way. Shas was not included in the governing coalition, and programs that favored religious institutions were scaled back, only to be partially restored after the 2006 elections in which Shinui imploded and disappeared, and Shas was reinstalled at the table of government.

With 80% of the seats, it was numerically possible for nonreligious parties to form a winning coalition and legislate a secular platform. This has never happened—nor is it likely to happen. It is more acceptable for large parties to compromise over matters dear to the religious than to negotiate with a rival party on opposite sides of the political spectrum.

On the whole, religious groups came to terms with Zionism late, if at all. While Jewish religious symbolism was part of Zionism from its inception, the most vocal opposition to Zionism among Jews came from religious circles. It is therefore ironic that today's religious parties are among the most stable political groups competing in Israeli politics.

All of the religious parties are Orthodox Jewish parties. The uninitiated should be warned that we are discussing distinctions among Orthodox, ultra-Orthodox, and ultra-ultra-Orthodox Judaism. Reform and Conservative Judaism are simply not in the picture, although both of these groups make efforts, especially through the courts, to win approved status.

When it comes to differentiating among these Orthodox religious parties, three topics are useful: (1) their willingness to cooperate in the Zionist enterprise;[10] (2) the representation of Sephardim within each party (all three were largely formed and run by Ashkenazim); and (3) the party's degree of militancy regarding the occupied territories.

Religious separatists, including the *Eda Haharidit* and other extreme elements, pursue a policy of non-contact with Zionists, whom they perceive as a threat to religious purity. Neturai Karta, a small group of a few hundred families in Jerusalem and Bnei Brak (a religious suburb of Tel Aviv), refuses to recognize the legitimacy of the State of Israel and accuses those who do so of blasphemy. There have even been reports that members have conspired with elements in the Arab world to rid themselves and their Jerusalem of the Zionist oppressors.

Of all the parties, the National Religious Party (NRP) was most willing to cooperate in the Zionist enterprise, as its name attests. It fully cooperated with the secular Zionist parties in building the Jewish state; its sons (and some daughters) serve in the armed forces; and the party itself joined in the "historical partnership" with Mapai and Labor in the formative years and then in a government coalition with the Likud. The members of NRP blend their religious fervor and Zionist zeal into a potent mix. This is why the unilateral separation from the Gaza Strip came as such a blow to them. Not only did Ariel Sharon renege on his historical support of the settlers and the settlements, but he also ceded territory from Biblical Israel.

At a lower level of cooperation are three haredi parties: Agudat Israel, Shas, and Degel Hatorah (the Torah Flag). The word *haredi* connotes awe-inspired, fearful of God's majesty; Christian Quakers and the Shakers use the term similarly. The haredim maintain separate organizational and social structures, although they agree to limited political participation, such as chairing influential economic committees in the Knesset (parliament). Their religious belief is that Israel will be restored by a divine act—not human acts. Accordingly, their religious beliefs do not drive their political positions, which makes them endlessly flexible and often cooperative coalition partners, no matter which party is in control. They do not consider themselves Zionists, nor do they participate in Zionist institutions such as the World Zionist Organization. Instead, they see their role in influencing the Israeli government as similar to their role in influencing the local government in Boston or Brooklyn, where some of them also have large numbers of followers. To ensure their support, Israeli governments (led by either Labor or Likud) have allowed them unusual privileges, such as exempting their sons from army service (daughters are completely exempt) and allowing their sons to study in yeshivas instead, and allowing them to maintain an "independent" school system partly funded by public monies yet not controlled by the ministry of education.

The 2006 election results for the religious parties (12 seats for Shas, nine for the NRP-National Union, and six for the combined list of Agudat Israel and Degel Hatorah), continued the pattern begun in 1988, when non-Zionist religious parties won more seats than Zionist religious parties. Until 1988, the Zionist religious parties had bettered the non-Zionist religious parties by a ratio of 2 to 1; in 1988, the NRP—the only Zionist religious party to win representation that year—won only five seats, while the three non-Zionist religious parties won 13. In 1996, the division was nine for the NRP and 14 for the others (10 for Shas, and four for the joint list).

The religious parties in Israel today are the clearest cases of total interpenetration of religious, social, cultural, political, and often economic life. Their members tend to live in religious districts, send their children to religious schools and youth groups, and read religious party newspapers and journals. They tend to pray together and vote together.[11] Their organizations provide housing, schools, and even food to their members. In the pre-state period, this interpenetration existed among socialist groups, especially in kibbutzim. One of the last sizable communities in which political affiliation is still so intertwined with social life, however, is the religious community. It is evident in their neighborhoods. The religious parties' educational activities are much more clearly identified with their political parties, both organizationally and in terms of social and political values, than is the case in parallel secular neighborhoods (less so in the state-religious school system controlled by the NRP, more so in the "independent" school systems of the haredim, which receive public money without being supervised by the state). Religious youth groups are more successful in recruiting and conveying a clear social, cultural, and political message; the unifying effects of national sovereignty have only partially penetrated their value structure. Whereas statism has tended to blur differences among parties in the secular camp, especially in schools and youth groups, members of the religious parties have retained a central core of religious belief that distinguishes them from the general population. This particularistic orientation is reinforced by the social, educational, and political structures that exist in their environment.

A community's separateness is reflected in the dress of its adherents. In modern Israel, it is likely that a man whose head is covered (unless he is in the sun) is religious and supports a religious party. But the differentiation is likely to be even finer: a knitted *kipah* (skullcap) has become a symbol of the NRP and especially of its youth movement; a non-knitted *kipah,* by extension, often indicates support for the religious point of view but probably not for the NRP. Black wide-brimmed fedoras and suits generally identify non-Zionist Orthodox supporters—popularly known as "black hats" in Israel—while the more traditional garb of long-flowing robes and fur hats[12] identifies the dress of the Aguda and their supporters and separatists. Different subgroups also have different colored socks, gowns, and other identifiable garments.

As one would expect, the competition among religious parties is intense. Each group grades the others in terms of categories important to it. The Aguda argues that the NRP is not religious enough, citing the NRP's record of compromise and cooperation with secular governments and policies. The NRP emphasizes its record of contributing to the Zionist cause and education, arguing that a separatist Aguda can have no impact on the larger society and its values. The rabbis of the Council of Torah Sages, the spiritual and ideological guides of the Aguda, Shas, and Degel Hatorah, sometimes chasten the chief rabbis associated with the NRP for their interpretations and scholarly exegesis of the *halacha* (Jewish religious law).

The secular are often unable to deal with this competition. One example of their exasperation: A law making it illegal to try to influence voters by promising to provide a blessing; or by threatening to withhold a blessing; or to curse someone for voting or for not voting for a specific party (just as it is a crime to buy votes with money or favors). Despite this legislation, the fierce competition for votes continues, and the use of amulets and promises of blessings for "correct" voting is reported to be widespread.

The success of the religious parties (and they clearly have succeeded politically) rests on their pivotal role in coalition formation. Laws and administrative rulings on various issues—abortion, marriage and divorce, public transportation on Sabbath and holy days, enforcement of the Jewish dietary laws, and the definition of Who is a Jew?—have gone in the direction desired by the religious parties. The NRP's goal was to have religious institutions, which might have been temporary or voluntary in the past, become permanent fixtures of the religious community. That is, to have them established, and funded, by law. The party expended great efforts to promote this legislation and dominate institutions such as the Ministry of Religious Affairs, the chief rabbinate, the rabbinical courts, and the religious councils.

As we have seen, the foundation of their success is cultural, based on the symbol system and the basic premises on which Israeli society rests. But would things change drastically if the religious parties were no longer needed in the government coalition? To what extent is the Jewish character of Israel a matter of political expediency, and to what extent is it part of Israel's civic culture? There is no definitive answer to this hypothetical question, but it seems likely that the forms of religion and religious usage that have evolved in Israel are more permanent than many secularists would like to think.

There have been attempts to bridge the gaps among the various positions without forcing any side to surrender cherished principles. One such example is the Gavison-Medan Covenant, which tries to provide a basis for a new social covenant between observant and secular Jews in Israel.[13] This project addresses many of the basic issues confronting the two groups, including the Law of Return, the right to marry and establish a family, and the observance of the Sabbath and holy days. Such efforts reflect an awareness of the deep divide between the two sides and the importance of seeking consensual solutions. A solution proposed by The Israel Democracy Institute's Constitution by Consensus draft leaves many of the Orthodox' cherished goals in place, but submits future legislation to the draft constitution's bill of rights and to judicial review.[14] This proposal does not seem to go far enough to win the support of the religious. Meanwhile, civil rights groups, feminists, egalitarians, and Reform and Conservative Jewish groups all see it the opposite way—as *too* accommodating to the religious.

The arrangements in place, as a result of the status quo, are more flexible than is commonly thought. Local authorities have leeway in how strenuously they apply laws concerning both commerce and entertainment on the Sabbath and holy days; in both cases, the strength of the religious parties in the local jurisdiction plays an important role in determining local rules. On national issues, uniformity is maintained. All institutions that receive money from the public treasury—including the army, schools, hospitals, universities, and government missions abroad—must observe Jewish dietary laws. The issue of whether El Al, the national airline, could operate on the Sabbath and holidays occupied the country's attention in 1982 until the government decided, in accordance with the demands of the religious parties, to halt these operations. Recently, the privatized El Al faced a consumer's boycott because of claims that the airline had begun to operate on the Sabbath in certain locations. The solution to that crisis kept El Al grounded on the Sabbath, its seats crowded with religious passengers.

Many Israelis would support a pluralistic approach that would allow both types of "religious" freedom: freedom *of* religion and freedom *from* religion. The problems begin when one group begins to believe that the other group is impinging on its rights. Typically, the Israeli political system has legitimized both the role of Orthodox religion and the ethic of a single Jewish people; these are important political issues because it is so difficult to achieve these goals simultaneously.

ENDNOTES

1. Menachem Friedman, "The Structural Foundation for Religio-Political Accommodation in Israel: Fallacy and Reality," in *Israel: The First Decade of Independence,* eds. S. Ilan Troen and Noah Lucas (Albany: SUNY Press, 1995), 51–81.

2. Baruch Kimmerling, "Between the Primordial and the Civil Definitions of the Collective Identity: 'Eretz Israel' or the State of Israel?" in *Comparative Social Dynamics*, Erik Cohen et al. eds., (Boulder: Westview Press, 1985), 262-83.

3. (N=1050).

4. Asher Arian, David Nachmias, Doron Navot, and Danielle Shani, *Auditing Israeli Democracy* (Jerusalem: Israel Democracy Institute, 2003 [Hebrew]), 229-234.

5. Jews only; N=940.

6. See the discussion in Michal Shamir and Asher Arian, "Collective Identity and Electoral Competition in Israel," *American Political Science Review* (1999).

7. The distributions for the 2006 sample were:

    Value Priority. "In thinking about the various paths along which Israel can develop, there seem to be four important values which clash to some extent, and which are important to different degrees to various people: Israel with a Jewish majority, greater Israel, a democratic state (with equal political rights to all), and peace (that is, a low probability of war). Among these four values, which is the most important to you? And the second? And third? And fourth?" [Respondent's choice was used, generating a 4-value variable. First choice for a given value – 1.]

	1st choice	2nd choice	3rd choice	4th choice
Jewish Majority	36%	22%	29%	12%
Peace	33%	35%	28%	16%
Democracy	20%	36%	26%	16%
Greater Israel	11%	17%	17%	56%
	100%	100%	100%	100%
N	1,619	1,591	1,552	1,539

Identity. "Among the following four categories, which best describes the way you identity yourself? Jewish, Israeli, ethnic classification (Ashkenazi or Sephardi) or religiosity (observant or secular)." [Only first choice was used since 88% chose "Israeli" or "Jewish."]

	1st choice	2nd choice	3rd choice	4th choice
Jewish	46%	30%	17%	5%
Israeli	42%	37%	16%	7%
Religious/secular	10%	27%	41%	22%
Ethnic	2%	6%	26%	66%
	100%	100%	100%	100%
N	1,616	1,533	1,429	1,418

State-Religion Issue. N = 1,622. "In your opinion, should the government of Israel see to it or should it not see to it that public life be conducted according to Jewish religious law (Halacha)?"

Definitely yes: 28%; Yes: 20%; No: 32%; Definitely no: 20%.

Primacy of Democracy or Jewish Religious Law. N = 1,612. "To what extent do you agree or disagree with the statement that when democracy and Jewish religious law (*halacha*) are in conflict, Jewish religious law should be preferred?"

Halacha – 26%; middle 24%; democracy 50%.

8.   *Haaretz*, May 27, 2004, 13A.

9.   Central Bureau of Statistics, Monthly Report, March 2004, vol. 55, table 3G.

10. Gary Schiff, *Tradition and Politics: Religious Parties of Israel* (Detroit: Wayne State University Press, 1977); and Menachem Freedman, *Society and Religion: Non-Zionist Orthodoxy in Eretz Israel, 1918-1936* [in Hebrew] (Jerusalem: Ben-Zvi Institute, 1978).

11. For geographical insight into the competition, see Yosseph Shilhav, "Spatial Strategies of the Haredi Population in Jerusalem," *Socio-Economic Planning Science* 18, no. 6 (1986): 411-418.

12 . Common to nobles in Poland in the Middle Ages.

13. Yoav Artsieli, *The Gavison-Medan Covenant: Main Points and Principles* (Jerusalem: Israel Democracy Institute and AVI CHAI Foundation, 2004).

14. *Constitution by Consensus* (Jerusalem: Israel Democracy Institute, 2007).

7. Egypt: Secularism, Sharia, and the Prospects for an Inclusive Democracy

Manar Shorbagy

Introduction

The relationship between religion and politics is at the top of the political agenda in Egypt, and, as I shall argue, it has important implications for the political rights of Egyptian women and minorities. However, the issue is not a simple secular/religious divide. It is, rather, the problem of how to define the nature and characteristics of a civil, democratic state that is neither a theocracy nor an Islamically "naked" public space. The Islamist/secularist dichotomy is a false one; it has little or no relevance to actual political processes and possibilities in Egypt, where a middle ground is both theoretically and practically conceivable. Such a middle ground, however, must be deliberately sought and found by Egyptians, so that a national consensus on the relationship between religion and politics can emerge.

For a brief time, such a consensus seemed possible. Hopes were high between 2005 and early 2007. But those possibilities collapsed in 2007. This paper examines the reasons for this collapse. Reasons, I will argue, that lie in correctable political failures of actors across the board, rather than any inherent impossibility of creating an inclusive democracy in a Muslim society.

Understanding Egypt's Current Predicament

2005 was an unusual political year in Egypt. Many taboos were broken in street protests and by the independent press. Domestic political pressure to begin democratic reform was mounting to unprecedented levels. Moreover, in their confrontation with the regime, many political forces shrewdly took advantage of the U.S.'s democracy rhetoric without buying into the Bush agenda or allowing themselves to be exploited by the Bush administration.

One of 2005's most promising developments was the public acknowledgement, for the first time, that a generation of young activists and intellectuals had succeeded, over more than a decade, in acting across ideological lines. The Egyptian Movement for Change, also known as Kefaya,[1] was one manifestation of these efforts and an important illustration of the possibilities of this new politics.

At the dawn of the 21st century, Egypt's political system has reached a dead end. The opposition political parties are locked in their headquarters, unable to communicate with the public. Having virtually acquiesced to an arsenal of restrictive laws, those political parties have for years suffered from ever-dwindling membership, lack of operational funds, and internecine feuds. The "illegality" of the Muslim Brothers (MB) had paradoxically liberated that organization from restrictions that come with governmental licensing. However, the ideology, posture, secrecy, and political tactics of the grassroots-based MB have all engendered the mistrust of many political forces, including some Islamists. At the same time, the secularist/Islamist polarization has hindered the possibility of reaching any meaningful consensus on critical issues. This blockage is not lost on the regime—which has clearly benefited from such divisions among its adversaries—and it does not augur well for the future of the Brotherhood as leaders of Egyptian political life.

With the seething political discontent on the one hand, and the ideologically based mistrust among oppositional political forces on the other, Egypt needs—now more than ever—a new form of politics that unites diverse forces from across the political spectrum to forge a new national project. Kefaya has been one step in that direction. It represents a resounding success for the cross-ideological interactions that date back to the early 1990s. Back then, a group of young activists noticed that the ideological animosity among the older generations had hindered efforts to reach a national consensus. It took that ideologically diverse group of young activists (which included Marxists, Islamists, Nasserists, and liberals) years of formal and informal dialogue to explore both their differences and common goals. By the end of the 1990s, this group was able to collaborate only on issues of foreign policy, since a widely shared platform already existed. However, the trust that was established over years of joint action enabled them to successfully launch the Kefaya movement, which represented a clear national project of political transformation.

However, this success, embodied in Kefaya, remains only the first step. The challenge for that generation is to both expand and deepen this cross-ideological, interactive politics. At the heart of the national project envisioned by different democratic forces in today's Egypt is the establishment of a civil, democratic state that respects the rights and freedoms of all citizens regardless of religion or gender. However, democratization efforts in Egypt have faltered. The reason is not simply the ruling party's monopoly of power and its repressive tactics; equally important is the fact that the regime's adversaries are deeply divided over the nature of the envisioned civil, democratic state. There are bitter disagreements over core issues such as the socioeconomic character of that state, the nature of its political system, and, above all, the relationship between religion and politics, for religion is central to the state's democratic citizenship.

Thus, a national consensus must emerge on such issues. Without a consensus, Egypt's democratic forces will remain hindered by the ideological differences among its various groups; the struggle may devolve into another round of bitter Secularist/Islamist conflict. The latest such polarization, in the early 1990s, distracted both sides from the real democratic challenge, and the regime was the sole beneficiary.

The experience of the founders of Kefaya indicates that there is far more common ground among Egypt's political forces than either the regime, or the MB, have led us to believe. The challenge, therefore, is to carry the experience further—to open a new national dialogue on important issues such as the relationship between state and religion and, until the beginning of 2007, the political stage seemed ripe for such a national consensus.

Fertile Ground, Paradoxically Abandoned

Egypt, like the U.S., has an elite dominated by secularists and a highly religious population of Muslims and Christians alike. However, unlike the U.S., the Egyptian secularist elite, with a few marginal exceptions, does not really call for the exclusion of religion from the public arena. Rather, it aims to regulate the role of religion, particularly as far as the state is concerned.

The cosmopolitan image of Egypt in the media was designed to attract tourists to its historical treasures. But it often obscures the deeply ingrained religious heritage of the country. Islam, and to a lesser extent Christianity, is present in public spaces, and the Egyptian public discourse is highly infused with religious rhetoric, symbols, and narratives.

This reality has perhaps shaped the national project of mainstream secularists. It is a project that tends to adopt the narrow definition of secularism—as simply the separation of religion and state—rather than the broader definition, which regards the transcendent realm as "entirely irrelevant to the concerns of the visible material world."[2]

This is actually good news, given Egypt's current political condition and predicament. Egypt has a powerful yet diverse Islamic population and a mainstream secularist elite that does not insist on a "naked" public space;[3] therefore, a national consensus on the role of religion becomes all the more possible. And because it is impossible for a democratic national project to be built on political exclusion, the Islamic trend, the most powerful in today's Egypt, must be involved in any national dialogue in order to have a political consensus. The mainstream secularists who rightly call for regulating the role of religion, therefore, need a reasonable Islamist partner that recognizes the need for such regulation.

Fortunately, such a partner does exist. It is an important force within the broader Islamic trend, and it has made a major intellectual contribution to Egypt (and beyond). Thanks to this relatively small and independent—yet highly influential—group of intellectuals, there is today a considerable body of new *Fiqh* (interpretations of Sharia) that has put forward new, important, highly progressive interpretations of Islam. Their project of interpretation—which they perceive as unfinished, a work-in-progress—has, for example, redefined, on the basis of Islamic Sharia, the role of women and non-Muslims.[4] More important, this group recognizes that the relationship between religion and politics needs to be discussed in Egypt—and regulated.

Additionally, this force of moderation has impacted the world of activism. It is a new generation of Islamist activists who were attracted to this body of scholarly work and who aim to bring it into the real world through a political party, the Islamist Wassat party. The party's platform clearly states that women shall have "equal political and legal rights." It stresses freedom of religion, and states in unequivocal terms that Christians in Egypt have full citizenship rights and obligations. For more than a decade, the Wassat activists have been applying for a legal license—but to no avail.

Yet this moderate force within the Islamic population is usually ignored by secularist Egyptians—as well as Westerners—who tend to ignore its significance, focusing, instead, on the alarming interpretations of the militant factions within political Islam. Secularists' responses to this moderate Islamist force have varied: they range from questioning its very moderation to belittling its weight to ignoring its contribution altogether. Questioning the moderation of this force is perhaps the most extreme response, for it denies the differences among the Islamists and insists that, regardless of their differences on specific topics, they are all still "fundamentalists" who seek to create a religious state.[5]

Some secularists, however, recognize the differences among the Islamists, and even applaud their positions as highly progressive, while still seeing them as a marginal force within the broad Islamic population, with far less weight than "organized"[6] Islam. What matters, they argue, is the Muslim Brothers, and not those moderates who are simply individuals with few followers.[7]

This argument leads to the third response, which tends, on different occasions, to ignore the scholarly work of moderates altogether.[8] Such responses, by secularists, occasionally inflame the secularist/Islamist divide. While the case for moderate Islam has been made by many scholars, these secularists' responses carry their own *political* peril. By failing to appreciate the differences among the Islamists, the secularists may inadvertently be helping to strengthen militant Islam. The Islamic moderates have embarked on a battle within their own community. Questioning the long-held (and very popular) views of organized Islam—and doing so on Islamic grounds—is both a difficult and important task indeed. Accusations from the militants of "selling out" continue to swirl around the moderates; and so the attacks from the secularists only help the militants. Besides, the moderates' battle has in fact been fruitful on many levels. For example, new generations of Islamist activists, armed with progressive interpretations of the Koran, are now capable of real political activism on Islamic grounds; they are also capable of interacting with other political forces. Secondly, to argue that this movement is unimportant is to ignore that their scholarly work has supported the cause of both Christian rights and women's rights in Egypt (as will be discussed in more detail below).

No less important, the independent moderate Islamists have attempted to soothe the Islamic/secularist divide—an example of the group working beyond its own constituency.

The last decade has witnessed the success of such efforts in the nationalist-Islamist rapprochement and in the Kefaya movement.

In post-Nasser Egypt, the most intractable ideological conflict seemed to be the one between the nationalists and the Islamists. The Nasser regime's brutality against imprisoned Islamists had exacerbated the seemingly intractable conflict between Arabism and Islam. By the end of the 1980s, a group of independent Islamists and nationalists embarked on a series of internal dialogues, both formally and informally; and they ended up establishing the Islamist-Nationalist Conference. This rapprochement created a new political environment in which Arabism and Islam were perceived as compatible. The two movements found common ground in resisting imperialist threats and working together for a democratic project.

The Islamist/nationalist rapprochement is clear evidence that independent moderates, rather than "organized" Islam, can make a real difference. Kefaya: The Egyptian Movement for Change is an example of a group overcoming the secularist/Islamist divide. The founders of Kefaya, who worked together towards a democratic, peaceful change in Egypt, included Marxists, Nasserists and moderate Islamists. In other words, the contribution of independent Islamists makes clear that the obsession with organized Islam fails to appreciate real achievements that have left their mark on Egyptian public life.

By early 2007, new efforts by Egyptian intellectuals and activists had started renewing the dialogue, and with it, chances for a national consensus. On their agenda, among other issues, was the issue of religion and state. Clearly, therefore, by the beginning of 2007, Egypt seemed poised to enter a new and crucial phase in its progress toward a serious, and long overdue, dialogue on the role of religion in politics and public life. But suddenly those hopes were dashed; the opportunity was lost. Instead, Egypt today has embarked on yet another round of bitter secularist/Islamist battles.

What Happened?

The president of Egypt had proposed the amendment of 34 articles of the Egyptian Constitution. However, among them was not Article II of the Constitution which states that "the principles of the Islamic Sharia shall be the main source of legislation." But in 2007, immediately before constitutional amendments were proposed[9] by the ruling party, a group of secularist intellectuals and activists launched a media campaign demanding the amendment of Article II. They pushed their case with a series of articles, press releases, and TV shows, and a statement was signed by almost two hundred secularists "calling on the president" and parliament to amend the article, and "hoping that the president of the republic and the legislative bodies would include this demand among the currently proposed Constitutional amendments."[10]

The electoral victories of the MB in the parliamentary elections of 2005 fueled the argument that what matters is organized Islam. This environment exacerbated the secularists' responses (mentioned above) toward the Islamist moderate forces, with whom they were already in dialogue on other issues. Adding fuel to the fire were dubious actions by rank and file members of the MB, as well as extreme statements by prominent figures within that organization.

For example, in the winter of 2007, amidst the battle over repressive actions by the regime during the student unions' elections, a group of students, affiliated with the MB, wearing militia-like dresses, demonstrated fighting skills in front of the office of the president of Al Azhar University. The parade against this symbol of authority[11] caused alarm across the Egyptian political spectrum. It was immediately linked to an earlier statement by the MB Supreme Guide that his organization was prepared to take on Hezbollah with thousands of fighters. Many people had legitimate fears that the MB was reviving its 1950s secret military wing.

If that were not enough, Muhammad Habib, the MB deputy Supreme Guide, was quoted as saying that the MB would propose a special tax for Christians "equal to what Muslims pay in zakat."[12] This would have clearly undermined the notion of full citizenship for Christians. These developments, coming as they did from "organized Islam," have together raised legitimate concerns about the future of Egypt in the event that the MB wins a majority in a free election.

Such concerns, however, were channeled simply into a call by some secularists to amend Article II of the Egyptian Constitution, which states that the "principles of Sharia are the main source of legislation." While the wording of the statement proposed an alternative phrasing—that "religion(s) shall be (a) main source of legislation"[13] (hardly the language of a naked public space)—the fact that the proposed plank deleted any mention of Sharia, per se, was enough to rile moderate Islamists, who perceived the campaign as an attack on Sharia in particular. A new round of polarization ensued.

In a sense, the secularists picked the wrong battle at the wrong time. To be sure, given the alarming positions of the MB, the relationship between religion and politics indeed needed serious consideration. However, reducing the issue to the argument over the article on Sharia—already in the constitution since 1980—was an unhelpful diversion. The logic behind that proposed amendment, it was argued, was to eliminate any possibility that the article would be abused should the MB reach power in a free election. However, since the point is that the Muslim Brothers cannot be trusted, there is no reason to believe that the organization, once in power, will keep the current constitution intact in the first place! Focusing, therefore, on that article in the current constitution for the sake of such a hypothetical situation only distracts the nation from its critical task of forging a real national consensus on the issue of religion and politics. The presence of such a consensus is the only thing that guarantees that elected force cannot govern against its very principles.

Furthermore, such a call clearly alienates the very forces in the Islamic movement that are needed to reach such a consensus. In other words, the secularists might have taken these alarming positions by the MB as new evidence that a national consensus is long overdue, and actually embarked on that dialogue with the best forces in the Islamist movement (who in fact spoke out against such positions).[14] But instead, the secularists simply chose to short-circuit the process by seeking a solution from above. By calling on the president and the parliament to act, the secularist intellectuals have actually resorted to the very undemocratic means they have been loudly opposing with regard to how other constitutional amendments were handled by the regime.

The reaction of the moderate Islamists to the campaign against Article II was not helpful either. They reacted angrily, and they used a discourse at odds with their moderation. Immediately, some of them decried the campaign against Article II as "an attack against Islam"[15] and described the secularists involved as "extremists" who only represent themselves.[16]

To be fair, it is important to note that just five months before this episode, Selim Al Awa, one of the most prominent Islamist independent figures, had publicly called for a "reconsideration" of Article II[17]—clear evidence that there is indeed common ground with even the secularists who launched the campaign. But apparently, in times of tension, each side's position pushes the other side to take positions it wouldn't have taken otherwise.

Just as the secularists' tendency to exclude the Islamists altogether has contributed to the current polarization, the Islamists' angry response has further exacerbated the divide. The moderate Islamists failed to appreciate that it was, after all, a wing in the broader Islamic movement—the Muslim Brothers—which raised legitimate concerns on the part of many people, including intellectuals who were never hostile to the Islamic movement. The moderates, in their anger, used a discourse that abetted the (false) perception that "all Islamists are the same." Many of those moderates argued, for example, that what the secularists call for is an elitist position "against the will of the majority of Egyptians."[18] This was the same argument arrogantly used by the MB, an argument that alienated many political forces, including those independent Islamist moderates themselves.

Clearly, the Islamists tend to perceive Egypt's increasing religiosity as a sign of public support. However, until there are live political forces capable of competing peacefully in an open and free environment, Egyptians' real "political" preference remains virtually unknowable. In other words, while the secularist democratic forces need to live up to their own values of non-exclusion and recognize that Egypt needs a new, inclusive mainstream that welcomes all political forces—including the Islamists—the Islamists need to abandon their arrogance, their sense of power, based on the public's apparent religiosity, for this religiosity is a highly complex phenomenon that does not necessarily translate into support for a particular political group.

Amidst this noise, the issue was indeed reduced to a simple constitutional article—whether to keep it, delete it, or change it. For one camp, the Islamists, an article in a "positive" document became a red line, not open for discussion, while for the other camp, the secularists, the article became the source of all ills, the main obstacle to real citizenship and democracy. Neither perception is true, of course.

In such a context, the chances for a serious national dialogue about how best to regulate religion in politics and public life became as remote as ever, to the detriment of the country's democratic future. Moreover, although progress has been made, particularly on minority rights, that progress has now stalled. In a society that is becoming increasingly religious, it is important to argue for minority rights on both secular as well as Islamic grounds.

For example, as a Muslim woman, I find it extremely helpful to be able to argue for my equal rights on Islamic grounds. On the one hand, it is far easier to expose and confront sexism when it is deprived of its false religious cover; political battles can thus be won on a cross-ideological basis. On the other hand, I am convinced that I do not have to choose between my full rights and my religion. Women who argue for their equal rights on Islamic grounds have only this group of centrist Islamists to rely on. Their Islamic scholarship and activism is the basis of their call for women's equality within the Sharia itself.

This moderate group—unlike all other Islamists in Egypt, including the Muslim Brothers—argues that Islamic Sharia is fully compatible with women's right to vote, run for election, participate fully in public life, and assume all public offices including the highest executive office and judgeship positions.[19] According to them, Sharia also guarantees women's right to work, own property, and receive an education. Marriage is valid only upon the full consent of the woman (who also has the right to divorce). Of all the different elements in the broad Islamic movement, it was only the centrists who spoke out against female circumcision, calling it a "crime."[20]

This centrist group sees the face veil as a Gulf-area tradition that has nothing to do with Islam so they downplay the headscarf controversy as of secondary importance. Hoda Hegazy, the unveiled professor of literature, is one of the founders of the Islamist Wassat party.

Those positions clearly make such Islamists full partners for those who both struggle for women's rights and come from a secular background. Similarly, those working for full citizenship rights for Christians in Egypt find those same Islamists as their full partners. Again, they base their positions—including the position that Egyptian Christians have full citizenship rights, including the right to run for and assume the office of the President of the Republic[21]—on Islamic Sharia.

In our rapidly changing world, new issues involving minority rights are constantly emerging. The contribution of the moderate Islamists is thus crucial in order to strike the balance necessary for building a modern Egypt that guarantees equal rights for all its citizens without abandoning its rich heritage. But because the moderate Islamists perceived the latest round of polarization as a direct attack on the principles of Sharia, the centrist Islamists have put their public interventions on hold.

Two negative developments that would have normally triggered a reaction from the centrists occurred, and their silence was keenly felt. In the summer of 2007, the media reported several fatal cases of female circumcision, as well as an alarming new level of Muslim/Christian tension. In both cases, when the only group that might have decried these acts as "un-Islamic" was instead silent, that silence certainly exacerbated both problems.

Conclusion

Today, Egypt's biggest political dilemma is that its formal political system does not represent the country's political realities. Legal licenses for political activity are denied to some important groups, while licenses are granted to elements that have no political base whatsoever. Among the forces denied legal legitimacy— foremost among them, in fact—is the Islamic group, with all its stripes and variations. The politics of exclusion, however, has failed to stem the grassroots power of the Islamists, who sometimes use a deliberately generalized discourse to attract more followers. The best hope for Egypt is to reach a point where the Islamist project is simply "one" among many others, without the current mystique surrounding it. Then it can be contested in reality, and thus challenged by other groups and scrutinized by the public.

In today's political environment, a free election would probably lead to a victory for the MB. Given the organization's tactics and attitude toward other political forces, Egypt would then be vulnerable to yet another monopoly of power, this time by the Muslim Brothers instead of the current ruling party. In order to avoid such an outcome, it is not enough to call for an open environment in which all political forces can compete on equal footing. What is more important is a serious national dialogue that would lead to a consensus on the nature of the civil democratic state envisioned by all democratic forces in Egypt. Only when a consensus is reached can a new constitution, embodying fair, agreed upon principles, be drafted.

ENDNOTES

1. Which was announced in late 2004.

2. Wilfred M. McClay, "Two Concepts of Secularism," in *Religion Returns to the Public Square, Faith and Policy in America*, eds. Hugh Helco and Wilfred M. McClay (Washington, DC: Woodrow Wilson Center Press, 2003), 31-61.

3. Abdel Wahab El Messiri, al *'Almaneyya al Juz'eyah wal 'Almaneyya al Mutlaqa*, Absolute Secularism and Partial Secularism (Cairo: al Sherouq Press, 2002).

4. For an illustration of the scholarly contribution of these moderates, see Raymond W. Baker, *Islam Without Fear: Egypt and the New Islamists* (Cambridge, Mass.: Harvard University Press, 2003).

5. See, for example, Abdel Mone'im Said, Heen Usbih al Usuli Dimocrateyyan, "When the Fundamentalist Becomes a Democrat," *Al Ahram*, (April 23, 2007).

6. In Egypt's public discourse, the term "Organized Islam" by no means refers to state religion or to religious institutions. Rather, it refers to the organizations of political Islam, particularly the Muslim Brothers, which is a highly sophisticated, well-organized group.

7. Interviews by the author with the Nasserist Amin Eskandar, and the Marxist Ahmed Bahaa Din Shaaban, Cairo, May 10, 2007 and May 13, 2007, respectively.

8. Tarek El Malt and Lemaza la Yarawnana, "Why Don't They See Us?" *Al Wassat Party Website*, http://montada.alwasatparty.com/showthread.php?+=699 (accessed May 8, 2007).

9. They were later passed.

10. See the full text of the Statement: *Al Ahaly*, March 14, 2007.

11. "Iste'iradat Ikhwaneya le fenoun el qital fi Jame'at al Azhar"(Ikwani Militias Show Fighting Skills at Al Azhar University), *Al Masry Al Youm*, p. 1, Dec. 11, 2006.

12. *Nahdat Masr*, p. 1, January 21, 2007.

13. Ibid.

14. Essam Sultan of Al Wassat Party, for example, stated that Habib's statement on extra taxes means the MB has "got F in the citizenship exam": *Al Wafd*, March 4, 2007.

15. Abul Ela Mady and Bayna al Muwatna wal Sharia, "Between Citizenship and Sharia," *Al Wassat Party website*, www.alwasatparty.com/modules.php?name=News&file=article&sid=5300 (accessed April 28, 2007).

16. Ela Mady and am Naqs Islam, "Citizenship or Less Islam," *Al Wassat Party Website*, www.alwasatparty.com/modules.php?name=News&file=article&sid=5536 (accessed April 13, 2007).

17. Public Symposium titled "New Political Parties," Sept. 9, 2006.

18. Mady and Islam, "Citizenship or Less Islam," from the *Al Wassat Party website*.

19. Abul Ela Mady, Ru'yat al Wassat fil Syassa wal Mujtama, *Al Wassat's Vision for Politics and Society* (Cairo: al Sherouq, 2005), 104-110.

20. M. Selim Al Awa, al Islameyoon wal Mara'a, *The Islamists and Women*, (Cairo: Dar al Wafaa, 2000), 59-76.

21. Tareq Al Bishry, Al Muslimoon wal Aqbat fi Itat al Jama'a al Wataneyya, *Muslims and Copts within the National Community* (Cairo: al Sherouq, 1988), 677-688.

8. Algeria:
Prospects for an Islamic or a Secular State

Kada Akacem

What are the prospects for an Islamic state in Algeria nowadays? Before we can answer that question, we must first understand the political, economic, and social developments that have recently taken place in Algeria. These events will shed some light on the decline of the Islamist movements.

Soon after independence, Algeria adopted an inward-oriented "socialist" system. Its economic development model depended on revenues from hydrocarbons, mainly oil. Additionally, the public sector dominated the economic activities through the State Owned Enterprises (SOEs) that were supposed to catalyze the economic and social development of the country. The government was the main supplier of subsidized food, utilities, housing, education, and jobs. In this first phase of the socialist experience, the government successfully faced "the problems of development," and it could deliver the just-mentioned goods and services as long as oil prices and oil revenues were high enough.[1] The government, however, failed to face "the development of problems" during the second phase of its socialist experience. A huge decrease in the price of oil in the mid-1980s, from around $40 to around $6 a barrel in few weeks, left the government unable to provide better living standards for a population that had doubled in size since independence. Since oil revenues were, and still are, the most important source of foreign currency for the country, the drastic decrease in crude oil prices had several consequences. First, it led to a severe foreign debt crisis. Second, there was a dramatic reduction in the volume of imports—in particular, food products. Third, the government's budgetary resources were reduced by about 50%. Finally, there was a severe economic recession that led to social protests that led, in turn, to "bread rioting." All of this culminated, in October 1988, with violent demonstrations throughout the country; a few hundred citizens lost their lives.

The social unrest and the economic crisis of the late 1980s were coupled with a severe foreign debt crisis, which led to IMF conditions for its financial assistance. These factors explain why, in late 1988 and early 1989, the country was forced to initiate a series of unprecedented political and economic reforms. The reforms included the adoption of a new constitution, the introduction of a multiparty system, and the establishment of a free written press (radio and television are still state-controlled) and a market-oriented economic system (however, the economic "liberation" is still yet to be associated with a true political liberation).

Shortly after allowing multi-partyism, over 50 parties were created. Only a handful of them survived. The government encouraged the creation of parties through subsidies, hoping to dilute the power of both the National Liberation Front (FLN) and the Islamic Salvation Front (FIS, an Islamist party).

The Rise of Islamic Movements

Between independence and 1989, the only legal political party in Algeria was the FLN, a "secular" party that presided over the independence war and which is nowadays a kind of a melting pot, comprised of many political tendencies. The FIS was allowed to participate as a counterweight to the FLN, despite the fact that the constitution forbids parties founded on a religious basis, a rule intended to weaken the vested interests within the FLN that opposed the new political and economic reforms.[2] The FIS was the strongest of the new parties, with support across all population groups: adults, youth, students, teachers, businesspersons, intellectuals, public employees, and women. It even had supporters among the police and the armed forces.

From the beginning, the FIS was the most popular opposition party—and one of the few parties considered credible by the general public. Algerians were attracted to its strong anti-government stance. It opposed, openly and vehemently through the mosques and charitable organizations, the prevailing political system, which it accused of incompetence and corruption. To solve Algeria's political problems, the FIS promised an Islamic state based on justice, fairness, and Islamic values.

In the 1990 local elections, the FIS won 54% of the votes. In the legislative elections of December 1991, it got 47% of the votes in the first round. The second round was supposed to be held in January 1992, but was cancelled after a military "coup." Given the electoral rules at the time, however, the FIS had won the majority of the seats already, in the first leg: 188 of 231 total seats.

The FIS was banned in March 1992, after the bloodless military coup of

December 1991, which saw the resignation of the President, Chadli Bendjdid, and his replacement by the HCE (High State Council), a collegial entity. The FIS leaders and the core of its members were imprisoned, forced into exile, or forced into hiding underground.[3]

Civil strife began soon after the FIS was banned. Several armed Islamic groups were created to continue the struggle, supposedly with the purpose of establishing an Islamic state and promoting more justice. The most important of these movements was the Islamic Salvation Army (AIS), the armed branch of the FIS, and the much more violent and radical Armed Islamic Group (GIA), which split from the FIS and the AIS. The cost of the civil strife was very high in all regards: politically, economically, socially. Between 150,000 and 200,000 people died during the war. Hundreds of schools and dozens of factories were burned.

Even though most Algerians opposed the bloody violence, the country adopted a kind of neutral (if not sympathetic) position toward the armed groups. The general feeling was that the ongoing war between the armed forces and the Islamic groups was not the people's fight as long as the general public was not specifically targeted by either faction. Consequently, the public hardly supported the regime, especially in its struggle against the urban guerillas. However, an important minority of the population (including many women) was providing logistical support to these armed rebel groups.

That explains why, until 1995, the FIS was still somewhat popular despite the increasing number of casualties: till that point, the main targets of the armed groups were the police, military or paramilitary personnel, young conscripts, veterans of the independence war, journalists, intellectuals, artists, and any person who was actively or publicly opposed to their objectives and methods—but not random civilians. There were, in other words, no random mass murders. It was during this period that the Islamic groups were the strongest in terms of 1) membership and 2) their relative success against the inexperienced police forces.

The Decline of Islamic Movements

However, if the reputation of the Islamic movement, particularly the FIS, was not yet tarnished, its popularity had begun to decline as early as December 1991. This was after the legislative elections, when the FIS lost 7% of the popular votes in fewer than two years (following the local elections of 1990). According to political analysts, the decline was due to public disappointment over the mismanagement of local resources (in some of the communes), plus the somewhat dishonest behavior of some FIS elected representatives, especially since Islamists had an honest reputation. In fact, the FIS was potentially weak from its very inception because it was a "front" comprised of a very diverse population: devout Muslims from different Muslim schools, opportunists, and infiltrators from other parties.

The presidential election of November 1995 was organized and won by L. Zeroual, a retired general who had been appointed President of Algeria by the HCE. This was a key turning point in Algeria's recent history.[4] L. Zeroual wanted, among other things, to "electorally" legitimize his appointment and pursue his peace initiative through political dialogue with the Islamist movements. Besides giving Algeria its first elected president since the "resignation" of President Chadli in 1991, these elections marked the start of the downfall of the Islamist movement and all its diverse groups, political as well as armed. It marked the starting point of a decisive rupture—a divorce between the Islamist movement and its grass roots—and the decline of popular support for the Islamist movements, particularly the GIA.

These elections were important for the prospects of an Islamist state for several reasons. First, there was a record turnout of 75.7% despite security concerns and, more important, death threats from the GIA to anyone who decided to vote. This was due mainly to the public's desire to put an end to the ongoing violence. Peace, which was President Zeroual's main promise, was the people's top priority, above material and spiritual needs.

The runner-up in the election, M. Nahnah of the Islamist Movement for a Peaceful Society (MSP), received roughly 25.6%[5] of the vote. Political analysts attribute this low vote total to the fact that many of those who voted for Zeroual, instead of Nahnah, did so in order to avoid a crisis similar to that of December 1991, when the legislative elections were cancelled, with deadly consequences.

Nahnah's low vote total also highlighted an incipient trend: many people had begun to defect from the FIS. (These were moderate and peace-seeking supporters who blamed the FIS's armed branches for the atrocities and violence.) It also bespoke a clear disapproval of the methods used by the armed groups. Additionally, because of the huge turnout, and because Algerians defied the GIA by ignoring its threats and its warning "not to vote," the GIA believed thenceforth that all Algerians were "unbelievers" and unfaithful (to them or to God?).

From then on, the GIA started a long campaign of random, atrocious mass killings. This was a huge mistake. The general public stopped considering the "war" between the army and the Islamist groups to be a just war, and it began backing the police forces in the urban warfare by giving them precious information about the whereabouts of the terrorists.[6]

This assistance was important for the army, which needed it badly for its urban guerilla warfare. By 1997, the big urban centers had become relatively safe again from terrorist attacks, and by September 1997 the AIS had declared a cease-fire because, among other reasons, it wanted to distance itself from the atrocities committed by the GIA, which had become gradually isolated and weakened in the whole country.

The GIA's ranks have shrunk dramatically, from about 30,000 (between 1993 and 1996) to about 24,000 (after 2002). This can be attributed to two main factors: the successful actions of the armed forces; and the general amnesty, granted by President A. Bouteflika, to terrorists who surrendered to the police forces. This was done in early 2006, through the National Reconciliation Law.[7]

In terms of security, "the army succeeded in 'neutralizing' the threat that violent Islamism represented for the state. At that point the international community still had not recognized the legitimacy of 'all-out war' against violent Islamist," on the basis of human rights violation by the armed forces. However, the September 11th attacks on the United States effectively reversed international opinion, and the strong anti-terrorist military campaign in Algeria was indeed, *a posteriori*, legitimized.

The Future of the Islamic Movement

Two legal and somewhat moderate Islamist parties remained politically active after the banning of the FIS in early 1992: the MSP and Ennahda. After fairly good performances in different elections, their influence and strength have diminished because their supporters have come to consider the parties' cooperation with, and participation in, the government as a form of a useless "collaboration" that neither improved the people's material and spiritual needs, nor solved the multiple crises of the Algerian society. Of the two parties, Ennahda's loss of influence was particularly dramatic; it is today practically wiped off the political map, after having won just 0.6% of the vote and 4 seats in the May 2007 legislative elections.[8]

The MSP's fall has not been quite as dramatic. It received 13% (52 seats) of the vote in the 2007 legislative elections. Still, it fell short of the 30% predicted by its leader. Another party, El Islah, which was the third strongest party in 2002 (43 seats) has had the same fate: El Islah was founded after a split with Ennahda, and it was the only Islamic party that wasn't "collaborating" in the ruling coalition. However, it was basically wiped out after the 2007 elections.

Finally, Wafa[9] could have had a brighter future and a bigger role than El Islah, Ennahda, and the MSP for many reasons. First, it is a moderate and liberal Islamic party whose grassroots are midway between the ex-FIS and the FLN.

Second, it has a competent, moderate, and experienced leadership, starting with its founder and leader, Ahmed Taleb Ibrahimi (who has been a minister several times). Third, because it is a moderate party and does not call for an Islamic state, Wafa was able to draw support from moderate members of the MSP and El Islah.

However, it seems that Wafa will be unable to participate because it is considered a surrogate for the FIS (which has been banned). In 2004, the Interior Minister declared, "I will never give an authorization to a *FIS-bis* [a second FIS]." Moreover, its founder is too old to be a candidate in the 2009 presidential elections. And so the fate of the party could be the same as its founder (that is, a politically bleak future). That is the tradition in Algeria.

All that the Islamists promise is an Islamic state—but they do not say much about the nature of this future state. The Algerian people do not know what type of Islamic state to eventually expect—a state according to the vision of the ex-FIS, or of the MSP, or of El Islah, or of Ennahda, or a Saudi-state (Wahabit) or the Pakistani, or the Iranian type? Or a state of the Afghani (Taliban) type, which existed before 9/11 and in which there was continuing civil war between two groups—each fighting in the name of Islam—and in which women in particular were denied almost all rights, including the simple but very important right to be educated? All this makes Algerians deeply afraid of finding themselves in a situation à la Libanaise or à la Taliban. Thus, from the above developments, we can conclude that the divorce between the Algerian public and Islamist movements—the radical and violent ones in particular—has been final.

In conclusion, we can say that the answer to our question concerning an Islamic state has been given recently by the head of the MSP (which is a part of the new government coalition). Not long before the legislative elections of May 2007, he said that:

"*The dream of an Islamic state is not on the agenda anymore...* The philosophy of the road map of our party consists in [our] *participation in all the state institutions*: the government, the parliament, unions...We are for peace, *against the use of force to take the power or to use it to stay in power.* This vision requires the neutrality of four institutions, namely: the administration, *the mosque*, the school, and the barracks [the military]... The people should be the sole arbitrator in the elections [that should be held] in all transparency." (Our translation).[10]

The Prospects for a Secular State

What are then the chances for a secular state in Algeria? None, if we consider a secular state in its strict sense—a state entirely separated from religion and in which religion is entirely free from government interference. Strict separation of state and religion cannot be implemented without serious and dangerous consequences for both the government and the stability of the whole country; it should not be contemplated at all. No one will be bold enough to propose a strict separation of the state and the Muslim religion: the consequences of such a decision could be devastating, leading to more civil strife or even a civil war. Why?

The Role of Islam in Contemporary Algeria since Independence

Islam provided moral support to the independence war. At the time, Algerian nationalism and Islam were so intertwined that individuals who drank alcohol, smoked, or did not fast during Ramadan were considered traitors to the national cause. The link between nationalism and religion is presently so strong that it is out of the question, at least in the foreseeable future, to "privatize" the Muslim religion, or to remove it from the political space, without serious consequences. Molokotos-Liederman (in this volume) has observed similar tendencies in Greece, where society is so profoundly religious that "religion is not confined to the private sphere" since it "has never really left the public sphere." Shorbagy (in this volume) reached a similar conclusion regarding Egypt.

The FLN, among others, has played, and still plays, the largest role in shaping the nature of Algeria. Many members of the party are devout Muslims and some of them are moderate Islamists. The FLN's present General Secretary (and Prime Minister) is a very devout Muslim, who, when he was the President of the parliament, introduced the recitation of verses from the Koran at the beginning of every session. A recent bill concerning the family code, based partially on the Sharia, became a law thanks to support from the FLN.[11] Hence, Islam is and will remain the state religion for years to come. Reflecting on the use of "symbols and markers of Islamic identity" to help define the state, Charles Tripp says the following about the pre-independence FLN: "[a]lthough ostensibly secular in intent... [and] aspiring to statehood on the basis of a distinct national identity [it was] unable—possibly also unwilling—to separate [its] definition of the community [the state being defined as distinct community] from distinctively Islamic aspects of its character."[12]

The FLN was intended, from its inception, to be a large tent where any Algerian, regardless of political affiliation, was welcome to volunteer in the war of independence. The strong link between Islamic affiliation and national affiliation is evidenced by the re-appropriation of the churches, after the independence, and their conversion into mosques. This is similar to the situation in Russia, where a re-territorialization and revitalization of many Orthodox national churches took place after the fall of Communism. Another example of the ambiguity between Algerian national identity and religious affiliation is that conversions into Islam by non-Muslims in Algeria are regularly reported as a major event by the "secular" media; the converts are heralded as heroes.

Since independence in 1962, all governments have included a Ministry of Religious Affairs. This ministry is so important, at least symbolically, that its elimination could have serious consequences for the stability of the nation. Former Primer Minister Mouloud Hamrouche, the "father" of the economic and political reforms in Algeria, learned this the hard way when he dared to do away with the Ministry of Veterans Affairs, much less important and much less symbolic for the general public. The decision cost him his premiership.[13] As someone said, it is dangerous nowadays to be honest!

There are at least two reasons why the Ministry of Religious Affairs is symbolically important to Algerians. First of all, the population in general,[14] being somehow profoundly pious, will not accept any politician who seeks to abolish it: this would be interpreted as a move away from Islam, or even as a move against Islam, against their faith, and hence a dangerous (and improbable) move. Any such move would sooner or later lead to an opportunistic military coup. Political observers claim that even at the height of his rule in 1988, President Chadli—who was a pretty strong president—could not easily switch from the socialist economic system to a market-oriented economic system. Instead, he had to "provoke," to trigger, social unrest and street riots, and then use this social unrest as a pretext to introduce political and economic reforms in early 1989. That is the reason it has been claimed that when the people *demonstrated for bread* and a better material life they *got democracy instead* (narrowly defined as a multiparty system with a free press).

Second, dissolving the Ministry of Religious Affairs will certainly be exploited by radical movements seeking to increase their ranks, and/or by any opportunist seeking power, since we all know that religion still plays a significant role in the private as well as in the public space. Finally, Islam has been the official state religion ever since the original post-independence constitution.

The Sustainability of the Current State of Affairs

The only type of state that Algeria can have, at least for the foreseeable future, is a hybrid state with Islam as an established religion, a state in which the government regulates religious affairs while staying far away from religious interference—in other words, the type of state that Algeria currently enjoys. However, the present type of state is still sustainable, even in the long term, if certain conditions are satisfied.

There is reason to believe that the relative decline of the Islamist movement in general, and the radical Islamist movement in particular, may well be temporary. This is because even though there has been a divorce between the people and the Islamist movements, there is also an increasing divide between the public and the government. This rift was evidenced by the high abstention rate (64.5%) in the 2007 legislative elections.

Today, all sectors of the population evince a deep dissatisfaction. Social unrest is increasing among unemployed young people. Protests are taking place on almost a daily basis. Although these protests are not violent and have not yielded human casualties yet, they often result in significant material damages. (The economic cost of which is often very high, something Algeria cannot afford.)

For the time being, these young people are demanding only part of the cake, over time, but if not satisfied, they might very well demand the "whole" cake. For example, if these protests last too long and spill over, the protestors might be manipulated and taken advantage of by an opportunistic group. Over time, this social unrest could become a very serious threat to the social stability of the country and an unnecessary constraint upon economic growth. The growing inequality in Algeria constitutes a real time bomb.

So unless the government finds acceptable solutions for the *economic* and *social* problems of the country, as well as the problem of unemployment among the youth, social unrest will increase. The unemployed and desperate youth will then be relatively easy to brainwash and manipulate and will be vulnerable to radical recruiters, who will also exploit the youth for logistic support. The public's discontent—and the youths' discontent—has been exploited in the past by radical Islamists, and the same thing could happen again either by Islamists or another opportunistic group. If this does happen, it could lead to another cycle of bloody violence, destabilizing the entire country.

Therefore, one of the best solutions to the threat of radical Islamists is a sustainable and reasonably high economic growth rate that will curb unemployment drastically. However, this growth should have a minimum of equity; it must deal not only with the problem of youth unemployment, but also with the problems of poverty and inequality. The latter is increasing dramatically, in all aspects (rich versus poor, young versus adults, men versus women); and, as a result, social unrest is increasing as well, dangerously threatening economic growth (a potential vicious circle).

Right now, Algeria is enjoying a golden period of relative peace that should be used not only to solve the present social and economic problems, but also to prevent future problems insofar as possible. For this to happen, however,

Algeria desperately needs successful economic reforms. Even more urgently, the government should engage—vigorously, persistently, and as soon as possible—in institutional reforms,[15] which are the *sine qua non* for successful economic reforms, political reforms, and social reforms. To decrease feelings of unfairness and injustice, among other things, the government should also vigorously fight the endemic corruption in Algeria.[16] The government should also have a fair income distribution policy and a fair and transparent judiciary system; in short, a true democracy where the rule of law prevails.

Finally, the government should promote gender equality through, among other means, universal primary and high school education. Gender equality should not only be an objective for its own sake; it also helps to reduce poverty, infant mortality, and even promotes economic growth, as evidenced by the tremendous benefit of women's education on children as future human capital (a very important factor of economic growth). In addition, gender equality "in access to opportunities, rights, and voice can lead to more efficient economic functioning and better institutions."

Moreover, the authorities should try to isolate the radical core of the Islamists by cutting or weakening their logistical links with the general public. Authorities should have an inclusive policy toward moderate Islamist movements and give them non-violent avenues to address their grievances and demands. The government should allow all types of parties. Why permit Communist, Trotskyite, and secular parties and not permit moderate Islamist or simply Islamist parties? Islamist parties should be permitted as long as they pledge to respect the democratic rules—rules that can be enforced through a system of checks and balances. After all, these types of parties are based on some type of ideology: some might call them secularized religions. Islamism should not be used as a bugaboo or a scarecrow by the authoritarian regimes in Algeria or other Muslim countries to head off reform pressures.

In any case, religious and political Islam, especially the moderate and nonviolent versions, "are there to stay as a permanent part of the Algerian political landscape."[17] Therefore, it is better and much wiser to integrate them into the political system than to exclude them and thus push them into the arms of the radicals. In fact, this integration is now explicitly (and implicitly) being demanded by the leaders of the ex-FIS. Leaders of the ex-AIS are publicly demanding that the Islamists be integrated into the political process, in spite of the fact that they have been stripped of their civic rights and that some of their former colleagues now oppose them. Actually, the disintegration of the ex-FIS family proves that their earlier shift from the political field to the battlefield has been a failure. The pressing demand for their reintegration into the political arena is rather a struggle for their political survival and a readiness for compromise. Manar Shorbagy makes similar observations and suggestions concerning Egyptian moderate Islamists.

Many people and many officials (even within the U.S. government and Congress) favor, and have called for, an inclusive policy towards moderate Islamists. For instance, in an analysis of the 2007 Turkish elections, which were won by the Islamist party AKP with a record participation of 85% (and which doubled the number of women represented in parliament: 50 women won a seat), *The Economist* wrote: "Islamist parties that declare themselves willing to abide by the [democratic] rules ought to be allowed to participate fully in electoral politics" and "should be allowed to win elections."

The secular fear about the authoritarian nature of a Muslim State—as illustrated by the Iranian, Saudi, and Taliban examples—is understandable. However, a true democrat, a true human rights activist, anyone who is truly anti dictatorship and true to himself, should condemn equally all types of dictatorships, be they clerical, secular, or Communist.

In conclusion, for the sake of a peaceful society and for the social and political stability of Algeria—which are necessary for economic growth—moderate, rule-abiding Islamists must be accepted as full participants in the political space. If they are squeezed out, they will sooner or later join the armed group—with dreadful consequences. The call for an inclusive policy makes sense, since many Islamist movements around the world are becoming more and more moderate, more politically mature, and have renounced violence.

ENDNOTES

1. K. Akacem, "Economic Reforms in Algeria," Conference Paper, *"Islam, Democracy and the State in Algeria,"* CMENAS, University of Michigan, (Ann Arbor, Michigan: September 2002) p. 9.

2. A. Richards and J. Waterbury, *A Political Economy of the Middle East* (Boulder: Westview Press 1996).

3. K. Akacem, "Islamist Opposition in Algeria: Recent Development" in ed. Amy Hawthorne, *Arab Reform Bulletin*, Vol. 2, Issue 2 (February 2004) Carnegie Endowment for International Peace: www.carnegieendowment.org/arabreform.

4. Akacem, 2004.

5. Le Quotidien d'Oran: http://www.lequotidien-oran.com/; all statistics about the different elections have been taken from this daily Algerian newspaper.

6. Akacem, 2004.

7. In contrast with the relative amnesty that was given in 1999 through the *Concorde Civile*: A Law on Civil Harmony.

8. Le Quotidien d'Oran.

9. Akacem, 2004.

10. *Le Soir d'Algerie*: daily Algerian newspaper, 03/03/07, p. 3.

11. A recent bill concerning the family code, based partially on the Sharia, became a law mainly due to the votes of the FLN.

12. Charles Tripp, "States, Elites, and the 'Management of Change'" in *The State and Global Change: The Political Economy of Transition in the MENA* eds. H. Hakinian and Z. Moshaver (Richmond Survey: Curzon Press 2001) p. 217.

13. There were other factors contributing to his departure: He had also published, in the media, the list of beneficiaries of the "privatization" of the state's lands and farms—a list which included some very high ranking public employees.

14. Or, as some call it, *L'Algerie Profonde* (mainly the rural population).

15. K. Akacem, "Des Reformes Economiques pour la Promotion des PME," Conference Paper, "*Les exigences de la réhabilitation des petites et moyennes enterprises (PME) dans les pays arabes*," la Faculté des Sciences Humaines et Sociales de l'Université de Chlef (Chlef, Algeria: Avril 2006).

16. Akacem, 2006.

17. Akacem, 2004.

Women & Society

9. Women and Demography in the Mediterranean States

Ariela Keysar

> The social position of women in any land is evidence of the country's cultural state.
>
> —*Joseph Klausner (1874-1958)*

Introduction

The goal of this chapter, drawing on recent statistics collected by the United Nations, is to explore the extent to which state secularism and private secularity across a range of Mediterranean states affect the socioeconomic status of women through the mediating factor of demographic processes, mainly reproductive patterns.

Religion in its various forms, Catholicism, Eastern Orthodoxy, Islam and Judaism, plays a major role in shaping Mediterranean societies and national cultures. The Mediterranean countries today have a wide range of socioeconomic development. Adding to the complexity, mass migration of Muslims to France, Italy and Spain, and migration of non-Jews to Israel, is altering the fabric and characteristics of the host societies and challenging their dominant culture and political institutions. Several authors in this volume describe how debates over the role of religion develop into debates over women's roles in society. For example, in Turkey, France and Algeria, there are ongoing controversies over women's wearing of head scarves in public schools and in universities. In other cases, women are challenging traditional social norms by resisting the dependence of women on men, and by demanding power in domestic decision-making, and so defying dominant religious practices and traditional lifestyles.

Socioeconomic transitions have strong effects on demographic behavior. One key transition is the shift in the locus of control over fertility from society to the individual.[1] Many social and economic studies show that as women increase

117

their educational attainment they tend to delay getting married[2] and decrease the number of children to which they give birth.[3] Today, individual family planning preferences can be accommodated by modern and efficient contraceptives that allow women to regulate fertility and limit their family size.[4]

Religion affects both the demand for and the supply of children. On the supply side are the non-monetary costs and constraints associated with contraceptive use. Traditional religions, through sanctioning of life, prohibit the use of modern birth control and abortions. On the demand side, religious worldviews restrict procreation to married couples but encourage large families in keeping with the biblical injunction to "be fruitful and multiply." Consequently, religions have a special interest in the family, and religious institutions and authorities are pro-active in reproductive issues. Exposure to religion starts in the home with family upbringing. Religious authorities of all the Mediterranean faiths endorse the norms and lifestyles associated with the traditional family (married couple with children). As a result, traditional families are usually more involved in religious activities and influenced by religious values than are single people or divorced families.

Women's Status as Human Rights Issue or as "Culture War"

Each Mediterranean country in our study has unique constitutional and societal characteristics. Political scientists often compare the political systems and socio-economics of the Mediterranean countries but a comparative analysis focused on demography, the family and the status of women is rare.

Historically, women have been socialized into specific gender roles but every religion has its particular set of constraints and prohibitions with regard to women and reproduction. They have been given role models to imitate and follow among family members, particularly mothers and grandmothers, as well as kin and others who live in their neighborhoods. The more conservative creeds set strict rules on family formation and gender roles, whereby women are expected to be homemakers and the primary caregivers of children and family. As a result, religion influences demography. In the other direction, demography helps to shape the religious landscape[5] through differential fertility and mortality across religious groups.

Across the Mediterranean region, these themes play out differently in each country. Modern secularly oriented societies regard women's rights as part of basic human rights. In various modern and transitional societies there are constant battles over attempts to diminish gender gaps in educational levels and in labor force participation rates. The goal of the reformers is to achieve equal pay for equal work and to assist women to climb to high positions in politics and government. These rights are now guaranteed by law and custom within the countries of the European Union but debates continue to rage within Islamic countries in the Mediterranean region between modernizers and traditionalists, the secular progressives and the religious conservatives. Women have tightly circumscribed roles in the more conservative Islamic societies. In contrast, moderate Muslims argue that Islamic Sharia is fully compatible with women's right to vote, run for election, participate fully in public life and assume all public offices including the highest executive office and judgeship positions. According to this interpretation, Sharia also guarantees women's right to work, own property and receive an education. Marriage is valid only upon the full consent of the woman (who also has the right to divorce).

Hypothesis

The hypothesis of this chapter is that the status of women is higher in more secular states because of the influence of state secularism and private secularity on demographic policies. According to this hypothesis, state secularism and private secularity influence the proximate determinants of fertility such as age at marriage and the usage of modern contraceptives. These demographic factors in turn affect the profile of educational attainment and the rate of labor force participation of women. These two markers are used to measure the overall socioeconomic status of women in each state. The hypothesis rests on the theory that modernization encourages women to seek economic rewards in non-domestic activities.[6] As women's human capital increases, it promotes economic growth and reduces poverty, further benefiting all of society, women and men alike.

Testing the Hypothesis: Demographic Factors

Population

Mediterranean nations vary widely in population size; Egypt, Turkey and France each have over 60 million inhabitants, while Israel, Libya and Lebanon have fewer than 10 million people. (See Figure 9-1.) The ratio of females to males also varies widely by country. A ratio of 1 indicates a gender balance while a ratio bigger than 1 indicates a surplus of females and a ratio lower than 1 points at a surplus of males, due primarily to differential mortality and migration. The range of F/M ratios shows a shortfall of women in Libya (F/M=0.93) and the opposite in France with shortfalls of males (F/M=1.05). Imbalance in the gender ratios has critical consequences for the marriage market in the population.

Annual population growth is an indicator of the socioeconomic factors shaping population increase or decline. The Mediterranean countries represent a wide range in rates of population growth, from Italy, with an annual growth rate

Figure 9-1
National Population, Ratio of Females/Males and Population Growth

Mediterranean Country	Population (In Millions) 2008	Ratio F/M	Annual Population Growth (%) 2005-2010
EGYPT	76.8	0.99	1.8
TURKEY	75.8	0.98	1.3
FRANCE	61.9	1.05	0.3
ITALY	58.9	1.05	0.1
SPAIN	44.6	1.02	0.4
ALGERIA	34.4	0.98	1.5
MOROCCO	31.6	1.03	1.4
SYRIA	20.4	0.98	2.4
GREECE	11.2	1.02	0.2
TUNISIA	10.4	0.98	1.0
ISRAEL	7.0	1.01	1.7
LIBYA	6.3	0.93	1.9
LEBANON	4.1	1.04	1.1

Source: United Nations Statistics Division http://unstats.un.org/unsd/demographic/

close to zero, to Syria with annual population growth of 2.4%—over 20 times that of Italy and 12 times the annual growth rate of Greece. Population growth is determined by demographic processes, namely mortality, fertility and migration. National statistics on these indicators tend to reflect the balance between the religious and secular segments of the population and to overall national attitudes towards women's roles in the family and in society.

Age Composition

Age composition is created by demographic patterns, such as fertility and mortality, as well as migration patterns. The age composition of a country's population is an important predictor of future demographic processes. For instance, the size of cohorts of women of childbearing age will determine the potential number of children in the future. The age composition by gender has major consequences for the future marriage market as it affects the number of potential couples of marrying age. Naturally, larger age groups in the upper part of the population pyramid indicate an older population and lower fertility for the population as a whole.

Figure 9-1a
Percentage of Population Under 15 Years of Age (2008)

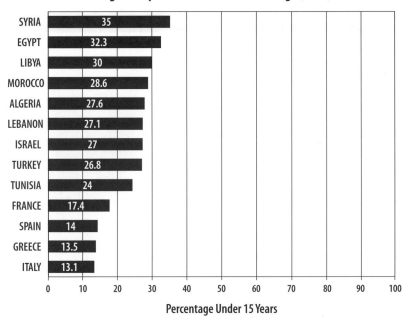

Percentage Under 15 Years

Figure 9-1b
Percentage of Population Over 60 Years of Age (2008)

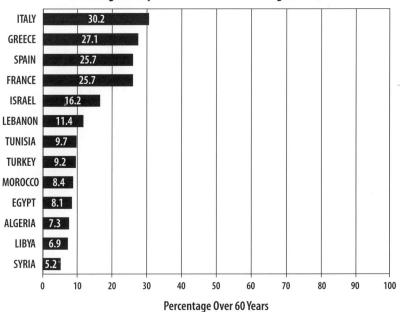

Percentage Over 60 Years

Source: United Nations Statistics Division

The age composition of the Mediterranean populations in Figures 9-1a and 9-1b follows two distinct patterns. There is one pattern for North African and Middle Eastern countries with a large portion of young people (those under age 15 years) and a small segment of older people (60 years old and older), such as Syria and Libya. The other pattern is the reverse, small portions of young people and many older people, such as in the European states of Italy, Greece and Spain. A small base is a consequence of low fertility rates. Interestingly, Israel lies in the middle between the "Christian/Secular" and the "Muslim" patterns in the two parts of Figure 9-1.

Both the young and the old are considered economically dependent sub-populations since they are not included in the current labor force. However, the young people at the base of the population pyramid are the future generation of adults and the future labor force. The aging of countries like Italy, Spain and Greece has major social and economic consequences. The elderly population cannot be fully replaced by the country's own young labor force, which requires the import of foreign workers. Yet, anti-immigrant sentiments often lead to conflicts between migrant workers and native citizens. The core of some of these conflicts between secular Europeans and North African and Middle Eastern immigrants stems from different social and religious norms, including attitudes regarding the status of women.

Mortality

Infant mortality is an important indicator of the overall standard of health of a country's population and the quality of its medical system. It is generally correlated with the wealth and standard of living of a country and per capita spending on health.

Three clusters emerge in Figure 9-2: low, middle and high infant mortality rates. At the lowest end are France, Spain, Israel and Italy, representing modern and industrialized countries. At the other extreme are Algeria, Morocco and Egypt. Their infant mortality rates are almost seven times the rates in the advanced countries. In the middle range are Syria, Libya, Tunisia and Lebanon.

Life expectancy at birth is another major indicator of the level of social and economic advancement of a country, its health system and standard of living. Due to differential mortality rates by gender, life expectancy is usually presented separately for men and for women.

Figure 9-3 shows that life expectancies for women are higher than those for men in every Mediterranean country. Morocco, Egypt and Turkey, followed by Lebanon, Algeria, Tunisia and Syria have the lowest life expectancies at birth, trailing the high-life-expectancy countries by almost 10 years among women. Israel has the highest longevity among men while Spain and France lead among

Figure 9-2
Infant Mortality Rate (2005-2010)

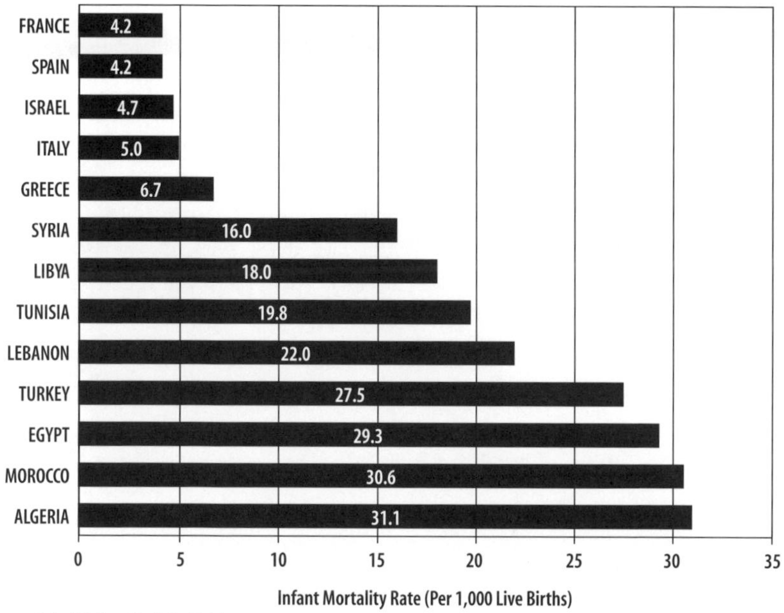

Infant Mortality Rate (Per 1,000 Live Births)

Source: United Nations Statistics Division

women. It is noteworthy that these latter countries, France and Spain, exhibit large gender gaps (6-7 years). One explanation could be the large number of male immigrants in France and Spain who are originally from North African countries with lower rates of life expectancy.

Contraceptive Prevalence

Using modern means of birth control, a woman can efficiently plan the timing and spacing of the children she bears and the size of her family by preventing unwanted pregnancies. Contraceptive prevalence among women of fertile age is an indicator of the availability, feasibility and desirability of effective family planning.[a] Family planning services are usually supplied or supported by national governments as part of social policy.[b] (See Figure 9-4.)

Religious teachings and norms affirming the "value of human life" discourage

---

[a] Note that modern methods refers to the use of female and male sterilization, the contraceptive pill, the intrauterine device (IUD), injectables, implants, female and male condom, cervical cap, diaphragm, spermicidal foams, jelly, cream, sponges and emergency contraception, and thus they exclude traditional methods which might be more available and acceptable in traditional and religious societies.

[b] The United Nations data in Figure 9-4 assembled figures from different years and some earlier points in time, in order to compare the same measurement. For Greece and Israel see http://www.un.org/esa/population/publications/contraceptive2007/contraceptive2007.htm.

women, especially unmarried women, from the use of modern contraceptives and abortion. A conservative religious attitude generally opts toward a "pro-life" rather than "pro-choice" approach in reproductive decision-making. Even in a modern market economy like the United States, the availability of advanced medical technologies and efficient birth control does not prevent the existence of a "pro-life" movement which strives to limit the reproductive rights of women especially at young ages. Therefore, the low rates of modern contraceptive use in a Muslim country, Libya (only 26%); an Orthodox country, Greece (with 34%); and a Catholic country, Italy (with only 39%) are probably attributable to religious influences on public policies and the suppressing of information and access to family planning. Nevertheless, Spain is an example of a mainly Catholic society which is also quite liberal regarding contraception (See Fulco, 2009 in this volume), with a high 67% usage rate of modern contraceptives in 1995. Interestingly, France, the most secular society in the region, has the highest rate.

Age at Marriage

The timing of marriage is presented here by the singulate mean age at marriage,[c] which is a summary measure of differences in the timing of first marriage. Figure 9-5 focuses on the singulate mean age at marriage for women.[d]

Generally, the younger the woman gets married the earlier she starts to have children. Early motherhood is usually associated with lower educational attainment for women as the burdens of raising a family preclude devoting time to schooling and developing a career. In traditional societies, mothers must also take care of older relatives in the extended family and are discouraged from working outside their home.

Advocates of women's rights support creating and enforcing a minimum legal age at marriage, which prevents the custom of arranged marriages of teenage girls and boys in traditional religious societies. The minimum legal age at marriage for women at the beginning of the 21st century in most Mediterranean countries is 18. It is 16 in Egypt and 17 in Turkey. Figure 9-5 shows that these official marriage laws seem to be working to delay marriage age for women into the early twenties even in the more traditional societies.

Nevertheless, the Mediterranean countries presented here belong to three clusters: early marriage under age 25, in Egypt and Turkey; the Western European

---

[c] The singulate mean age at marriage is an indirect measure based on the percentage of people reporting they are single (i.e., never married) in different age groups.

[d] Marriage data for Lebanon and Syria are available only for 1970 and 1981; therefore these countries were excluded from the analysis. http://www.un.org/esa/population/publications/worldmarriage/worldmarriage.htm

Figure 9-3
Life Expectancy at Birth for Men and Women (2005-2010)

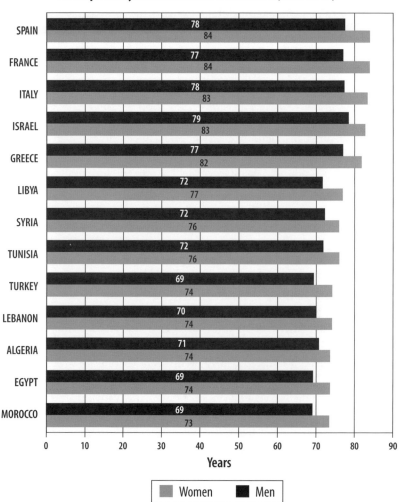

Source: United Nations Statistics Division

late marriage pattern (around 29 years) with a high proportion of women who never marry, in France, Spain and Italy; and a middle group represented by Greece and Israel among others. Libya is somewhat a puzzle with its high age at marriage that contrasts with its placement on other demographic indicators. This may reflect an imperfection in the calculation of Libya's singulate median age at marriage, possibly because of incomplete or incorrect data.

Fertility

The average number of children a woman has, defined as the total fertility rate, is determined by both biology and individual choice. Marriage patterns, usage of birth control and social norms regarding family size and infant mortality[e] are among the determinants of fertility.[7] The differences in the timing of nuptiality in Figure 9-5 are mirrored to some extent by the differences in the average number of children per woman shown in Figure 9-6.

As discussed earlier, a critical factor is distributing the power over reproductive choices. The interests of grandparents, in extended families for instance, favor higher fertility than the usual preferences of parents, while husbands typically favor higher fertility than wives.[8] Therefore, emancipation of women in reproductive decision-making may explain some of the declines in fertility levels.

The differences in fertility rates among the Mediterranean countries are quite striking, with total fertility rates at the top of Figure 9-6 (in North Africa and the Eastern Mediterranean) double those at the bottom (in Northern Mediterranean or European countries). Egypt and Syria have about 3 children on average per woman. Greece, Italy and Spain have about 1.4 children on average. This is below replacement level of 2.1 children. In these countries many women are childless.

The general inverse relationship between modernization and economic development and fertility levels is evident in the Mediterranean, with one clear exception. Israel is a unique example of an advanced country with a modern health system (See Figures 9-2 and 3), high educational attainment of women (Figure 9-7) and high level of female labor force participation (Figure 9-8), and yet a high total fertility rate of 2.8. Israeli data are for Jewish women only (Figure 9-6). DellaPergola showed major differences in fertility patterns by religiosity among Jewish women in Israel. In 2005, the most religious Jewish women had 4.7 children compared with only 1.7 children for secular Jewish women. DellaPergola[9] attributed the large gaps to "powerful differentiation of family norms related to religious norms and religiosity."

After the population losses of World War I, France prohibited abortion and the promotion of contraception. After World War II, it adopted a pro-natalist national population policy which aims at encouraging more births through financial incentives, such as maternity grants, paid maternity leave and tax benefits to parents. It is associated with the relative high fertility in France as

---

[e] The infant mortality level determines how large a surplus of births is required to produce the normative number of children. Yet, this factor is less important in a modern society with advanced health system and low infant mortality levels.

Figure 9-4
Contraceptive Prevalence

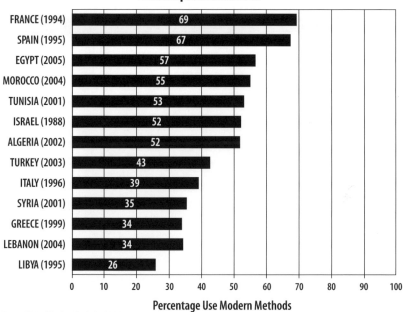

Source: United Nations Statistics Division

Figure 9-5
Singulate Mean Age at Marriage of Women

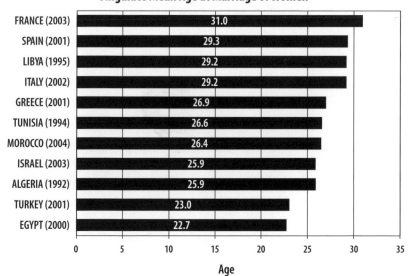

Source: United Nations Statistics Division

Figure 9-6
Fertility Rate by Country (2005-2010)

Country	Fertility Rate
SYRIA	3.1
EGYPT	2.9
ISRAEL	2.8
LIBYA	2.7
ALGERIA	2.4
MOROCCO	2.4
LEBANON	2.2
TURKEY	2.1
TUNISIA	1.9
FRANCE	1.9
SPAIN	1.4
ITALY	1.4
GREECE	1.3

Average Number of Children per Woman

Source: United Nations Statistics Division

compared with Italy and Spain.[10] Foreign women, mainly Muslim immigrants, have higher fertility rates than native French women, but there are not enough to significantly influence the overall French fertility rate.

Testing the Hypothesis: Socioeconomic Factors

Educational Attainment of Women

At the beginning of the 21st century, only 43% of women in Morocco are literate. The majority are deprived of the right to learn to read and write. In Egypt, Tunisia and Algeria, illiteracy is not as dire, yet only 60-70% of women are literate (Figure 9-7). Not only do these North African women trail substantially behind women in France, Italy, Israel, Spain and Greece, where 98-99% are literate, but they also lag behind the men in their own societies. Large gender gaps in literacy rates distinguish the low-educational-level countries, leaving women in these societies further disadvantaged.

The statistics on secondary education for girls in Figure 9-8 explain the data on literacy in Figure 9-7. Only one-third of the girls in Morocco are enrolled in secondary education. This extremely low level of educational attainment is

Figure 9-7
Literacy for Men and Women (1995-2005)

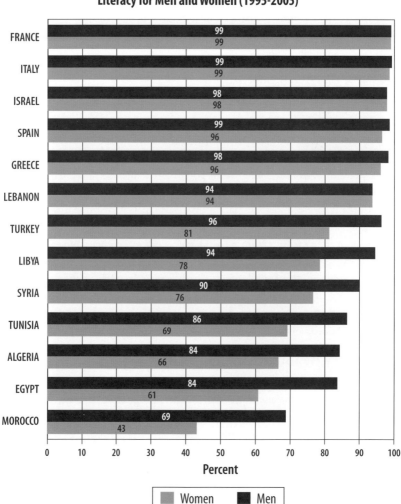

Source: United Nations Statistics Division & CIA World Fact-book (France and Lebanon)

rare in the Mediterranean region. In the rest of the countries, more than half of the girls are enrolled in high school. Although in Turkey, Tunisia and Algeria, secondary education enrollment is more than double the rate of Morocco, still more than one-third of the girls are not granted that opportunity. In Egypt and Lebanon about one-quarter of the girls are not even enrolled in high school, let alone graduate high school. Consequently, these girls face limited employment and career options and will unlikely gain freedom or economic independence.

An essential first step to empowerment of women is building security and independence through education. Needless to say, women today require education to compete in a modern society and global economy, as exemplified by France, Spain and Italy.

Women's Labor Force Participation

Labor force participation is an indicator of women's engagement outside the sphere of the extended family and the traditional homemaking environment. It provides women with opportunities to develop special skills and to earn money to become financially independent. In many ways, this is the triumph of egalitarianism as in the long run it potentially reduces gender inequality and empowers women.

In many modern societies, labor force participation of women is associated with lower fertility.[11] However, the rank order of states in Figure 9-9 is not an inversion of the order in Figure 9-6. The percentage of women in the adult labor force[f] is the lowest in Egypt (only 22%) and highest in Israel (47%) and France (46%), countries with middle range fertility regimes. Part of the explanation rests on the relationship between public policy and economic conditions relating to flexible work practices. However, it is noteworthy that in no country are women a majority of the work force.

Testing the Hypothesis: Religious Attitudes

The World Values Surveys www.worldvaluessurvey.org and Gallup World Poll https://worldview.gallup.com provide us with comparative data on values and cultural attitudes worldwide. Unfortunately data are not available for all the Mediterranean states we have presented so far. But the patterns that emerged for the demographic behavior closely mirror religious attitudes in most societies.

Figure 9-10 shows the level of importance religion has in people's lives and it sheds light on their socialization—religious versus secular. The more salience religion has in their lives, the more traditional their worldviews are and subsequently their social behaviors. The Mediterranean countries, shown in Figure 9-10, represent a wide range of levels of religiosity, from Egypt where people almost universally (97%) say that religion is "very important" in their lives to France, where only 11% of people say so. This enormous range highlights the vast cultural differences between these two societies. Below Egypt is Algeria, where over 90% of people claim that religion is "very important." In Italy and

---

[f] The share of women in the adult labor force refers to the percentage of the economically active who are women.

Figure 9-8
Girls Enrolled in Secondary Education

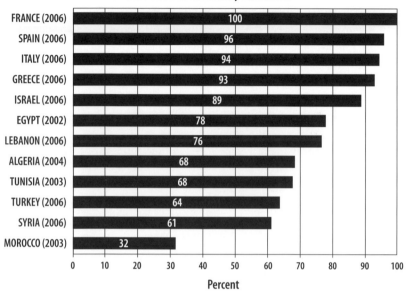

Source: United Nations Statistics Division & CIA World Fact-book (France and Lebanon)

Figure 9-9
Women Labor Force Participation

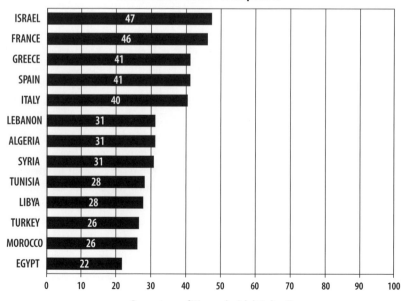

Source: United Nations Statistics Division

Greece a high importance of religion is claimed only by about one third of the people. This indicator shows a clear bifurcation between "secular" Europe and the Muslim nations since there is no middle ground.

A more theological question about the importance of God in people's lives follows a similar pattern but with more gradations. At the bottom of the ladder of belief is France, where only 8% say that God is "very important." For Italians and Greeks, God's importance is about four times higher than in France. In the middle stands Israel with about half of the population saying that God is important to them. In Egypt and Turkey, about 80% say that God is "very important" and in Algeria it is almost universal.

Rank order patterns in Figure 9-11 echo the patterns of infant mortality shown in Figure 9-2 and they are quite similar to the patterns of total fertility shown in Figure 9-6. Countries with high levels of secularity and low levels of religiosity such as France, Spain, Italy and Greece, have by far lower infant mortality levels than Algeria, Egypt and Turkey. Fertility levels in Spain are among the lowest in the world (1.4 children on average) and indeed only 22% of Spanish people view religion as "very important." At the other end of the Mediterranean in Egypt, the total fertility rate is double that of Spain with 2.9 children per woman, and religiosity is also high with 97% claiming that religion is "very important."

The Rise of Secularity

The empowerment of women requires a nation's society to adjust in many realms. Take Algeria, for example. While women are granted opportunities to attain education and job training, and they benefit from health advancements in society, in the domestic realm decision-making is assigned to men (See Cheriet in this volume). Consequently, women are deprived of reproductive decision-making because their status is perceived primarily as wife or mother. The Family Code enacted in Algeria in line with Islamic principles limits women's equality and denies them full citizenship, according to Cheriet.

The tension between advancing women's status and religious norms does not pertain only to Muslim societies. The Catholic Church's views of the "natural" family are in sharp contrast with the reality of the typical Italian family at the beginning of the 21st century. The data presented in this chapter indicated extremely low total fertility rate for Italy (TFR= 1.4) and delayed marriage (average age at marriage for women is 29 years old). Sansonetti (2009) in this volume points also at other controversial family issues prevalent in Italy today, such as cohabitations, divorce and use of birth control, all of which challenge church teachings.

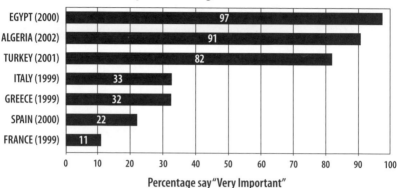

Figure 9-10
How Important is Religion in Your Life?

Percentage say "Very Important"

Source: World Values Survey and Gallup World Poll

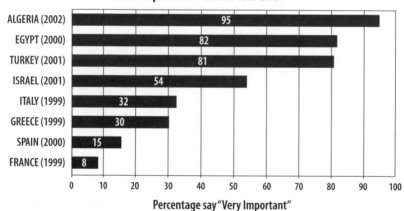

Figure 9-11
How Important is God in Your Life?

Percentage say "Very Important"

Source: World Values Survey and Gallup World Poll

All the Mediterranean countries experienced substantial declines in fertility levels compared to the 1970s levels, with the exception of Israel and France, which had only moderate decreases. The most notable declines were in Syria and Algeria, where fertility rates in the mid-1970s were about 7.4 children per woman on average. In Morocco TFR was 6.9 and in Turkey it was 5.8 at the beginning of the1970s. These rates are more than double the rates of the 1990s and the rates presented in Figure 9-6 for the beginning of the 21st century. This suggests that Mediterranean populations are shifting from high to low fertility regimes and that Muslim societies are switching from 'natural fertility' toward fertility control. Reducing the levels from TFR of 7 to 3 children per woman requires widespread use of contraception or abortion to limit family size. This involves critical shifts in individual attitudes and behavior primarily in women's preferences for family size and structure.

One would argue that freedom of choice is a secular value. Women's rights and freedom of choice in reproductive decision-making require access to information, availability of health services and openness in society to reshaping views about the family by allowing women to exercise their individual choices. The declines in fertility in Muslim societies provide clear evidence that women have begun to take some control of their lives. These demographic shifts create circumstances that will assist women to further increase their socioeconomic status. It shows that the modernization process that began in France more than a century ago has spread in different degrees across the Mediterranean. France is the most prosperous nation in the Mediterranean region, with the most advanced social welfare system. The French Enlightenment values that nourished an egalitarian society also produced a societal secularity and a secular state (*laïcité*) that is the model for many advocates of women's emancipation in the region.

Still, in European Mediterranean countries such as Greece and Italy the family remains an important agent providing essential needs of the individual. In times of economic crisis the family is required to "pitch in" and take a leading role in providing the needs of the individual where the government fails. Thus young-adult men and women return to their parents' home, delay getting married and postpone building a family. Demographic behavior (marriage, fertility and mortality) is directly linked to economic factors although their responses might lag economic trends. Yet their lasting effects both on demographic rates and the size and age composition of the national population have direct consequences for the status of women in society.

The structural challenges required to modify patriarchal societies are vast. When men are the controlling power, women traditionally need their fathers', brothers' or husbands' permission for participation in public activities. It requires normative shifts and cultural changes as necessary steps towards an egalitarian society. The case of the Women of the Wall, described by Raday in this volume, highlights the clashes within a Jewish state over equal rights for women. Although what these women are demanding is the right to pray in a public space, an issue that is particular to Israel, their fight exemplifies the universal struggle of women for empowerment and the universal religious obstacles, whether the society is Muslim, Catholic, Greek Orthodox or Jewish.

The conclusion that emerges from this analysis is that religion negatively influences the socioeconomic status of women across Mediterranean countries. Supporting our hypothesis on the relationship between the level of secularity of the state and the proximate determinants of fertility, we found that in general, women have made the greatest advances in the countries where religion has the smallest influence over demographic decision-making, especially reproduction. Yet fertility rates are falling throughout the region, suggesting that even in those countries where women remain oppressed, positive change may be coming.

ENDNOTES

1. Richard A. Easterlin, "An Economic Framework for Fertility Analysis," *Studies in Family Planning*, Volume 6, Number 3 (1975): pp. 54-63.

2. Arland Thornton, William G. Axinn, and Jay D. Teachman, "The Influence of School Enrollment and Accumulation on Cohabitation and Marriage in Early Adulthood," *American Sociological Review*, Volume 60 (1995): pp. 762-774; Carmel Chiswick, "The Economics of Contemporary American Jewish Family Life," in *Coping with Life and Death: Jewish Families in the Twentieth Century,* Medding, P.Y. (ed.). (Oxford: Oxford University Press, 1998); Evelyn Lehrer, "Patterns of Education and Entry into First Union among American Jewish Women," *Contemporary Jewry,* Volume 20 (1999): pp. 99-118.

3. Ronald Freedman, "The Sociology of Human Fertility," *Current Sociology,* Volume X/XI (1961-62): pp. 35-68 (reprinted in Ford & De Jong, *Social Demography,* pp. 44-53).

4. Donald J. Bogue, "Normative and Psychic Costs of Contraception," in *Determinants of Fertility in Developing Countries,* Bulatao, R.A. and R.D. Lee (eds.), Volume 1 (New York: Academic Press, 1983).

5. Michael Hout, "Demographic Methods for the Sociology of Religion," in *Handbook of the Sociology of Religion,* Michele Dillon (ed.), (Cambridge: Cambridge University Press, 2003).

6. Christine Oppong, "Women's Roles, Opportunity Costs, and Fertility," in *Determinants of Fertility in Developing Countries,* Bulatao, R.A. and R.D. Lee (eds.), Volume 1 (New York: Academic Press, 1983).

7. Rodolfo A. Bulatao and Ronald D. Lee, "The Demand for Children: A Critical Essay," in *Determinants of Fertility in Developing Countries,* Bulatao, R.A. and R.D. Lee (eds.), Volume 1 (New York: Academic Press, 1983).

8. Bulatao and Lee, 1983.

9. Sergio DellaPergola, Actual, Intended, and Appropriate Family Size in Israel: Trends, Attitudes and Policy Implications: A Preliminary Report, Presented at the Annual Conference Population Association of America – New York, March 29-31, 2007.

10. Marie-Therese Letablier, "Fertility and Family Policies in France," Journal of Population and Social Security (population), Supplement to Volume 1 (2003); Jonathan Grant, Stijn Hoorens, Suja Sivadasan, Mirjam van het Loo, Julie DaVanzo, Lauren Hale, Shawna Gibson, and William Butz, *Low Fertility and Population Ageing: Causes, Consequences, and Policy Options*, by MG-206-EC, 2004.

11. Constantina Safilios-Rothschild, "The Relationship between Women's Work and Fertility," in *The Fertility of Working Women*, Kupinsky, S. (ed.) (1977).

10. Social Indicators of Secularization in Italy

Silvia Sansonetti

Introduction

Secularization is a multidimensional and complex social process. The Critica Liberale Foundation and the CGIL (the largest Italian trade union) Sezione Nuovi Diritti have jointly sponsored research on the secularization process in Italy since 2005. The results, which are presented in this paper, have been published yearly in a special volume called *Quaderno Laico* of the Critica Liberale, the Foundation's review, together with the complete data-base.[1]

As a recent study has confirmed, Italy is a predominantly Catholic country.[2] Thanks to this religious homogeneity, exploring the secularization process in the country does not require making distinctions among different groups within the nation. Various social indicators concerning the Italian population covering the 14 years 1991-2004 are analyzed here including demography, health, and education, as well as participation in Catholic religious rites, public financing of religious groups, and statistics of the Italian Catholic Church and its organizations. The aim of this chapter is to juxtapose results and indicators from various studies and to reinterpret them from the point of view of the secularization process. The sources of the data are: the Vatican State (which publishes a statistical yearbook), the Italian Episcopal Conference (CEI), the Italian Institute for Statistics (Istat), the Italian Department for Education, and the Italian Department for Health and its research institute (Istituto Superiore di Sanità).[3]

Public Religious Practice and Religious Affiliation

Before presenting results regarding public religious practices and religious belonging in Italy, it is worth clarifying the relation between the sense of religious belonging and religious practice. This issue has been widely debated among scholars. Some have argued that religious practice does not necessarily follow a sentiment of belonging, since the practice may aim at gaining some social advantage. On the other hand, empirical studies have shown that practice and the sense of belonging are deeply interlaced. This is the case especially in advanced societies where religion has lost its value as a formal convention. For this reason, religious practice is commonly adopted as a key indicator of religious belonging, although it should be considered together with other indicators concerning the choices, behaviors, and beliefs of individuals.

Religious practice can be of two different kinds: the visible and the invisible. Visible practice consists of rites celebrated in public and for this reason it is also defined as public practice. Invisible practice concerns activities such as praying which take place in the private sphere. The first type can be studied by observing participation in public rites; in this case data collection can be carried out indirectly. In the second case, the investigation can be carried out only directly with individuals, using qualitative (interviews) as well as quantitative methods (questionnaires).

Here only the public practice is analyzed, more specifically, participation in rites of passage: baptism, first communion, confirmation, and marriage (see Figure 10-1). By and large, participation in life cycle rites has decreased in Italy during the years 1991-2004. The percentage of children aged one or less who have been baptized of the total children born alive in a year fell from 89.9% in 1991 to 77.5% in 2004. Two factors may explain this fall. One is the contribution of non-Catholic immigrants to the birth rate. However, the influence of this factor is small.[4] Secondly, the phenomenon may be related to a new attitude of Italian parents towards baptism. In the past, the rite was considered of an urgent character due to the belief that children who died without being baptized— who are bearers of original sin—would have been left for eternity in purgatory. Nowadays, this belief seems in decline and Catholic parents delay the rite so that the number of children baptized after age one is increasing as well as are baptisms among adults. Furthermore, the Church, after more than seven centuries, has reconsidered this issue.[5]

The first communion rate (per thousand) and the confirmation rate (per thousand) of Italian Catholics diminished during 1991-2004: communions from 9.9 to 8.4 and confirmations from 11.1 to 8.6. These decreases were partly influenced by the aging of the Italian population, since rates are computed for the entire population, but they also represent symptoms of a decrease in religiosity.

The percentage of Concordat[6] marriages among all marriages registered by the Italian state—i.e. concordat and civil marriages—is constantly decreasing: in 1991 it was 82.5% and in 2004 it was 68.8%. This trend suggests that public

Figure 10-1
Public Religious Practice 1991-2004

Years	Indicators			
	% children aged less than 1 baptized / children born in the year	FIRST COMMUNION Rate per thousand Catholics	CONFIRMATION RATE Rate per thousand Catholics	MARRIAGES % concordat marriages/ total marriages
1991	89.93%	9.93%	11.07%	82.53%
1992	86.42%	12.95%	10.97%	81.75%
1993	87.61%	9.34%	10.61%	82.09%
1994	89.41%	9.23%	10.25%	80.93%
1995	89.73%	9.17%	10.12%	80.02%
1996	85.81%	8.86%	9.27%	79.64%
1997	86.19%	9.05%	9.05%	80.68%
1998	89.21%	8.96%	9.11%	78.64%
1999	86.63%	8.99%	8.97%	77.03%
2000	85.34%	8.9%	8.78%	75.58%
2001	83.74%	8.57%	8.5%	73.16%
2002	82.15%	8.66%	8.52%	71.86%
2003	80.68%	8.52%	8.69%	71.46%
2004	77.46%	8.43%	8.56%	68.83%
Source: Quaderno Laico, 2007				

religious practice has continuously decreased in Italy during the 1990s.[7] This result contrasts with higher figures on the frequency of religious service attendance in Italy reported by other researchers.[8] However, rates of participation in rites of passage are often a better indicator of the degree or depth of the secularization process.

Family and Family Planning

Deep changes in how Italians experience their intimate lives can be observed from other indicators concerning family life choices such as cohabitations, separations, divorces, abortions, the adoption of contraceptive methods—all issues that challenge the Catholic ideal of "natural" family.[9] The absolute number of cohabitations[10] is increasing, according to survey estimates by the National Institute for Statistics, from 207,000 in 1993 to 556,000 in 2003. Another indicator is the number of children born outside marriage as a proportion of all children. Between 1991 and 2004, the percentage more than doubled, from 6.7% to 14.9%. Separations—both from concordat and civil marriages in 2004 numbered approximately 80,000, while they were only about 60,000 in 1991. Divorces too have almost doubled; there were 23,000 in 1991 and 45,000 in 2004.

These results point to the emergence of a new family model in Italy, which is completely opposite to the one promoted by the Catholic Church. There are increasing numbers of couples without children, single parents, and divorced parents who remarry or choose to cohabit. Family formation is changing and following the pattern of other advanced Western countries. Parenthood especially is becoming a deliberate choice rather than a fortuitous event. The data concerning all oral contraception (unfortunately these are the only data available) indicate an increasing rate of usage from 10.3% of fertile women in 1991 to 18.4% in 2004.

These changes in Italian society have been influenced by legal reforms during the 1970s, due to the increase of awareness concerning civil rights. In 1970, a divorce law was passed although it was strongly opposed by the Church and the Christian Democratic Party. It was confirmed by a referendum in 1974. One year later, in 1975, the New Family Law, promoted by a large majority in parliament including the Christian Democratic Party, was issued. In the same year, another law set up public Family Health Centers to promote the use of contraception. The Fascist law that prohibited them was abolished in 1971 by the Constitutional Court. These reforms have modified the relationship between individual and social group rights within the family by attributing to both husband and wife the same rights and responsibilities.[11] Another contributor to the change of the Italian society was the law on abortion passed in 1978 and confirmed by a referendum in 1981. This law stresses women's freedom of choice. It not only allows abortion but also promotes the diffusion of knowledge concerning means of contraception in public Family Health Centers. In the same year, finally an important reform concerning criminal law was issued: the abolishment of honor as a mitigating factor in cases of homicide, uxoricide, and infanticide. No doubt, all these reforms have greatly contributed to the reshaping of Italians' views about family, children, and marriage. They advance Italian women's rights in relation to men's rights. It is interesting to note that the Catholic Church strongly opposed the approval of divorce and abortion laws and it supported two referenda promoted by Catholic organizations and Catholic political parties aimed at abolishing them. Yet both referenda failed.[12]

The commitment of the Catholic hierarchy to actively oppose the changes in societies led to increased activism by Catholic organizations promoting the "natural" family. In particular, the Centers for the Defense of Life and Family (there were 487 in 1991 and 1,785 in 2004) have flourished, as well as Catholic family health centers (467 in 1991 and 517 in 2004). These organizations support couples and families in difficulties and promote the use of natural means of contraception. They are also committed to dissuading women from abortion.

The abortion rate (number of abortion per thousand fertile women) actually decreased between 1991 and 2004. It diminished from 10.9 in 1991 to 9.1 in 2001—and since then it has fluctuated around the annual average of 9.2. The slowing of the downward trend was mainly caused by immigrant women.[13] Many live in marginal conditions, especially the illegal immigrants, and ignore the opportunities to prevent pregnancies.[14] For this reason, Italian epidemiologists recommend a stronger commitment of the National Health Service to spread information on contraception among immigrant women, a strategy to prevent abortions that has been successful among the Italians.

Variations in the abortion rate may depend on the availability of facilities. Their availability is in turn also related to the presence of gynecologists, anesthetists, and nurses who are willing to practice abortion in those structures. The Italian law for abortion allows conscientious objection for employees of gynecological surgeries with regard to abortions. The personnel can change their mind as many times as they want during their professional lives. Unfortunately, there are no mechanisms to prevent employees misusing this opportunity which is common, especially among gynecologists.

Figure 10-2 shows the percentage of health professionals who refuse to practice abortion. For gynecologists, it diminished very slightly between 1991 and 2004 (from 60.4% to 59.5%). It was 67.4% in 2000 which was a holy year for the Catholic Church. Similar results emerge for anesthetists and nurses, but for them the decline between 1991 and 2004 was much steeper: for anesthetists from 60% to 46.3% and for nurses from 45.7% to 39.1%. The discrepancies among the percentages of the three different groups of professionals may be related to differing career strategies. Gender may also influence this phenomenon. We may hypothesize that women and men have a different attitude towards women's freedom of choice and therefore the number of conscientious objectors differ among the three groups according to the presence of women in each of them (there are more women among nurses than among doctors). Unfortunately, we are not able to test this hypothesis since data concerning doctors or anesthetists and nurses by gender are not available.

Education of Children

Choices regarding children's education can be considered a good indicator of secularization. The percentage of enrolled pupils taking Catholic religious classes at any level in public schools is worth analyzing. As far as the Catholic religious classes are concerned, it is first necessary to briefly review how they are organized. The first Concordat established that Catholic religious classes had to be compulsory for all Italian students. It was only in 1985 with the revision of the Concordat that Catholic religious classes became optional and an "alternative curriculum" for students who do not want to participate in Catholic religious classes was established in the official school timetables. Despite the agreements signed by the Italian state with representatives of other religious denominations, which established that Catholic religious classes have to be given in a way that does not discriminate against non-Catholic pupils, the "alternative curriculum" has never been taught in many schools. After years of debate with the representatives of other religious denominations as well as the representatives of associations for the promotion of secularism, and thanks to the positions taken by the Constitutional Court, alternative solutions were proposed. Pupils who do not want to take Catholic religious classes are allowed to study on their own, enter later, or leave school earlier. Notwithstanding this court decision, the Department of Education has issued many ambiguous rules concerning the evaluation of Catholic religious classes, so that the easiest way to cope with uncertainty for both parents and pupils seems to be conformism. Thus the vast majority of Italian pupils (over 90%) choose to attend religious classes.

Another indicator is the proportion of pupils enrolled in Catholic schools. This is continually diminishing (see Figure 10-3). In 1992, it was 9.1% and in 2004 it was 6.9%. This downward trend is similar for each school level. For the years 1992 and 2004, it was 28.1% and 21.2% in preschools, in elementary schools 6.5% and 4.9%, and in secondary schools it was 4.8% and 2.8%.

All religious schools in Italy are private. Therefore, the evolution of the phenomenon can be better explored by comparing pupils in Catholic schools with pupils in all private schools. The percentage of pupils in Catholic schools compared to pupils in private schools diminished from 67.2% in 1997 (first year for which data are available) to 51.5% in 2004. Just like the previous indicator, the trend is common to all educational levels. This result is even more interesting if we consider that during the same period the overall national share of pupils enrolled in all private schools increased: from 12.5% in 1998 to 13.4% in 2004. Thus, we can conclude that the proportion of Italian parents who prefer private schools is increasing whereas the number of those who choose Catholic schools is decreasing. This result reflects three different factors: first, a change

Figure 10-2
Percentages of Gynecologists, Anesthetists, and Nurses Working for the Italian National Health Service Who Refuse to Practice Abortion, 1992-2004*

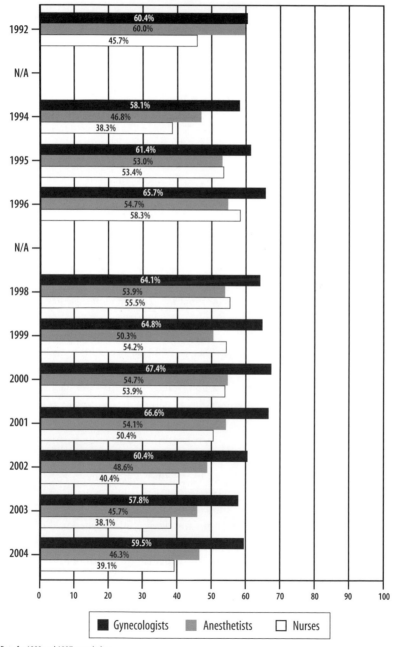

*Data for 1993 and 1997 are missing.
Source: Quaderno Laico, 2007.

in the perception of the sense of belonging among Italian parents; second, an increasing mistrust of the quality of education given in Catholic schools; third, at the secondary level in some private schools, other than Catholic, it is easier to obtain the final leaving qualification. The picture is rather different as far as Catholic universities are concerned since the number of students enrolled grew between 1999 and 2004, from about 52,000 to 56,000.

The Italian Catholic Church in Numbers

If a secularization process is proceeding in Italy, it should directly affect the Catholic Church as a social organization. The numbers of priests, deacons, nuns, monks, lay-brothers, and lay-sisters are recorded in the *Annuarium*, the official yearbook of the Catholic Church (Figure 10-4). Between 1991 and 2004, the number of priests in Italy fell from 57,200 to 51,600; monks fell from 5,000 to 3,500, nuns from 125,800 to 102,300, lay-brothers from 500 to 200, and lay-sisters from 13,500 to 10,100. Only the numbers of deacons and catechists have increased. Deacons, in 2004, were triple the number in 1991. Catechists were 202,000 in 2004, but were only 75,000 in 1996. This counter-phenomenon is probably related to the chastity vow, which is not required for deacons and catechists. Meanwhile, the great difference in numbers between these two roles (only few thousands for deacons and hundreds of thousands for catechists) may depend on the level of personal involvement and on gender: deacons are men, catechists can be either women or men.

We can observe disequilibrium in the proportions between women and men in general. Nuns and lay-sisters together in 2004 were 112,400, while priests, monks, deacons, and lay-brothers were about 62,100. Women are found at the lower level of the hierarchy of the Catholic Church, whereas men can ascend to higher offices, becoming bishops or cardinals. Although there are many opinions inside the Church in favor of access to sacerdotal orders and to positions of higher responsibilities for women, these voices are constantly silenced by the establishment.[15]

The incidence of Catholic clergy in the adult population residing in Italy shows that in 2004 there were two priests for every 1,000 men, one deacon and one monk for every 10,000 men, and a lay-brother for every 100,000 men. With respect to women, we found four nuns for every 1,000 women and four lay-sisters for every 10,000 women. Catechists who may be either women or men in 2004 were four for every 1,000 Italian residents. The continuous decrease of vocations is also reflected among the teachers who give Catholic religious classes in Italian public schools, where lay teachers are constantly increasing.

Another dimension that is worthy of consideration are the numbers enrolled

Figure 10-3
Percentages of Pupils in Catholic Schools
(Pre-schools, Elementary Schools, Secondary Schools) in a Year, 1992-2004

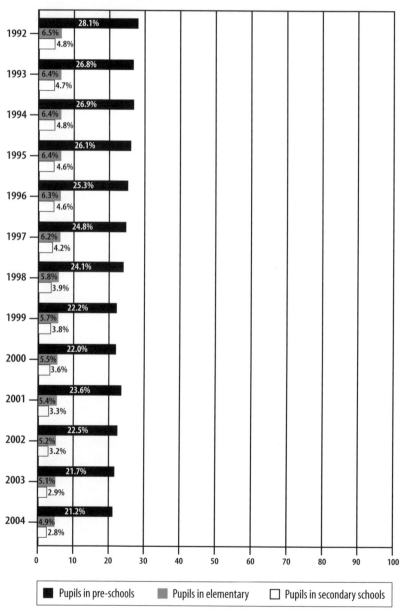

Source: Quaderno Laico, 2007.

in seminaries. Pupils who study in secondary schools were 7,000 in 1991 and 2,661 in 2004. The number of students enrolled in theological facilities has been stable (around 6,000 each year). Students in theological schools (in comparison to the number of pupils in second level school seminaries) may not be only Italian. They may come from other countries, while pupils in secondary schools are mainly Italian. If this holds true, then the stability in the total number of students in theological schools hides a decrease of Italians. Therefore, the continuous decrease of personnel in the Catholic Church organization in Italy may be actually higher than the data reveal. The nationality of clergy women and men is in fact unknown, and some of them may well not be Italians but foreigners living in Italy.

Catholic Institutions in Italian Society

Although a secularization process seems to be under way in the country, Catholic institutions are still very active in sectors such as education, health, caring and social services. In some cases they are charities or volunteer organizations; in other cases they operate as private companies. The percentage of Catholic schools among all schools in Italy slightly diminished between 1992 and 2004 to about 1.5%. Until 2004, the number of Catholic universities did not vary, although since then, it has increased. Investing in education is not as profitable as it used to be. First, because in Italy as in most advanced countries, fertility is decreasing and therefore the demand for child education is generally low. Second, the number of vocations is diminishing, and therefore the labor costs of Catholic education have risen so that Catholic schools have lost their competitive edge.

The same situation holds for the activities in the health sector, which are generally decreasing, with two exceptions. First, the Church has endorsed the opening of health centers for marginal people like the homeless and illegal immigrants. There were 168 in 2000 and 152 in 2004. They are organized by Catholic associations on a volunteer basis, often with funding help from local public institutions. Second, the Church supports the opening of Catholic family health centers and Centers for the Defense of Life and Family, which are aimed at promoting the positions of the Catholic Church regarding abortion and contraception. The commitment in favor of families emerges also in day-care centers for children up to three years of age (130 in 1991 and 221 in 2004). However, the greatest demand for care in Italy is related to the older retired population. As with many other advanced societies, Italian population is aging and even more so the Italian religious population[16] because of the decreasing trend in vocations. Offering care of the elderly is therefore not only a promising investment for Catholic religious organizations (old people's homes are often

Figure 10-4

Number of Priests, Monks, and Nuns in the Italian Church, 1991-2004

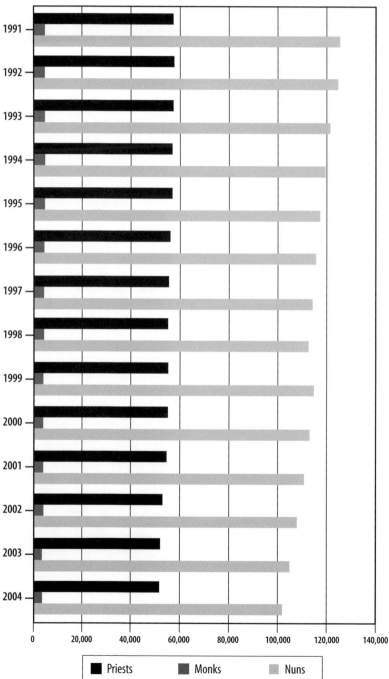

Source: Quaderno Laico, 2007.

run by nuns), but it is also a way to provide care for retired members of Catholic religious orders. Homes for elderly people, in fact, often accommodate religious people at a reduced rate, too. This is the reason why these kinds of services increased between 1994 (1,791) and 2004 (1,830).

With regard to social services, the issue is deeply interlaced with the activity of volunteer organizations and more generally of the non-profit Third Sector. The proportion between the number of non-religious volunteers and religious volunteers—which represents how many non-religious are found for every religious volunteer—has varied between a minimum of 79.0 in 1997 and a maximum of 145.4 in 2001. In 2003, it was 111.5.

The reorganization of Catholic agencies providing social services and care should be considered also in relation to wider reforms of social policy that have been implemented in the country in the last 15 years. This has involved the reform of the Third Sector and the rules concerning their collaboration with the public sector, as well as reform of social services aimed at establishing a minimum level of services to be granted to all citizens in need. All these innovations have tried to integrate the non-profit and the private sectors with the public sector in order to favor their cooperation and to increase the total supply of services to citizens.[17] As a result, many Catholic organizations and orders adjust their legal status to access direct and indirect public funding.[18] Another reform that has influenced the opportunities in terms of services provided by Catholic organizations is the reform of social policies for children and young people, according to which orphanages were closed down and replaced by other smaller structures. Although these reforms did not really affect the Italian welfare system as a whole, which is still conservative[19] and traditionally family-based, they have introduced, at least in the field of social services, small adjustments towards equality.

With regard to the Italian welfare state in general, scholars in the field of comparative welfare studies commonly acknowledge that it relies on the male bread-winner model and full employment scheme. As Hornsby-Smith[20] has stressed, Catholicism has played a role to determining its structure, at least from a cultural point of view. It assumes a family-oriented role for women that is common to other Catholic countries[21] and coheres with the religious ideal of the family proposed by the Catholic Church. Despite the acknowledgement that women must have: "the same right as men to perform various public functions,"[22] the Church advocates a society that:

> Must be structured in such a way that wives and mothers are not in practice compelled to work outside the home, and that their families can live and prosper in a dignified way even when they themselves devote their full time to their own family.[23]

It seems that the Catholic Church discourages the adoption of incentives to favor female access to the labor market. In spite of this, some measures that go in this direction have been adopted by the Italian state according to the policy guidelines established by the European Union that favor women's participation in the labor market. (For instance, widening the total supply of care service available to families goes in this direction.) All in all, Catholic institutions remain active in Italian society in the provision of services and, during the last decade, they have taken advantage of the reorganization of the welfare system especially in the fields of social services and care. Their presence is sustained by the Christian ideal of mercy and is aimed at promoting Catholic ideas regarding the family, children, and the role of women in the society.

The Italian Catholic Church and the Mass Media

Modern society communication represents an important way to be present and influence the society, and the Italian Catholic Church as an organization is aware of this. In Italy, the Catholic Church directly controls one national radio (*Vatican Radio*), one satellite television (*Sat 2000* owned by the Italian Episcopal Conference) and two national newspapers; *L'Osservatore Romano*, the official Vatican newspaper, and *L'Avvenire,* the official newspaper of the Italian Episcopal Conference. In addition, Catholic organizations control other national mass media such as a national radio station (*Radio Maria*), magazines, and periodicals at national or local levels. Besides this, representatives of the Catholic institutions are often present on public and private media on news as well as on entertainment programs. Available statistics show that news programs on the three public channels of the public Italian broadcasting company RAI devoted an average of 5% of their time to the Catholic Church in 2004.[24] Besides television, the world of communication includes publishing. The percentage of religious printed writings among the total of works published every year can be considered as a proxy for the influence in the publishing industry of Catholic Church. The time series shows growth between 1996 (5.8%) and 2000 (8.3%) and then a decrease until 2003 (6.7%).

Conclusions

The data gathered together in this chapter show that a process of secularization is taking place in Italy that is slow, but continuous. The process of transformation is oriented towards a more flexible attitude in applying the Catholic precepts and sometimes a growing disinterest towards these precepts by the Italian people. This trend towards greater secularity is suggested by the generalized decrease in the participation in public religious practice and in particular in rites of passage.

There appears to be a diminishing appeal of Catholic ideas as regards family life and children's education, as well as a decrease of religious vocations. The analysis shows the emergence of higher rates of autonomy and more individual responsibility in everyday life experience—phenomenon that can be traced back to processes of wider individualization in the society.[25]

As far as the Catholic Church is concerned, this analysis also shows a general readjustment of the institutions of the Italian Catholic Church towards becoming active in society through supplying welfare services and towards being present in the public sphere through using mass-media communication. Like soldiers who close their ranks, the Catholic Church is reorganizing its presence in the lives of Italians.

ENDNOTES

1. The Report on Secularization and the Observatory on Secularization have been published in *Quaderno Laico, 'Critica Liberale,'* the Review of the Foundation 'Critica Liberale':

   vol. XI I n. 111/2005

   vol. XIII n.123-124/2006

   vol. XIV n.135-137/2007

   Maria Gigliola Toniollo (CGIL 'Nuovi Diritti') and Enzo Marzo (Fondazione Critica Liberale), are the principal investigators. The team are: Laura Caramanna, Renato Coppi, Mario Di Carlo, Giulio Ercolessi, Silvia Sansonetti, Mirella Sartori, Marcello Vigli; the data collection was carried out by Alberto Emiletti.

2. A recent large study has estimated that only 1.9% of Italian citizens (that corresponds to about 1,124,300 individuals) do not self-define as Catholic (CESNUR, *Le religioni in Italia* (Torino: Ellenici-Velar, Leuman, 2006). Among immigrants who are not Italian citizens, non-Catholics (including Muslims, Orthodoxies, and Protestants) are estimated as 1,539,000. Among them the majority are Muslims (850,000) followed by Christian Orthodox (420,000), and Christian Protestants (150,000).

3. Please note that all the official documents of the Vatican State are available on the Vatican State website. Documents written by popes are available at the address: http://www.vatican.va/holy_father/. As to other documents of general interest like The Vaticanum II Concilium documents, the Canonical law, the Catechism, and related documents, they are available at the address: http://www.vatican.va/archive/.

   Data concerning passage rites, the Catholic welfare measures for families and numerosity of the clergy in Italy *Annuarium Statisticum Ecclesiae.*

   Data concerning pupils taking Catholic religious classes: the Cei-Italian Conference of Catholic Bishops.

Data concerning pupils in Italian schools: Italian State, Ministry of Education.

Data concerning abortion and contraception: Italian State, Ministry of Health, and Highter Institute for Health.

Demographic data: Istat: National Statistical Yearbook years: 1991–2004.

Istat has also published in depth research on:

families: Indagine Multiscopo sulle famiglie italiane and Statistiche giudiziarie

the volunteer association: Indagine sul volontariato.

4. Only 13% of children born in 2005 had at least one parent who was not an Italian citizen while 87% had both parents who were Italian. The second percentage is ten points above the number of baptised children with an age of 0-1.

5. A theological committee established in 2004 decided that the concept of limbo reflects an 'unduly restrictive view of salvation.' This decision is probably aimed at strengthening the position of the Catholic Church on abortion. The so called 'unborn children,' in fact, 'largely contribute to the increase of the unbaptized,' the commission wrote, thus granting that fetuses are human beings.

6. Concordat marriages are recognized within the Italian Republic-Vatican State Concordat agreement. The relations between the Italian Republic and the Vatican State are ruled by an international concordat, which also regulates many other aspects of the relations between the two States. Concordat marriages are religious marriages with civil effects, celebrated by a parish priest or one of his delegates. Concordat marriages present some problematic aspects, among them the issue of nullity. Italian Catholics can opt for religious marriage, which has no legal value for the Italian state. It is often chosen by old people, especially by widows and widowed who do not want the marriage to affect the legal assets of their descendants or who do not want to loose reversionary pensions (C. Saraceno e M. Naldini, *Sociologia della famiglia* (Bologna: Il Mulino, 2001)).

7. Research based on representative samples has shown similar results regarding baptisms and marriages (C. Lanzetti, "I comportamenti religiosi," in *La religiosità in Italia*, V. Cesareo, R. Cipriani, F. Garelli, C. Lanzetti, C. Rovati, p. 71-98 (1995); C. Chiara Canta, "La pratica religiosa," in *La religiosità a Roma*, R. Cipriani ed.: p. 87-106 (1997)).

8. P. Norris and R. Inglehart, *Sacred and Secular, Religion and Politics Worldwide*, (Cambridge University Press, 2004).

9. This is the family based on the religious marriage, which is a sacrament—i.e. an act done in the name of the supernatural reality of God. It is valid thanks to the 'conjugal act'—i.e. sexual act, which has two supernatural meanings: the unitive and the procreative. There are two consequences of the sacrament of marriage. On one hand, to dissolve the union, a declaration of nullity by an ecclesiastical court is needed because humans cannot divide what God has united, although spouses can choose to live separate if living together has become unbearable for serious reasons (as a consequence, civil divorces have no value and divorced people who remarry civilly are considered as adulterers and excluded from the communion). On the other hand, the use of artificial contraceptive means is forbidden because it goes against the procreative aim of marriage. The allowed means of birth-control are the natural ones together with the exercise of chastity.

10. In Italy, there are no laws that regulate the relations between cohabiting couples. Recent attempts (in the first months of 2007) to fill this gap have been strongly opposed by the Catholic Church.

11. The husband, in fact, was legally the family-head and women, as wives and mothers could not make decisions on their own. The same held for girls, who as daughters were under the tutelage of their fathers, from which they could emancipate only throughout marriage (D. Vincenzi Amato, "Il diritto di famiglia," in *Lo stato delle famiglie in Italia*, C. Barbagli and C. Saraceno: p. 37-52. (1997)) which used to take place in early ages (M. De Giorgio, *Le Italiane dall'Unità a Oggi* (Bari: Laterza, 1992). In addition, the old law gave different rights to children born within and outside marriage. On the opposite, the reform gave equal rights to all children. ALSO—The encyclical letter *Casti Connubii* by Pio XI in 1930 recommended: 'Domestic society being confirmed, therefore, by this bond of love, there should flourish in it that "order of love," as St. Augustine calls it. This order includes both the primacy of the husband with regard to the wife and children, the ready subjection of the wife and her willing obedience.

12. The Catholic Church fixed the guidelines for the Catholic Church on all these issues in the apostolic exhortation *Familiaris Consortio* on the 'role of the Christian family in the modern world' signed by John Paul II and published in 1981. The document tackles the issues of family, marriage, birth-control, divorce, abortion, cohabitations, as well as the condition of children, women, men, and elderly in the family. It also discusses in depth the position of women in the society. It has since inspired further official documents (the 'Charter for Family Rights' published in 1983, the *Mulieris dignitatem* in 1988, 'The Letter to the Families' in 2003, the encyclical letter *Evangelium vitae* in 1995), as well as the 1983 canon law reform and the 1992 Catholic text for catechism—readjusted in 1997, and its interpretation contained in the 2005 Compendium.

13. M. Grandolfo, L'ivg in italia, paper presentato al convegno 'Interruzione di gravidanza tra le donne straniere', Roma, 15 dicembre 2005, Istituto Superiore di Sanità (ISS).

14. In general, immigrant women present higher levels of fertility, for instance, in 2005, their total fertility rate was 2.45 per thousand; for Italian women, it was 1.24 per thousand.

15. Especially in Italy it is very rare to find discussions about these issues outside of specialized reviews. By the way, there is an Italian association of women theologians (Coordinamento Teologhe Italiane) which is very active and, thanks to the publishing house Queriniana, many writings of internationally well-known scholars have been translated into Italian.

16. As also other studies have highlighted (F. Garelli, *Sfide per la Chiesa del nuovo secolo* (Bologna: Il Mulino, 2003); L. Diotallevi, ed., *La Parabola del Clero: uno Sguardo Socio-demografico sui Sacerdoti Diocesani in Italia* (Torino: Edizioni Fondazione Giovanni Agnelli. 2005).

17. U. Ascoli e C. Ranci, *Dilemmas of the Welfare Mix: the New Structure of Welfare in an Era of Privatisation* (New York: Plenum-Kluwer, 2002).

18. According to the concordat between Italy and the Vatican State, Catholic organizations such as religious orders have a special legal status ruled by the canonical law.

19. G. Esping-Andersen, *Social Foundations of Postindustrial Economies* (Oxford-New York: Oxford University Press, 1999).

20. M. Hornsby-Smith, "The Catholic Church and social policy in Europe" in *Welfare and Culture in Europe: Towards a New Paradigm in Social Policy*, P. Chamberlyne, A. Cooper, R. Freeman, M. Rustin (eds.) p. 172-189 (London: Jessica Kingsley Publishers, 1999).

21. Catholic countries are generally characterized by corporatist regimes where the entitlement to services and provisions is related to the participation to the labor-market. This model attributes to women a family oriented role while men are the bread-winners. Many factors contribute to its realization. First of all, the gender gap in wages, with women always earning less than men in similar positions. Second, the poor supply of care services for children and the elderly that pushes families to turn to the market to pay care services to satisfy their needs. Obviously, the higher the price, the more convenient it is for women to care rather than to work. Other women with a good position in the labor market or those with a strong motivation to work may decide to continue to work, although with many personal difficulties related to poor collaboration by their male partners at home.

22. Pope John Paul II in *Familiaris Consortio, part III,* section 1: paragraph 23 'Women and society.'

23. *Ibid.*

24. M. Staderini, "Le pallottole di televaticano," in *Critica Liberale* vol. XIV n. 135-137. p. 80-84 (2007).

25. R. Inglehart, *Modernization and Postmodernization, Culture, Economic and Political Change in 43 Societies* (Princeton: Princeton University Press, 1997).

11. The Ambiguous State: Gender and Citizenship in Algeria

Boutheina Cheriet

Introduction

What is the best way to examine the problem of citizenship and gender in the emergence of civil society and its dialectical relationship with a monolithic state in Algeria?

One way is to analyze the Algerian debates over personal status in order to capture the nature of the relationship that links the triad of state, civil society and citizenship. This allows us to investigate the ambivalence that characterizes the nature of the state and women's access to citizenship.

Indeed, women are caught between the ambiguities of modernity and the regressive local traditional values. This ambivalence has hindered women's access to a full-fledged citizenship based on the individualization of their allegiance to the state.

It is worth noting that the ambiguities are those of the political class. In Algeria this class is mainly represented by the state technocracy, a group which had proved instrumental in erecting the normative and institutional bases of the state structures after independence in 1962. Their characteristics and reflexes correspond most closely with Hishem Sharabi's concept of neo-patriarchy in the Arab region.[1] This argument purports to demonstrate that the ambivalent attitude towards modernity—which has been taken as a "technical" infrastructural device, rather than a total phenomenon—has sown the seeds both of radical Islamism and of a gendered notion of citizenship, instead of that of universal enfranchisement.

However, it is not in women's limited access to the public realm that the hesitations of the neo-patriarchal state are most cogent but rather in women's empowerment as individual decision-makers in the domestic realm of the

155

family that is the reproductive space par excellence. In this cloistered space, the ambivalent attitude of neo-patriarchy feeds into the resolve of resurgent religious fundamentalist claims in tailoring a lame or subordinated citizenship for women in Algeria. The end result was the promulgation, in the early 1980s, of a Family Code bill. These laws entrenched women within the confines of a "minority" status in exchange for their access to the polity. To be admitted to the polity as into the public space, women in Algeria are asked to sacrifice their majority status in the family, thus ensuring that their access to citizenship will not undermine belief in the conjugal and familial cosmogony.[2]

Debates over personal status started as early as 1963 and were, at first, dominated by the revolutionary euphoria of Independence. This was well illustrated by the adoption, on July 25, 1963, of a law (Loi 63-224) establishing a minimum age for marriage. The law was intended to curb the early marriage of young girls. However, the bill was never enforced, as conservatives in the legislative and executive bodies quickly denied its legitimacy and denounced it as a "secularist" move (secularism being understood as a menace to the social order). Further attempts at issuing progressive provisions favoring an individualized decision-maker status for women were made in 1966 and 1972. However, these too were aborted after negative reactions from conservative quarters. Most significant in this contest was the systematic ambiguity of the elite in power regulating the place of secularism, and that of women.

State and Kin vs. Women

The list of participants in the process of state- and nation-building in Algeria is by no means binary, and one could easily discern differences among revolutionary radicals, nationalist apparatchiks and technocrats, and religious conservatives as early as 1962. Despite a unitary façade and an obligatory post-colonial rhetoric, radical opinion seemed to dominate early socio-political and ideological discussions of the polity; this was demonstrated by populist measures such as agrarian self-management, free education and health care, and a widespread social security system. However, a 1965 coup d'état by Col. Boumediene (1965-1978) put a sharp end to the radicals' revolutionary euphoria. The coup marked the first rupture with the "ideological" legitimacy of national unity implied by the 1954-62 anti-colonial war, and replaced it with a "technocratic" legitimacy of state-building efficacy, sustained by a new discourse of "specific socialism."

For over a decade, a large consensus had apparently emerged in support of the vast populist measures undertaken by the state technocracy. Their signal achievement was co-option of all trends of public opinion in the name of economic efficiency and social egalitarianism. The most notable co-option was of targeted left-wing radicals (following a wave of repression in the mid and late 1960s), and women, who were integrated into areas of mass consumption such as education and health. Last but not least was the co-option of the advocates of religious conservatism, whose "cardinal sin"—the endorsement of socialist policies—was lavishly compensated for by the promulgation of Islam as the religion of the state and the establishment of colleges and institutes dispensing religious education. These educational institutions, by and large, constituted veritable breeding grounds for the later, more transparent fundamentalist claims of the 1980s.

The technocratic nature of state- and nation-building during that period has left a deep imprint on the later development of what I would call a "commodity" notion of citizenship. Indeed, within a dynamic of rapid social change, from a pre-industrial formation into a dependent post-colonial one, universal enfranchisement could not be incorporated as a gratuitous right of a transcendental Republic, but rather brandished as a "barter good" in exchange for carefully tailored allegiances. This is where universal access to the Republica is negotiated against the preservation of allegiances of an ascriptive type, specifically with regards to women's empowerment as individual decision-makers in the domestic space.

Article 2 of the 1976, 1986 and 1989 constitutions stipulates that Islam is the religion of the state. The heterogeneity of the official ideological discourse about Socialism and Islamism, and also about local traditional communitarianism, has abetted a growing individualism. It has also helped legitimize regressive conservative claims against the ideal of modern citizenship. Furthermore, the present economic liberalization has simply dragged along, as a corollary, a clear political and social fundamentalist expression. This has occurred notwithstanding the monolithism of the technocratic neo-patriarchal state, which has attempted to excoriate both conservative and radical progressive opinions, in an effort to maintain, indefinitely and exclusively, the mythical unitarianism of the nebulous notion of nationalism. In this, the Algerian case mirrors its sister Arab neo-patriarchies.

Indeed, contrary to the broad support for a) the confinement of Arab women to the private domestic boundaries of the family and b) the marginalization of Arab women from decision-making processes in the public arena, one has to marvel at the formidable monopolization of family and personal status legislation by exclusively male-dominated executive, as well as legislative and state structures.[3]

The classical typology, which draws a clear line between categorizations of "public" and "private," ought to be handled with care where the role and status of women in the Islamic discourse are concerned. The process of the Family Code enactment in Algeria shows, all too clearly, that women's involvement, as full-fledged decision-makers, in the management of family matters within the ideal type of the individualized citizen, with direct allegiance to the state and the new national space is perceived as the factor most threatening domestic stability and social cohesion.[4]

Whereas women's participation in areas of public activity has been accepted as a social structural change, bestowing women equal decision-making powers in the family has not. It is perceived not only as sacrilegious, but threatening for the traditional predominantly patriarchal order, whose best guarantor remains the relational dynamics of the family unit. As paradoxical as it may sound, an active role of women in this domestic arena would entail the attainment of decision-maker status for them. This would promote their individuality but, by the same token, undermine the harmony of the Islamic dual cosmogony, on the one hand, and patriarchal power, on the other hand.[5]

The idiosyncratic tension between ideal womanhood and ideal citizenship came to the fore with the legislature of 1982. The National Popular Assembly (APN) was to examine a personal status bill regulating domestic relationships. Its purpose was to delineate the boundaries of women's status as wives and mothers, under the guardianship of their husbands and fathers. The bill was a very significant expression of the tentative preservation of the dominant agnatic and patrilineal familial structure, a structure largely ensured and protected by the subservient status of women. In addition to systematizing Shari'a provisions as those provisions are found in the Qur'an, Sunna and the dominant Maliki interpretations of the Islamic legal discourse—all of which give preeminence to the "male believer" above his female counterpart—the bill also introduced further limits on women's movements as participants in the public arena by conditioning their right to work. They can only do so with their husbands' permission. Rather than voicing a theological injunction, this last condition expressed the traditional local Algerian customs involving women's effacement and dependence on male kin. It is significant that most provisions of the bill were an expression of a misogynistic residual social order, which were conveniently added as legislative principles, since ones actually based on Shari'a would have necessarily introduced a debate along the more complex and most "fastidious" procedures of *Ijtihad* and *Taqleed* in the Islamic legal tradition. Neither the technocrats of the government who proposed the bill, nor the neo-patriarchs of the National Assembly, were ready to open any public forum on the matter. Recoursing to theological expertise was discreet, and limited to ad-hoc questions.

However, these legislative debates were far from unanimous, for the National

Assembly at that time included a few delegates with progressive views, who attempted to advance the concept of citizenship and individual allegiance to the state, comprised in the official ideological discourse of the modern nation-state. They were opposed by staunch conservatives who opposed equal legal status between men and women.

The Justice Minister, in his introductory talk about the bill, left no doubt as to the position of the modernizing state builders. He summarized the bill's mission as embodying "...the legislative reference within the framework of Islamic principles, which ought to guarantee woman her rights, her position as partner of man, and as mother in society." Following in the footsteps of the Minister, the Chairman of the Assembly's Administrative and Legislative Commission clarified women's status as subordinate in marriage, divorce and guardianship.

- Marriage is based on equality between husband and wife, except in legal responsibility, and familial authority, a natural prerogative of the husband.

- Divorce [read: repudiation in the Arabic text] is the exclusive faculty of the husband.

- Guardianship [over women and children] is an imperative injunction of Islamic legislation to insure the protection of incapacitated people [*qusara* in Arabic].

Accordingly, the die was cast with regard to the nature of the legislation to be issued by the Assembly. Although about ten delegates tried, in vain, to remind their peers of the Constitutional provisions on sex equality and the universality of citizenship for both sexes (Constitution, Article 58), the Assembly's arena turned into a veritable inquisition court against women's right to decision-making in familial matters, and a venting-session about the threat it posed to social stability.

The intervention of the conservative delegates left no doubt as to the values informing their positions. Some excerpts from the January 1982 APN minutes can be quite telling. Some saw in the bill: "a riposte against those impregnated with secular views" while others clearly affirmed that the bill represented an opportunity for "rejecting secularism because it has made of woman a merchandise, by prohibiting polygamy and encouraging the separation of bodies as well as adultery." Obviously, fear of secularity eloquently summarizes a fear of individuality and the ensuing sexual and social empowerment of women. This was clearly expressed in the allegory of "the separation of bodies."

The bill was not enacted by the 1982 legislature, and was discreetly withdrawn because of the conservative onslaught throughout the debate and the protest marches organized by independent women from professional circles and war veterans, protesting the promulgation of such retrograde provisions. It is worth noting that these protests were a first in the annals of "civil disobedience" in post-independence Algeria.

However, in the grand tradition of neo-patriarchal maneuvering, the then-Chairman of the National Assembly issued the following warning to both progressive and conservative delegates of the Assembly: "The Algerian Revolution is at the avant-garde of the Arab-Muslim nation. One of its most outstanding achievements is equality between man and woman in the acquisition of knowledge, and access to work....but...Algeria firmly opposes secularism."

In January 1992, on the eve of the first multi-party legislative elections following the overwhelming landslide victory of the Islamists in the 1990 local municipal elections, the Islamist parties, headed by the Islamic Salvation Front, went a step further, and announced in their campaigns a doomsday for secularism in Algeria and the promise of an Islamic Millennium. The organic ties binding the particularistic nostalgia of the discourse of "specific socialism," as dispensed in the 1960s and 1970s, and the more recently avowed puritanism of the Islamic fundamentalist claim, have by now been brought into the open. Rather significantly, the process was advanced by the representatives of the civil society in the guise of delegates at the National Popular Assembly. And, even more significantly, the main catalyst remained family legislation and women's status. In one word: gender.

Women's "Commodity" Citizenship

Notwithstanding the withdrawal of the 1982 Personal Status bill, pressure was mounting from conservative quarters to issue a family and personal status legislation, in accordance with Shari'a injunctions, and some traditional mores, especially those pertaining to the predominance of kin over females. This was achieved in June 1984, when Qanun al Usrah (Le Code de la Famille/The Family Code) was enacted, and became Loi (Law) no. 84-11.[6] The more recent, amended version of the law (codified in 2005) was a missed opportunity to grant Algerian women full equality because it retained polygamy, albeit a conditional "modernized" version, as well as the matrimonial legal guardianship.

All provisions of the Code, and indeed the Code itself, confine women to a relational model of citizenship by assigning them the status of a dependent, incapacitated being, be it in marriage, divorce, legal representation or in matters of inheritance.

Of particular interest to the present contention of women's marginalization from "domestic decision-making" was the desperate maneuvering of conservative delegates during the 1984 National Assembly debates. The point of this maneuvering was to impose polygamy as an unconditional provision in the Code. It is worth noting that polygamy is hardly a widespread practice in Algeria. Both local customs, as well as a post-independence growth of atomization of the family structure under the pressures of merchandization and urbanization, were not favorable to polygamous unions. In fact, polygamy was introduced as a Qur'anic injunction and the passionate defense of the sacred verse (Qur'an, Women: verse 2)[7] in the National Assembly was more informed by tentative trepidations to constrain women's empowerment and enforce social control around them. The most effective means to this end, it seemed, was to encourage polygamy so as to ensure the permanence of the extended family, and, henceforth, the primary role and status of women as reproducers.

In most of its provisions pertaining to marriage, divorce, child custody and inheritance, the 1984 Family Code was a moribund reproduction of Shari'a injunctions, without a specific reference to the Maliki trend, which has deeply informed the socio-legal organization of the Maghreb at large. However, while leaving most of the provisions of the Shari'a intact, the government bill made polygamy conditional upon the consent of the first wife as well as the second. This was sufficient to provoke so great an uproar in the Assembly that the debates were virtually turned into a conference on polygamy.

The minutes of the *Journal Officiel* of the National Popular Assembly, reporting the plenary sessions of April 23-24, 1984,[8] disclose a veritable "crusade" against Article 8 and a staunch defense of polygamy. There was no trace of interventions by secularist members. Of 60 interventions reported in the minutes, 45 stood against the conditional terms on polygamy.

Of the most significant interventions, one could hardly miss the idiosyncratic one on the military purposes of polygamy:

> Polygamy is not to be disputed, whatever the case, for a Muslim state is one based on Jihad, and this calls for the involvement of men alone. To whom will the women be left in case of Jihad, and how to protect society from subsequent depravity, if widows cannot find parties to marry. Polygamy is therefore a must.[9]

This intervention remains very eloquent with regard the super-structural paradigm informing conservative public opinion in Algeria, be it in relation to social actors (women as reproducers, men as Mujahidin) or political legitimation (the state is implicitly based on Jihad, in reference to Article 2 of the Constitution). The idiosyncratic logic of patriarchal conservatism has had the last word.

Nevertheless, despite the aforementioned hysteria over the adoption of unconditional polygamy, representatives of the neo-patriarchal elite managed to outmaneuver the intransigent conservatives and include the government's proposed article. For instance, the Chairman of the Legislative Committee argued in favor of retaining conditional polygamy. He "scientifically" rationalized the provision, explaining that "...given that Algeria's population is constituted of 48% males, and 52% females, four girls out of 52 would remain unmarried, and would fall prey to non-Muslim unions or even depravation; therefore polygamy is justified in a statistical sense." This pseudo-scientific legitimizing of polygamy is but an example of the newly independent state using science as a legitimating discourse. This approach in Algeria is common to radical and conservative public opinion alike. The state erects itself as the "decider," because it is the "knower," relying on teams of technocrats and experts whose competence cannot be easily challenged by lay people. Neo-patriarchy in Algeria has in fact relied on the double-edged appeal to transcendent worldviews in their sacred religious aura whenever radical, secular opinion emerged; conversely, and upon technical, rational "proof" as an argument when resisting conservative opinion.

However, this typical maneuvering of the Algerian post-independence political class went unheeded as long as the processes of nation and state building concerned the infrastructural public arena, the main features of which appeared to be industrialization, urbanization, mechanization of agriculture and, above all, systematic socialization via extended schooling. Nonetheless, the process stopped at the doorstep of the domestic familial arena, where the mechanisms of mechanical solidarities stood firm before the incursions of the state.

In Algeria, by and large, the family confines are designated as *Horma*—that is, "sacred intimacy." Etymologically, *Horma* is derived from the Arabic *Haram*, meaning "sacrilegious," forbidden. *Horma* also means the wife, or invariably all the women of the family. It seems that gender, therefore, stood up to the confusing eclecticism of the state legitimation discourse, where other spheres of social organizing remained docile, or even welcoming.

We cannot help but note that the outcry is principally expressed as a protectionist reflex of women's reproductive role, and the implicit rejection of their sexual empowerment is seen as a menace to reproductive and relational statuses (i.e., wife, mother). This clearly indicates that women's access to citizenship is heavily jeopardized by the problem of reproduction.

In Algeria, the nation-state-in-making has mostly relied on an eclectic and somehow mimetic adoption of universal liberal criteria of citizenry. In particular, it seems that women's access to the public arena, that is to citizenship, holds sway within a clientelist dynamic. Hence the generally favorable integration of women in public processes, in particular education, health and services. The state sells these packages as "constitutional rights," but uses them as "favors," and they are perceived as such by a majority of women, who face a very reluctant, if not hostile, social context. In exchange, women are expected to endorse citizenship as a commodity, and not as an inalienable right, by accepting their effacement from the major decision-making processes, especially those decisions pertaining to personal status and family legislation.

Interestingly enough, female citizens tend to look upon the state as a liberator, despite the formidable regressions it has engendered in matters related to personal status. Today, feminists in Algeria continue to call upon the state to intervene by halting the fundamentalist upsurge and implementing a model of universal citizenship within the framework of the Republica. However, state legitimation has been seriously undermined by the more universal appeal of the pan-Islamic revolution. Accordingly, one might expect that the dominant national elite, in a last bid to maintain its political power, will continue to maneuver and cooperate within the realm of patrimonial and clientelist relations with the feminists and democrats alike.

Nevertheless, sooner or later, bids for power will have to come from various social groups within civil society at large, groups that will discard the state as the omnipotent decider-protector in Algeria. It is then that the bid for citizenship will be open for all. For women, this means a long and painful birth, but after all…a birth!

ENDNOTES

1. Hisham, Sharabi, Oxford University Press, 1988.

2. For a detailed account of the debates which surrounded the Family Code, see Cheriet, Bouthenia, "Feminism and Fundamentalism: Algeria's Rites of Passage to Democracy" in J.P. Entelis, and Naylor, P.C., State and Society in Algeria, Westview Press, 1992, pp. 171-215, with specific reference to the contestants involved in the legal battle over personal status, see pp. 188-192.

3. Fatima Mernissi, *Beyond the Veil: Male-Female Dynamics in Modern Muslim Society*, Al Saqi Books, London, 1985.

4. See Cheriet and Naylor.

5. Abdel Hameed al-Shawaribi, *al-huquq al-siyassia lil-mar'a fil-islem* (Women's Political Rights in Islam), Mansha'at al-Ma'arif, Alexandria, 1987.

6. The documents used for the present argument include: *Le Journal Officiel de la Republique Algerienne Democratique et Populaire, Loi no. 84-11 du 9 Juin 1984 portant Code de la Famille, no. 24, 12 Juin 1984*, Imprimerie Officielle, Alger.

7. The Koran, translation by N.J. Dawood, Penguin Books, 1981.

8. *Le Journal Officiel de'l Assemblee Populaire Nationale (JOAPN), Debats Parlementaires,* nos. 46, 47, 52, 1984. Imprimerie Officielle, Alger. This represents meeting minutes of the 1984 debates on the Family Code. All documents are in French. The translations are this author's.

9. JOAPN, 46: 19-21.

12. The Ambiguous Position of French Muslim Women: Between Republican Integration and Religious Claims

Camille Froidevaux-Metterie

T he "veils quarrel"—also known as the "scarf affair"—is a useful point of entry into the problem of *laïcité* in France today, not only because of its topicality, but also because the issue epitomizes the challenge to which the French State, in its secular form, is confronted. When approaching the problem of some young veiled girls in the public schools, our country must consider the five million Muslims who live in France, half of whom have obtained French citizenship.[1] Despite the fact that the right to family reunification—given to immigrants in 1976—has recently been repealed, and also that President Nicolas Sarkozy wants the process to be restricted,[2] we must keep in mind that its implementation has entailed the permanent settling of hundreds of thousands of families, whose children, whether born in France or not, do not want to go back to the country of origin of their parents. Contrary to what was expected—i.e., that the immigrants, who arrived in the 1950s to participate in the industrial boom would go back home once their work was finished—there is a strong trend towards permanent settlement.

From a religious point of view, this situation has important consequences: Islam is now the "second religion of France,"[3] and its members understandably demand the right to practice their faith under tolerant conditions. One specific demand is the creation of "Muslim sections" in French cemeteries;[4] this claim demonstrates Muslims' willingness to settle permanently, since they do not consider burial in Muslim soil to be essential anymore. In addition to the right to be buried facing Mecca, they call for more places of worship[5] and for the right to obey and practice their religion without being discriminated against. Here is our core observation: through being veiled in their daily life, and therefore at school, young Muslim women have come to be perceived—almost against their will—as the bearers of the claim to be recognized by the French State in their religious particularity. Now visible in the public square, the Islam of France requires that one ceases to consider it as foreign. Above all, the newfound visibility of Islam questions the secular system as it was erected one century ago, and which has proved unable to integrate the new Muslim population. In a way, it is as a symbol of the success or the failure of our integration process that the *hijab* stands in front of *laïcité's* advocates, and this is why the problem is especially delicate. The true question is how Islam can undergo the French secular system, given that this system is mainly conceived as closed and permanent. Given this conservative spirit, *laïcité* must enter an unavoidable process of change.

To gauge the prospects of such change, one must first consider the dual secular frames that were constructed at the end of the 19th century. Beginning in 1905, two (opposing) conceptions of *laïcité* were erected: a liberal one that has long dominated, and an authoritarian one that seems to get the upper hand in the "veils affair" context. These have indeed reactivated the rigid conception of separation of church and state and, in doing so, slowed down, if not prevented, the changes that our modern multicultural society demands.

There are not "Two Frances," but Rather Two French "*Laïcités*"

Considering France's history of secularism, one generally opposes the idea of "two Frances": a Catholic and anti-republican one, and a secular and republican one. This contrast allows a good description of the duality of political life as it has been revealed since the first days of the French Revolution, and as it has been permanently settled from the second half of the 19th century. But the contrast does not begin to explain the dissensions that have occurred in the secular camp itself since the 1850s, and which set the course of the secular debate, right up until today.

In the wake of the introduction of universal adult suffrage in 1848, French republicans aimed at perfecting the autonomization of politics by defining a sphere permanently removed from any Catholic influence. As Victor Hugo said to the members of the Assemblée Nationale in 1850: "Church in its home and State in its home." Yet the way this separation has been conceived is immediately dualistic, if not antagonistic. On the one hand, separation is linked to government control over religion, for the purpose of ensuring the whole and complete emancipation of every individual. On the other hand, it is a simple question of separating the two spheres, while respecting the rights and liberties of everyone. In the first case, secularism serves human rights in the name of universal republican values; it implies an *authoritarian* conception of the secular system, generally accompanied by an anti-clerical spirit, a conception that agrees to dominate civil society in order to protect its members from every threat of enslavement. In the second case, secularism has only to redefine the spheres of competence of each institution while guaranteeing political autonomy. This implies a *liberal* conception of the secular system, respecting everyone's full freedom of conscience and worship.[6]

It is the second option, the liberal one, which succeeded in 1905,[7] as the plural in the title indicates: the law of separation of *churches* and State refers to the necessity of public neutrality with regard to every religion. Its first article guarantees freedom of conscience and worship, abolishing the governmental appointment of bishops, which was a true means of pressure instituted by Napoleon I in the *Concordat* of 1802. Article 2 adds: "The Republic neither recognizes, nor salaries, nor subsidizes any religion"—thus establishing the separation of the Catholic Church and State, while allowing the public funding of schools and religious associations. It is indeed a "liberal separation," a separation that ensures effective freedom of conscience by establishing an additional day off, in addition to Sunday, in order to allow organization of catechism teaching.[8] For Ferdinand Buisson, the president of the parliamentary commission on Church-State separation, the law was not a "law for combat"; crucifixes would not be removed from classrooms before there is a general agreement, and "duties towards God" would still be taught in classes on ethics until 1923. Above all, despite the hopes of the advocates of authoritarian secularism, education would always be divided between public and private schools. The principle of a State education monopoly would never be established: there would always be Catholic schools in France. This point weakened the claims of authoritarian secularists as two great liberal successes will prove.

In December 1959, the Debré law allowed the State to offer financial support to private schools—which are then "under contract," in exchange for their acceptance of public education programs and for their respect of freedom of conscience. In June 1984, the socialist government facing a huge mobilization from Catholic schools (also called "free schools") had to give up its idea of a "unified and secular public system of national education" when over one million supporters protested against the "freedom killer's" law. Thus, since the 1990s, French secularism can be qualified as "open *laïcité*," as one used to say at that time. The sudden public bursting of the "veil's quarrel" reversed this trend by offering to the "closed *laïcité*" advocates a solid argument for their revenge.

How "Authoritarian *Laïcité*" Took its Revenge

Two teenage girls were excluded from a junior high school in 1989 because they refused to remove the scarves they wore as a sign of Muslim identity. The case immediately became the "scarves affair" and revived the struggle between the two conceptions of *laïcité*. One conception rejects any possibility of wearing a Muslim veil at school. This was in accordance with the "closed" vision, which forbids any appearance or visibility of religion in public institutions. The other conception of *laïcité* dictates that the Republic should not cast its children out even if they are obviously being influenced by radical Islam, since public schools are the proper place for resistance to fundamentalism to occur. In both cases, the presence of young veiled girls in the public arena is perceived as evidence of the failure of the French integration model. A failure to which many attribute—and deplore in the same breath—the phenomenon of "re-Islamization" of the suburbs.

The Secretary of National Education, Lionel Jospin, consulted the *Conseil d'Etat*, which advised, in October 1989, that "veil's wearing [was] not in contradiction with the values of the secular and republican school," and that the school's headmasters were free to make individual decisions. Some intellectuals then published a virulent call to resist "the fanatics," denouncing the advice as a true surrender.[9] A series of other cases fed the debate until September 1994, when the decree of the new Secretary, François Bayrou, established a differentiation between "discreet" symbols of religion (which can be worn at school as elements of a personal belief) and "ostentatious" ones that have to be forbidden as "elements of proselytism." In 1996, the Mediatory of the Republic, Hanifa Cherifi, addressed the veils question; she averred that the number of "veil" cases went down from 2,400 to 1,000 in two years time, and only a hundred cases involved a refusal to remove veils at school. While not legion, these cases nonetheless received great media coverage and thus stoked the argument of the most inflexible defenders of *laïcité*. Over a period of ten years, the political establishment has swung over to the closed side of *laïcité*.[10] Between August 2002 and November 2003, no less than seven private bills to forbid the wearing of the veil at school were introduced by members of Parliament from both parts of the political arena, left and right.[11] In December 2003, the parliament addressed the veils question with a report that included the following statement: "the secular principle is today really threatened."[12] The report has aided the argument made by those who were demanding the vote of a law, and who won the battle when the Stasi Commission on "implementation of the *laïcité* principle" made[13] the claim for such a law. On March 15, 2004, after long debates, representatives and senators approved a law forbidding any religious sign in public schools. A rigid and defensive version of secularism was thus succeeding, allowing the "closed" conception of *laïcité* to triumph over the "open" *laïcité* that had prevailed for a century. Like many other commentators and experts, we would like to suggest that this option is harmful, as it turns its back on the challenges that multicultural modernity poses to secularism. Most attention is focused on interpreting the choice of young French Muslim girls to wear the veil. However, things are not as Manichean as one might think when listening to the debate.

The Veil's Polysemy

Arguments for banning the veil are numerous and varied. Chronologically, the first and most popular argument is the one that says accepting veiled young girls in public school would open the door to fundamentalists and their claims (e.g., demand of *hallal* meat in school meals, requirement of non-mixed classes, refusal of some school programs, etc.). The second argument is essentially feminist: the veil being the sign of a patriarchal domination exerted on girls, tolerating it would create a zone of expression for the most ardent advocates of women's oppression. This argument sees the veil as a sexist discrimination, a symbol of the submission of women, and an offense against women's dignity; thus, allowing the veil would deny women their autonomy, and would place them into unavoidable subordination to fathers and husbands.[14] Arguments of this type have been often sharp, as the following statement shows: "*Hijab* is the yellow star of Muslim women, and every Muslim woman is a Jew that every fundamentalist would dream of deporting five times a day (...) Behind each veil, 3,000 years of hatred towards women is watching us."[15] To go beyond the Manicheanism of such a declaration, one has to understand the very nature of the choice made by young French Muslims when they decide to wear the *hijab* in the public arena. Some recent sociological studies allow us indeed to shade the veil's perception in terms of religious fundamentalism and denying republican values. Considering the veil as a polysemic sign would help us abandon simplistic analyses and open a path towards possibly reforming French *laïcité* and recognizing the new multicultural face of our society.

Interviewing young French Muslim girls, sociologists have revealed the deep polysemy of the veil. There is, of course, a proper religious dimension: to wear *hijab* is the immediate sign of Muslim practice. But, in the modern context of an individualization of beliefs and of a redefinition of religions as identities, through which strict obedience and the development of community membership trump true religious convictions,[16] the *hijab* is above all the means of an individual commitment, both towards society and family. For these young girls, it is not so much a question of Muslim membership as a way of asserting oneself—one's singularity and individual dignity. Nadine Weibel has underlined the crucial role of veil-wearing in the process of the emancipation of young Muslims.[17] Unlike Western society, which reduces women to sexual objects, wearing the veil allows women to take on their lives in the public arena while de-eroticizing social space:

"it cuts off women from the men's world and, by protecting their intimacy, it entitles them to acquire a proper place in contemporary societies."[18] In a way quite paradoxical way, one may consider the *hijab* as a means for emancipation from fathers and husbands insomuch as it reveals the emergence of a female individual, thinking of herself as a holder of rights, and getting involved in secular life. Against centuries of customs imprisoning women and keeping them ignorant, veiled Muslims are today claiming access to mosques, as well as their right to education and work. As Danièle Hervieu-Léger has put it, if the Islam of those young girls can express a reintegration of familial tradition, it also often implies a break from traditional Islam as a religion of constraints and prohibitions. The *hijab* allows the "conquest of their woman's identity by giving to fathers and brothers the fictitious guarantee of a submission from which they are precisely escaping."[19]

In a recently published study, Nathalie Kakpo makes the same acknowledgement: French Muslims' religiosity may serve autonomy. After succeeding at school and before going to university, numerous young women have made the choice to wear the *hijab* in order to reassure their parents, that they will maintain the family's honor.[20] Beyond this individual dimension of the assertion, the study demonstrates that even if claims about the veil conflict with republican principles, they also contribute to the political socialization of these young women. One would observe "the emergence of a new public figure, the veiled young woman seeking new rights."[21] Far from the stereotype of passive and submissive girls, sociological studies reveal the young Muslims ambition to "go their own way in the French society, between a quest of freedom and a loyalty to their origins."[22] This point of view has not been the prevalent one in the veils debate. Trapped in the vision of an archaic religion, the defenders of *laïcité* have been unable to see that the Islam which has been developing in our society, notably through the veiled young girls, has become gradually integrated into religious modernity. Most sociologists agree that the Islam of the diaspora proves to be a modern Islam inasmuch as it indicates the assertion of a Muslim identity. The young French Muslims' religion is much more chosen than inherited; it is part of a process of self-building, typical of the culture of individuality, and ideally fitting into the modern figure of the converted: the veil allows young women "to acquire self-esteem and a socially recognizable identity at the same time."[23]

The interpretation of *hijab* as a tool of submission and social exclusion is by no means denied. The whole problem is the huge variety of cases—which prevents generalizing. It is absolutely undeniable that, for some young girls, wearing the veil is not a true choice, and it is also absolutely undeniable that it thus expresses a fundamentalist option. In any case, French society and State are facing a dynamic "Islam of France" which must be taken into consideration; and, likewise, its claims must be taken into account in the public sphere.

Prospects: Toward "Reasonable Adjustment"?

The future of French *laïcité* thus depends on its capacity to establish a secular plan that addresses the double phenomenon of individualization of beliefs and *identarisation*, the creation of group or cultural identity on the basis of religion. The goal is to enable the public expression of the Muslim's religious identity, while keeping it in the frame of citizenship. In other words, one has to promote a new kind of citizenship, one that is compatible with pluralism. The historian of *laïcité* and member of the Stasi Commission, Jean Baubérot, has suggested looking to the Québécois system's principle of "reasonable adjustment." This notion refers to "the softening, if not to the change, of norms and practices in order to take the proper needs of minorities into account"; an adjustment that must be "reasonable," i.e., "which does not impose excessive constraints to institutions, State or companies, nor undermines others."[24] Every reasonable adjustment should consider indirect discrimination on religious grounds. There was a French precedent at the beginning of the 1980s, when workers from Maghreb, who were working in Peugeot's factories, went on strike to protest mass layoffs and demand more dignity at work. To everybody's surprise, the general management responded favorably to these religious claims by creating prayer rooms.[25] More recently, one can invoke one of the proposals made by the Stasi Commission aimed at allowing every worker to take a day off to celebrate either Pentecost, Aïd, Yom Kippur, or any religious holiday of his choice. It has also suggested that public schools might be closed not only for Christmas and Easter, but also Yom Kippur and Aïd. These suggestions have not been taken into consideration, probably because of the French people's reluctance, after centuries of religious monolithism and a century of conflict between Catholics and Seculars, to accept this kind of accommodation. In Québec, taking Sunday off is no longer mentioned in labor laws; managers are just compelled to make their employees work no more than six days in a row. Reacting to the refusal to change the school schedule, Jean Baubérot warns us: "waving the red flag of communitarianism as soon as one wants to give more pluralism in the context of a *catho-laïcité* condemns France to be a particularly corny country."[26]

What is undeniable is that Islam is not treated as a religion among others, as the following fact proves: there is a single private Muslim school in France, whereas Catholic, Protestant, and Jewish schools are numerous. One has to keep in mind that Catholicism is the only religion to benefit from the free public care of its religious buildings and monuments. We must also consider that the two *départements* of Alsace and Moselle are still today governed by the Concordat status as it was established in 1802 by Napoléon. The three religions, Catholic, Protestant, and Jewish, are established, and members of their clergy are salaried and paid by the State, while the archbishop of Strasbourg is appointed by the President. Today, Islam is excluded from this system, even though local laws are more favorable than national ones towards Muslim communities. One can also cite the very specific case of French Guyana, where a decree from 1828 established the Catholic Church. With no less than seven different statuses for religious denominations, *laïcité* in France is thus anything but standardized. Therefore it is unacceptable that Islam is not granted the same recognition as other religions.

In 2008, the crucial question is: What policy will the new government select? In 2005, when the 1905 law's centenary was celebrated, Nicolas Sarkozy favored a legal reform aimed at taking into account Islam, a religion that was not yet present at the beginning of the 20th century. Sarkozy has suggested that the law be adapted to the new religious and social frame, and the historic inequalities between Catholicism and "minor" religions should be ended. The main change would concern public funding of Mosques, which would then avoid foreign interferences. In October 2005, when he was Minister of the Interior, Nicolas Sarkozy ordered a report about State-Church relationships. The *"Rapport Machelon"* published in September 2006, advocated a reform of the 1905 law aimed at easing the public funding of worship and harmonizing the different statuses of religious bodies. Whether a legal reform is necessary is hard to say, but the issue remained unaddressed during the 2007 electoral campaign.

Can the State guarantee the free exercise of worship and, at the same time, proscribe public funding of religions? Will the new Minister of the Interior, Michèle Alliot-Marie, implement the changes sought by Nicolas Sarkozy? Will the problems of Muslim places of worship, and of the education of French imams, lead to a reform of the 1905 law? It is hard to say. What is obvious is that there is goodwill everywhere. A recent initiative by the Mayor of Paris, Bertrand Delanoë, shows the accord between political will and civil society commitment. The city council has planned, for 2011, the creation of an *Institute of Muslim Cultures (Institut des Cultures Musulmanes)* in La Goutte d'or—a working-class neighborhood where immigrants are in the majority. Its main purposes are to promote Muslim culture and to contribute to the reconsideration of Islam and its cultural and religious identity. This project will probably please those who believe that true change is not primarily political, and who reject any legislative reform in the name of the extremely widespread fear of a divisive communitarianism. As Jean Baubérot suggested, one should let the civil society actors be in charge of the creation of a "new secular pact." What exactly this would be is an open question.

ENDNOTES

1. This statistic has been much debated. The demographer Michele Tribalat has given the lowest estimate: 3.7 million "possibly Muslim" people in France, of whom 1.7 million are immigrants and as many are immigrants' children. See *Population*, INED, vol. 59, n° 1, Jan-Feb. 2004. The highest estimate is up to 8 million. For this discussion, see Jonathan Laurence, Justin Vaïsse, *Intégrer l'islam*, Paris: Odile Jacob, 2007.

2. A recent law (06/02/2002) states that family reunification is no longer a right, even for children and wives, but, rather, that each case should be considered individually. The new Department of Immigration, Integration, National Identity and Co-development has elaborated a pilot project (06/12/2007) that strengthens the conditions of family reunification while compelling the persons who wish to come to France to pass a test, in their native country, evaluating their knowledge of the French language and republican values. In September 2007, the Members of Parliament discussed an amendment that would impose an ADN test to persons wishing to join their families in France; the debate has been fierce, and no resolution has yet been reached.

3. According to 2002-2003 data, Islam is second to Catholicism (40 million members) and before Protestantism (1 million). Other sizeable religions are Buddhism (600,000), Judaism (525,000), and Christian Orthodoxy (150,000). These figures, too, must be taken with a grain of salt, as the "Informatique et liberté" law from 1978 forbids counting people based on ethnic or religious affiliation. Most of the time, estimates are made on the basis of the origin of the immigrant population.

4. The principle of cemeteries' religious neutrality is a legal one; mayors, the only ones who have authority in funeral affairs, are not compelled to, but can, concentrate the graves of the same religion together. There are only three full Muslim cemeteries and about 70 Muslim sections in France. Dalil Boubakeur, rector of the Paris Mosque and President of the *French Council of Muslim Religion* (*Conseil français du culte musulman*), believes that only 10% of the needs are satisfied.

5. There are about 2,150 places of worship in France, of which only 13, called "mosques-cathedrals" can welcome more than 1,000 people.

6. The notion of "authoritarian" and "liberal" secularism is borrowed from Jean Baubérot, *Laïcité 1905-2005, entre passion et raison* (Paris: Seuil, 2004).

7. In 1904, a first version of the law was clearly authoritarian. The text did not guarantee liberty of conscience and religion, churches were owned by the State (which rented them for 10 years), religious manifestations were forbidden in the public arena, and religious associations had to declare every meeting.

8. The major republican 1882 law (03/28/1882) established the principle of compulsory education for boys and girls aged 6-13, and defined the conditions of a secularization of teaching.

9. Entitled "Teachers, do not surrender!" the call was published by Elisabeth Badinter, Régis Debray, Alain Finkielkraut, Elisabeth de Fontenay, and Catherine Kintzler, in *Le Nouvel Observateur*, November 2-8, 1989.

10. In September 2004, 79% of French people favored a law forbidding ostentatious religious signs at school, whereas "only" 49% favored such a law in April 2003. Some commentators have thus suggested that the debate was media driven, accusing the political-journalistic sphere of pushing the public toward accepting the law, in a background of anti-Muslim sentiment. See Pierre Tévanian, *Le voile médiatique. Un faux débat: "l'affaire du foulard islamique"* (Paris: Editions Raison d'Agir, 2005).

11 . See Alessandro Ferrari, "La lutte des symboles et l'espoir du droit: laïcité et voile islamique en France depuis le début du nouveau millénaire," *Migrations Société*, n° 96, Nov. 2004. The authors of the private bills are, in chronological order, Jacques Myard (UMP), Maurice Leroy (UDF), François Aurtain, Jean-Yves Autexier and Paul Loridant (groupe Communistes Républicains et Citoyens), Michel Charasse (PS), Didier Julia (UMP), Serge Lagauche (PS), Jack Lang (PS), and Laurent Hénart (UMP).

12. Jean-Louis Debré, President of the Assemblée Nationale and of the Information Mission on Religious Signs at School. See the report given to President Jacques Chirac on December 5, 2003.

13. Among many other proposals aiming at "asserting a firm and embracing *laïcité*."

14. See the arguments presented by Florence Rochefort, "Foulard, genre et laïcité en 1989," in *Vingtième siècle*, n° 75, 2002: 149-151.

15. Mohamed Kacimi, "Voile, une antique aliénation," in *La laïcité dévoilée. Quinze années de débat en quarante "Rebonds" de Libération* (Paris: Editions de l'Aube, 2004: 70). The author is a Moroccan poet, storyteller, and theater writer.

16. See Marcel Gauchet, *La religion dans la démocratie. Parcours de la laïcité* (Paris: Gallimard, "Le débat," 1998).

17. Nadine Weibel, *Par-delà le voile. Femmes d'islam en Europe* (Bruxelles: Complexes, 2000).

18. Nadine Weibel,"Islamité, égalité et complémentarité: vers une nouvelle approche de l'identité féminine," in *Archives des sciences sociales des religions*, n° 95, 1996: 137.

19. Danièle Hervieu-Léger, "Le miroir de l'islam en France," in *Vingtième siècle*, n° 66, 2000: 86. See also, defending a similar thesis, Françoise Gaspard, Farhad Khosrokhavar, *Le Foulard et la République* (Paris: la Découverte, 1995); Leila Barbès, *L'islam positif. La religion des jeunes musulmans en France* (Paris: Editions de l'Atelier, 1997); Jocelyne Césari, *Musulmans et républicains. Les jeunes, l'islam et la France* (Bruxelles: Complexes, 1997); Nancy Venel, *Musulmanes françaises. Des pratiquantes voilées à l'université* (Paris: L'Harmattan, 1999).

20. Nathalie Kakpo, *L'islam, un nouveau recours pour les jeunes* (Paris: Presses de la FNSP, 2007), 114.

21. Ibid., 146.

22. Ibid., 177.

23. Danièle Hervieu-Léger, "Le miroir de l'islam en France," art. cit., 85. See also *Le pélerin et le converti. La religion en mouvement* (Paris: Flammarion, 1999).

24. Jean Baubérot, op. cit., 239. See also Micheline Milot, *Laïcité dans le Nouveau Monde. Le cas du Québec* (Turnhouts (Belgique): Brepols, 2002); Guy Durand, *Le Québec et la laïcité. Avancées et derives* (Montréal: Les éditions Varia, 2004); Christian Joppke, "The Retreat of Multiculturalism in the Liberal State: Theory and Policy," in *The British Journal of Sociology*, vol. 55, no 2, 2004.

25. See Gilles Kepel, *Les banlieues de l'islam* (Paris: Seuil, 1987).

26. Jean Baubérot, "La laïcité, le chêne et le roseau," in *La laïcité dévoilée, op. cit.*, 236-237.

13. Secularization Versus the Weight of Catholic Tradition among Spanish Women

Sofía Rodríguez López

Introduction

In order to measure the presence of secularism in Spain we must, first of all, consider the influence and impact of religion, in this case the established Roman Catholic Church, on civil society and public institutions, particularly as they affect the status of women. Then we shall analyze this problem by looking at the historical development of public services such as education and public health, which are traditionally considered to be the domain of the Church, and how they have undergone a process of secularization. Finally, we will determine the current relationship between women and the Catholic faith in Spain at the individual and collective levels.

The leading feminist theories are relevant to this question. They include *humanist secular feminism*, which tackles religion as a symbol of patriarchal oppression against women; and traditionalist feminism, which considers religion to be a moral guide for women. During the first half of the 20th century, the latter was the dominant type of feminism in Spain among Catholic women. Spanish women by and large have never embraced humanist secular feminism but have found opportunities for advancement under the umbrella of the Catholic Church. The secularist argument was a minority opinion limited to individuals with connections to Freemasonry, atheism, Marxism, and anarcho-syndicalism, which were prominent ideologies during the 1930s. Notable among this group of secularist women were Hidegart Rodríguez, a reformer of Christian moral sexuality, and Lucía Sánchez Saornil, the leader of *Mujeres Libres* (Free Women). However, a mutually hostile relationship with the Church impeded the establishment of partnerships with Roman Catholic feminists.[1] In the first half of the 20th century, religion was a tool for preventing the advancement of feminism but by the end of the century, religion served as a catalyst for a genuine women's movement. Still, in order to properly comprehend the development of political attitudes among Spanish women during the 20th century, we must take into account its social context.

The Emergence of a Women's Movement

During the Bourbon Restoration (1873-1923), the Spanish women's movement leaders, such as Concepción Arenal and Elmila Pardo Bazán had modest educational demands compared to those in France and the United States.[2] Women's suffrage was a chimera due to the inadequacies of the electoral system and a governing system based on back room deals between the dynastic political parties. Reformers criticized the monarchy's disdain for democratization and looked for support among the Church and the army. This was because, despite the differences among the reformers, there was no doubt that all republican factions were interested in social issues. This republican reform agenda incorporated the secularization of the state and educational reform, which included the education of women.

The first few decades of the 20th century witnessed measures implemented by the Liberal Government such as *la Ley del Candado* (the Padlock Law). In 1910, the government imposed a two-year ban on the establishment of new religious congregations. As a response to this government prohibition there was a mobilization of laymen[3] led by Cardinal Guisasola, which included lay women. The new relationship between women and the Catholic Church coincided with the publication of new social proposals in the encyclicals *Rerum Novarum* by Leo XIII (1891) and *Quadragessimo Anno* (1931) by Pope Pius XI. These opposed liberalism and included among their core principles were: the consecration of private property and the acceptance of inequality; a search for harmony and fraternity, as opposed to a Marxist class struggle; and the use of welfare as part of a social justice agenda based on Catholic dogma.[4]

Church doctrine was rooted in a patriarchal system that was redefined during the Industrial Revolution. It fostered a puritan discourse via the *Casti Connubii* (1930), which promoted the submission of women to God and husband. This meant a return to the baroque ideal of *La Perfecta Casada* (the Perfect Wife), which condemned sex equality and prioritized the family over civil rights.[5]

However, in the second half of the 19th Century, the influence in Spain of intellectual traditions and philosophies such as Krausism and Positivism hindered the implementation of the Protestant liberal, Anglo-Saxon model of the modern bourgeois "Home Angel" (*Angel del Hogar*). This middle class paradigm was also contested by the existence of the peasant and working classes, which threatened the prevalent morality of "separate spheres."[6]

The educators at the *Institución Libre de Enseñanza* (the Free Institution of Teaching), expressed an idealist rationalism that was rooted in Catholicism, and believed in the equality of the souls of both sexes and in the possibility of educating women. However, very prestigious scientists, philosophers, and men of letters doubted the intellectual capacities of women, and thus their need to be socially and legally equal to men.[7] This confusion between sociology and physiology, based on "biosocial" thought, contributed to the creation of a coalition of sexist prejudice based on the fear of socialist feminism and a misogynist pseudoscience detrimental to Spanish women.[8]

Among the leaders of that period, Carmen de Burgos distinguished herself as a symbol for women and writers influenced by *Blasquismo*, the idea of a minority socialist *coup d'etat*.[9] De Burgos's activism in favor of divorce, women's suffrage, and an active role for women in public life, was influenced by both her republican values and an anticlerical sentiment, which strengthened after a crisis of faith in 1905. Under the pseudonym of *Colombine*, de Burgos pursued an "enlightened feminism" to find solutions to the problems of Spanish women. Her proposals stressed access to a liberal and secular education, which was not at odds with the "mysticism of femininity."[10] Her mission was to eradicate illiteracy, which affected family relations, and was against the honor of women as mothers and ladies.

Moreover, *Colombine's* membership in the Freemasons is the quintessential example of the fusion of free thought, deism or atheist spiritualism, and feminism in the Spain between the 19th and 20th centuries. These were profoundly secular ideas found in exclusive social circles, but liberalism was as weak as the middle class in Spain. This alternative discourse attempted to go beyond the "battle of the sexes," proposing, instead, harmony and equality between the sexes. It aimed at preparing women intellectually to go beyond their current roles in the family and the Church.[11]

This struggle for women's individuality, according to Karen Offen, Mary Nash, and Susanna Tavera, appealed to bourgeois republican women, the Catalan vanguard, and the revolutionary anarcho-syndicalists. This minority of women attempted to break with a female identity based on the patriarchal model of the Catholic family and began to progressively internalize secular individualism.[12]

Myriad secular feminist groups began to appear in Spain around World War I. These associations, which sprouted in Valencia, Barcelona, and Málaga, were unique due to their strong support of women's education as a means to achieve autonomy. Eventually, after 1918, female suffrage was added to the struggle by organizations such as the *Sociedad Progresiva de Mujeres* (Progressive League of

Women), active between 1888 and 1926 and the *Consejo Supremo Feminista* (Supreme Feminist Council), founded as a coordinating organization in 1919. In addition, the *Asociación Nacional* (National Association of Spanish Women), the *Cruzada de Mujeres Españolas* (Crusade of Spanish Women), and the Lyceum Club were created with a full agenda of rights. This period also saw the founding of *El Gladiador* (*The Gladiator*), one of the first secular forums. Women involved in these groups were caricatured in pejorative terms such as *crazies, bimbos, she-husbands* (*maridas*), *Anglophiles, atheists,* and *enemies of the Christian family,* which were common insults for single and/or independent women.[13]

Paradoxically, Primo de Rivera's dictatorship (1923-30) was a period ripe for the development of this formula for women's independence, thanks to the expansion of formal education and a wage-based labor market. Between the first and second Republics, a new movement and a new model of femininity developed. This "new woman" was still a second class citizen, but one accepted by liberals and Catholic women as another dimension of the "social woman" and a new formula for feminism.[14]

However, not all of Spanish society was moving in the same direction. There was an increasing differentiation between sexes, particularly among the upper and middle classes, which led men to avoid liturgy and women to transform religiosity into a female characteristic.[15] This event, coupled with an explosion in the number of religious communities of French origin due to anticlerical legislation in the French Third Republic, tied women to a sort of "irrational mysticism." This mysticism and the "infantile and superficial spirituality" to which women were destined, ended up stigmatizing them as moral traditionalists and political conservatives.[16] The author Celia Viñas projected these qualities in her 1946 novel *Tiempo Levante* when one of the male characters stated: "In this, you win. You don't believe in ideals, or science, or love, don't even try to find a definition, or an understanding of the end of life. You care for our children and men, and go to Mass on Sundays without ever asking, without ever doubting."[17]

A Secular Republic, Secular Schools, and Some Secular Women

The 1930s brought an air of modernity to the country, due to the Republican attempts to introduce greater social justice by copying the secularism of states such as France and Weimar Germany. During the first Republican-Socialist term, girls were subject to the implementation of a new religiously neutral system of education that contradicted Pope Pius XI's 1929 encyclical *Divini Illius Magistri.* It was a very controversial decision, and the Church accused the government of being anticlerical and atheist. The state's religious neutrality was considered a betrayal of the traditions and the Christian character of the Spanish nation and the debate became polarized between the defenders of freedom of thought and conscience and the supporters of religion and the apostles of educational morality. The latter accused the secular schools of being immoral, a threat to academic freedom, and copies of those in the USSR or Mexico.

The implementation of religious freedom in schools and the symbolic removal of crucifixes were some of the boldest achievements of Manuel Azaña's government (1931-33). The government's confrontation with the Church peaked when it failed to condemn the burning of convents in several cities (such as Madrid, Málaga, Córdoba, Sevilla, and Alicante) during May 1931, and when it passed the Law of Confessions and Religious Congregations in 1933. The abolition and/or seizure of Catholic schools exacerbated the educational issue in the country. In addition, there were problems due to the loss or transformation of educational infrastructure, such as the prohibition against teaching by members of regular religious orders without teaching degrees. Moreover, articles 3, 26, and 48 of the Constitution dissolved the influential Society of Jesus (Jesuits), eliminated the teaching of religion in schools, and promoted the primary cultural role of the State.

These events prompted a swift reaction from the Pope and Spanish bishops. Their strategy was to mobilize Catholic families by invoking the threat to salvation of their children's souls, and by calling on Catholics to boycott the new secular public schools. After the seizure of Jesuit properties and their conversion into welfare institutions, the Church redoubled its efforts to create a private parallel system of Catholic instruction with parish schools under diocesan oversight.[18]

The Religious Backlash against the Republic

The educational secularization project was never completed due to economic limitations and local resistance to proposals such as the 1933 Law of Congregations. There was a deficit of national schools so they could not absorb the demand, and teachers had to expand their school day and work afternoon shifts. Additionally, aside from the opposition from bureaucrats and condemnation from the political right, there was an active mobilization of parents' associations, alumni, and Catholic women's organizations against the reforms. These groups collected money, signed petitions, and used propaganda campaigns to voice the citizens' opposition to the State's secularization process under the banner of freedom of religion.

Eventually, after the right came to power in December 1933, the work of the commissions in charge of replacing religious education was stopped and the

Catholic organizations kept running their educational centers. Several factors contributed to the triumph of religious traditionalism over liberal and secular feminism. Among these factors were the Church's quasi-monopoly on public education until the 1930s, the labor populism of Catholic trade unions, and mechanisms of apostolic "nationalism."

Moreover, laywomen became the main target of the campaign by the Church. It projected the female image as what one author called an "inferior, ignorant, naïve, and impressionable being that needs direction and protection from men."[19] Despite the exclusion of women from the Church's hierarchy, and from many liturgical ceremonies and secular associations, Spanish women took an active part in practicing religion and doctrinal obedience. This happened, not only due to the effect of the religious propaganda, but also because it was the only public space to which they had access and were encouraged to belong outside of the home.

The most dynamic Church institutions in the 1910s and 1920s had been led by the Jesuit priest Alarcón y Meléndez, who earned the support of a group of active Catholic women from the social elites. This was how the "charity ladies" (*damas de beneficiencia*) model was born. These women dedicated themselves to charity and the teaching of the catechism. This model lasted in Spain until the controversial "sexual revolution" in Spain after 1968.[20] These aristocratic and bourgeois women became "heroines of religion" (*heroínas de la religión*) by virtue of avoiding a frivolous use of their free time and by upholding the concept of "separate spheres."[21] Their energy was spent on charity work because this was work that they were gifted to do thanks to their supposedly selfless nature and sentimentalist socialization. They founded and/or promoted the creation of hospitals, elderly centers, orphanages, and Catholic labor unions. These institutions were used to introduce their mission of "moralizing the poor,"[22] and obtaining rights for working women and their children. These services, as Carmen de Burgos and socialists Margarita Nelken and María Cambrils claimed, were at odds with the role of the State and particularly with the Republican secularizing project developed in the Commission for Social Reforms.[23] Cambrils's *Socialist Feminism* was a result of her anticlerical opposition to the leading role that Catholic women such as María Echarri were gaining. Inspired by the ideas of Marx and Bebel, Cambrils opposed the concept of humanistic redemption and the ignorance and male-centeredness promoted by religious instruction.[24] She believed that despite Engels's warnings in *The Origins of the Family, Private Property, and the State*, women could make an "acceptable transition" from the home (and family life) to the public square fueled by the ideals of feminine excellence, social maternity, and the sexual division of labor.

Those in power did not take long to realize the need for legalizing the Christianizing and patriotic potential of women, which until the arrival of women's suffrage in 1931 was channeled through welfare in exchange for civil rights. This issue was debated during the Constitutional Convention of 1934 and it exposed the different positions regarding the electoral behavior of Spanish women and whether or not women were bound by "instructions from the confessional box."[25]

Women were attracted to religious political parties, which provided them with different opportunities for participation. In contrast, some labor organizations did not reach out to women because they were convinced of the conservatism of women.[26] Thus the "top-down revolution" proposed by Catholicism based on a large-scale social mobilization counted women among its most ardent supporters. Women joined a versatile social base in which they were able to be active in several political, labor, and trade organizations as part of the lay apostolic network. The Church supervised "freed" young women through the Theresian Insitution, which was active in teachers' colleges, and the Daughters of Charity, active in hospitals.[27]

Female chapters not only inflated the number of members but also played an important role in the propaganda campaigns of the main political organizations opposed to the secularization project of the Republican government. The members of the Traditionalist Communion (*Comunión Tradicionalista*) were an important group in the historical Carlist Party fief of Navarre and launched various women's groups onto the national stage.[28] The proselytism of the "*margaritas*" (named after Doña Margarita de Borbón, wife of Carlos VII) centered on elite women who were known (from the age of 16) for their charity work.[29] Using the slogan "*Dios, Patria, Rey*" (God, Fatherland, King), these women became the Traditionalist Women's Group, which was unique due to the Catholic/patriotic duality of their mission. Together with the Councils, comprised of priests, gentlemen, and pious ladies, they collected money to cover Church expenses after Azaña's secularization project emptied the Church's coffers by cutting public funding. The involvement of Catholic women in the struggle against Republican reforms developed under a guise of female "identity politics." The "agenda" was to defend those values that provided women with social authority as mothers and Christian educators and gave men the role of breadwinners using arguments that stemmed from liberal revolutions and the *Social Contract*.[30]

According to Helen Graham, the appeal of conservative solutions to the European crises of the 1930s was strengthened by conservatism's commitment to traditional gender roles and the family. These ideas promoted security in contrast to the apparent fickleness of bourgeois feminists and workers' organizations reforms. The latter offered little security to women across social groups, particularly rural women. The unpopular top-down approach to female enfranchisement and mobilization by an inexperienced ruling class, coupled with a state family policy that threatened people's values and belief systems (e.g., secular education, divorce, maternity benefits), allowed "the people and right-wing organizations to mount a blockade of the Republican secularization efforts."[31]

Despite their secondary roles as parliamentary players, the women's political chapters had the potential of being mobilized by the Republican government's aggressions against the Church. Many women, fueled by the Falange's populist concept of national unity as a grand family and its propaganda against the Republican government that represented secularism, sexual freedom, and federalism, dedicated themselves to oppose the government.

After the victory of the reactionary coalition in the 1933 elections and after the end of the Spanish Civil War in 1939, women supportive of male guardianship promoted "the return to the home."[32] Thus, according to the religious elements, the crises of the 1930s could only be solved by the re-Christening of Europe through an increase of charity activities, obedience to traditional authority, and lay missions.[33]

Francoism and Catholic Dominance

Given national conditions and the weight of the Catholic tradition, particularly among women, it appears that the "overloaded Republican agenda" ran out of time for educating and sensitizing the people with their neutral schools and other reforms.[34] In addition, the radicalization of the secularizing projects after the February 1936 triumph of the *Frente Popular Antifascista* (Popular Anti-fascist Front) and the anticlerical reaction at the beginning of the Civil War deepened the political and ideological cleavages of the Spanish into what can arguably be called a crusade.

During the war, the purges of the clergy started early. A large number of Church officials were assassinated while nuns became the objects of gendered violence. Acts of physical destruction and arson directed against artistic treasures of the Church became symbols of the revolution and the "bestiality of the Reds" which were much cited by Francoists over the years. The images of "burning saints" caused deeper wounds among the people than any of the Republican constitutional reforms. The dictatorship perpetuated these images as a means of consolidating its own legitimacy.[35] As a result, the legitimacy of the serious proposals for Church-State separation and secularization took a back seat.

As Rafael Cruz says, the Republic never articulated an authentically Republican culture able to substitute religious traditionalism and expel Catholics from the national community. Hence, the war was also a clash between "threatened collective identities" that were equally violent and intransigent.[36] After the end of the Civil War, all those opposed to the "National Movement" and, by association, the Church, were persecuted. This persecution involved the physical disappearance and administrative purges of many men and women who were not considered "religious, patriotic and proper."

Only a few intellectual Falangists dared to criticize aspects of the Spanish Catholic Church during the post-war period. The Catholic leanings of the Franco government's domestic policy agenda empowered sociopolitical sectors associated with the Church.[37] The Church became a guarantor of the traditional order during the dictatorship and the clergy organized "female elite supporters of the cultural Counter-reform."[38] After a period of high mobilization among Spanish women, *Sección Femenina* competed with *Acción Católica* in the 1950s for the fulfillment of their cultural mission. During these years the Mediterranean dictatorships of Greece, Portugal, and Spain destroyed the remnants of feminism. These years also witnessed the discrediting of independent women and a return to Baroque models of femininity based on the home, maternity, and Christian marriage.[39]

Until 1953 (when the Concordat with the Vatican was signed), the dominant values of spirituality and militarism imposed a Manichean ideology that pitted Nationalist-Catholic discourse against the Republican ideology. This discourse helped define the dictatorship as antithetical to the values once defended by the *Frente Popular*: centralization versus 19th century federal liberalism; capitalism v. communism; National-Catholic v. *laicismo*; confessionalism v. anticlericalism and "masonic" rationalism; traditionalism v. modernity and feminism. The mixture of these ingredients produced an "ideological cocktail" of Spanish myths and extreme nationalism that praised the peasants' and the military's values. It was based upon the imperial spirit of the medieval *Reconquista* and the Counter-Reformation that divided Spanish society between good and bad people and transformed individuals into useful subjects of the fatherland:

> The Spanish women under the autocracy and during the Cold War were represented as a "reservoir of Christendom" and "sentinels of the West."[40] Although a new period of openness was soon to occur, this openness did not stop the dictatorship using the Church to legitimate the dictatorial system and to continue using the anticlerical characterization of the Left as a weapon and public insult.[41]

The ideological reconstruction under Franco was matched by the tangible reconstruction of Church infrastructure. There were repairs to churches, rectors' houses, cemeteries, and chapels such as the ones dedicated to the Sacred Heart of Jesus. The government also encouraged the building of memorials for the fallen martyrs of the Civil War as well as new churches all over the country.

In the educational arena, there was a proliferation of parish school and youth groups. The Jesuits and Salesians took the lead among the religious congregations dedicated to these missions. The women's lay ministries dedicated great efforts to these spiritual exercises and the maintenance of public and private worship. For their part, *Acción Católica* gained a larger social base for their charity and relief activities.[42] However, the main service of the Church to the dictatorship was social demobilization. The Church did not hesitate to collaborate with the regime and kept silent about political repression after 1939 so it could enhance its own influence over the people.[43]

In the 1950s and 1960s, the dictatorship's new diplomatic and commercial treaties did not lead to a reduction in ultramontane Catholicism. Although there were dissident stirrings and small rebellions among the disadvantaged,[44] public meetings were still banned during the 1950s, especially those that could affect Church attendance. As Kaplan indicates, the government in Madrid "would have been happy" prohibiting all public celebrations, including funerals that risked becoming a demonstration or symbol of popular resistance against the Regime.[45]

The nationwide and dogmatic "crusade of decency" faced popular resistance because it censored carnival dances and the wearing of swim suits by female tourists. Both prohibitions were considered punishable offenses. Despite this, Franco was conscious of the value of preserving specific traditional festivities such as the Marian pilgrimages and processions during Easter week. These events were regarded as devotional expressions that did not lead to threats to the social order.[46] In the face of these prohibitions, the political, artistic, and confessional acts celebrated by the regime repeated a familiar ritualism. Even though the Church lost some degree of control over the meaning of these images, it won the capacity to influence life in the cities and new suburbs. The "*de-Christening environment*" of the workers' world made this necessary, because the population affected by the rural exodus stopped practicing their faith and instead acquired a model of consumer behavior opposed to Catholic spirituality.

The Political, Ecclesiastical, and Secular Transition

Pope John XXIII's Second Vatican Council made the 1960s a decade of symbolic changes aimed at getting the Church closer to the "people," for instance, by the substitution of the cassock by the clerical collar and the substitution of the Latin Mass by Spanish.[47] Beyond the position of the official church, the last decades of the dictatorship witnessed the expansion of the Catholic workers' movements represented by the youth, brotherhoods, study groups (GOES), and trade unions (CISC-USO). Together with the Workers' Commissions, these would show a clear anti-Francoism. They energized their bases with a class consciousness and by a movement to the political left. Women were participants in this, thanks to the political renovation of *Acción Católica*, the feminist impulse in social commitment, and the leadership of the Christian Democrats.[48]

In the years prior to Franco's death, Spain developed a social platform which made it possible to reconcile opposition to the regime alongside Church membership. Female mobilization groups were created in the parishes along with neighborhood services such as day care centers and hospitals. Improvements in the status of women occurred through organizations such as the Galician shellfish gatherers (*mariscadoras*) from the Popular Cultural Center of Yecla and groups from the Cordoba countryside.[49] There were demands for a non-sexist culture so women would no longer be used as pornographic media objects.[50] Other issues under debate concerned the family, prostitution, homosexuality, Church influence on the women's vote, and what the left was offering women compared to the right.

From the vantage point of gender as a social variable, the transition from Francoism made it possible to consider common and specific issues affecting women[51] both as anti-Francoists and feminists, and as housewives and workers. These multiple identities included their identities as Catholics. Others acquired autonomy through Catholic organizations and then moved to the political left, so establishing a conversation with Marxists (apostolic movements, Christians for socialism, and liberation theology) that preceded the secularization of lay men and women. According to Mary Salas, while there was no organized Catholic feminism, there were Catholic women in the feminist movement.[52]

Despite the generational differences there were moments when the old and the new guard joined forces among the Spanish population.[53] There was not, however, a generalized sentiment of anticlericalism among the generation of the transition because of the work of the new Spanish clergy and social doctrine represented by Cardinal Tarancón. The new clergy formed a sort of "Parallel Church" comprised of the "Christian Workers Front" and "red priests" from disadvantaged neighborhoods, who supported strikers and demonstrators during the disturbances during the Burgos trials of 1970 of Basque separatists.[54]

There was a demand for *laicismo* as the cornerstone of a new free and secular state. The Church was not a target because of its renovation exemplified by its preaching of liberation theology. This did not mean an official alliance with the democrats and feminists since the Church always opposed reforms related to family law and the advancement of women. The Episcopal Conference opposed the legalization of divorce, abortion, and the birth control pill in 1982 and today still opposes gay marriage. As late as 1987, the traditionalist University of Navarra published books about female secularism with antiquated views about feminism:

> There is also operating the misnamed "women's liberation" which emphasizes efforts to masculinize or assimilate to the male (attire, behavior, rights, etc.) rather than the authentic development and maturation of their female potentialities in the human and social spheres.[55]

Contemporary Spain

Such attitudes explain the anti-religious trend in recent times and the crisis of religious vocations (down from 91,000 to 76,000 religious women, between 1969 and 1980). There was also the appearance of the unusual phenomenon of Apostasy.[56] Indeed, currently there are more non-religious Spanish women than at the beginning of 20th century, and there are many more than in 1975.

On Sundays, most Spanish families no longer attend mass because they prefer the supermarkets, the new cathedrals of postmodernity. True, Spain is still not a secular nation. Although Spain's Constitution, passed just three years after Franco's death, claims it to be a secular and non-denominational state, the weight of the Catholic heritage is still evident. However, currently this Catholicism is not at odds with ecumenism, modernity, or equal rights and citizenship for women. Nowadays, religion-state debates center on the school curriculum, the financing of religion through the general fund, and tax exemptions. The clergy, Opus Dei, and a few monastic orders survive as primarily religious organizations, whereas the catechists, *Acción Católica* or Caritas, coexist in civil society with new non-governmental associations. However, worship is still alive in churches and households. Religion has become a more intimate privatized affair although it is still institutionalized in the swearing-in of public officials and State funerals. Recently, as Spanish Catholicism has been challenged by Muslim immigration, the Hispano-American immigrant community has reinvigorated it.

Today, Spanish women are not fully secular and the Church remains influential. Most women who get married still prefer a Catholic wedding ceremony and May is still the Marian month. But now, Church power is inferior to the State's and is no longer part of a traditional alliance of "the throne and the altar." Its capacity for social exclusion and of decision-making over society has been reduced considerably. This does not mean that the new generations of Spanish women have revived the lay and freethinking ways of the old 1930s radical feminism. The difference is that today's society possesses functionalist, or perhaps pragmatic, values that are less combative and spiritual. Other than some minor groups, the political left has not monitored and defended the lay state despite the constant deals between the government and the Church. Since there have been constitutional reforms correcting the inferior status of women on civil, labor, and education rights, politicians have ignored the misogynist environment still existent in the Catholic Church. Furthermore, there are no public discussions about the gender inequalities in the Church's hierarchy or of the prohibition on female priesthood, but also there is the impression that encyclicals are no longer a threat to gender relations.

Today's lay ministries are shaped around issues such as abortion and gay marriage. With these pro-life groups and "Family Forums," the heirs to the Catholic propagandists of the 1930s have revived in opposition to the socialist government. Paradoxically, 75 years after the Republican reforms, the insult remains the same for the Archbishops of Madrid, Toledo, and Valencia. They describe "secular culture" as "a fraud" that "leads to despair through abortion, express divorce, and ideologies that pretend to manipulate the education of the youth" and will end with the "collapse of democracy."[57] These statements that consider public education as anathema and abortion as a crime against "innocent saints" were made to over a million supporters. In Spain today, progressive women have abandoned the banner of *laicismo* and allowed a fearless conservative mobilization to monopolize the Christian definition of family under the Church's umbrella. Political speeches and social and cultural practices are more disconnected from each other than ever. Thus, it is clear that while secularity is dominant among the people, the actual secularization of public policy in Spain remains a work in progress.

ENDNOTES

1. Martha C. Nussbaum, *Las mujeres y el desarrollo humano, El enfoque de las capacidades* (Barcelona, Spain: Herder, 2002) pp. 239-246.

2. Mary Nash and Susanna Tavera, *Experiencias desiguales, Conflictos sociales y respuestas colectivas, Siglo XIX* (Madrid: Síntesis, 1994).

3. The Church defines the concept "layman" (*laico or lego*) as baptized. This is different from the current meaning influenced by the recent history of secularization. "Secularity defines the active and specific participation of laymen and women in the Church's mission. However, today's secularity is degenerating in secularism, precisely in historically Christian countries and at a time when there is talk of the lay leadership on issues concerning the Church." Manuel Guerra Gómez, *El laicado masculino y femenino*, (Navarra, Spain: Universidad de Navarra, 1987) p. 135.

4.   Mónica Moreno Seco, *La quiebra de la unidad, Nacional-catolicismo y Vaticano II en la diócesis de Orihuela-Alicante, 1939-1975* (Alicante, Spain: Instituto de Cultura "Juan Gil-Albert," 1998) pp. 80-167. The author analyzes the Thomistic conception of the Catholic Church which exalts inequality as the "perfect type of social relation, because it is the way God created the world."

5.   *Vid.*, Adela Oña González, "La literatura religiosa como conformadora de un modelo de educación femenina en la Restauración (1875-1931)" in *La mujer en Andalucía, Tomo I. Encuentro Interdisciplinar de Estudios de la Mujer en Andalucía*, Pilar Ballarín and Teresa Ortiz, eds. (Granada: Feminae-Seminario de Estudios de la Mujer de la Universidad de Granada, 1990) pp. 499-507; Frances Lannon, "Los cuerpos de las mujeres y el cuerpo político católico: autoridades e identidades en conflicto en España durante las décadas de 1920 y 1930," *Historia Social* 35, 65-81 (1999).

6.   *Vid.*, Nerea Aresti Esteban, "El Ángel del Hogar y sus demonios. Ciencia, religión y género en la España del siglo XIX," *Historia Contemporánea* 21, 363-394 (2000).

7.   For the positions of Krausists read: Rosa María Capel Martínez, "La apertura del horizonte cultural femenino: Fernando de Castro y los Congresos Pedagógicos del siglo XIX," in *Mujer y sociedad en España, 1700-1975* (Madrid: Ministerio de Cultura-Instituto de la Mujer, 1986) pp. 113-146; María Isabel Cabrera Bosch, "Las mujeres que lucharon solas: Concepción Arenal y Emilia Pardo Bazán," in *El feminismo en España: Dos siglos de historia*, Pilar Folguera Crespo, coord., (Madrid: Pablo Iglesias, 1988) pp. 29-50.

8.   Shirley Mangini. *Las modernas de Madrid, Las grandes intelectuales españolas de la vanguardia* (Barcelona: Península, 2001).

9.   M. Luz Sanfeliú Gimeno, *Republicanas. Identidades de género en el Blasquismo (1895-1910)* (Valencia, Spain: Universitat de Valencia, 2005).

10. Pilar Ballarín Domingo, Maestras, innovación y cambios," *Arenal* 6 (1): 95 (1999). See also: Helena Establier Pérez, "La evolución del pensamiento feminista en la obra de Carmen de Burgos Seguí," in *Pensamiento, imagen, identidad: a la búsqueda de la definición de género*, María José Jiménez Tomé (Málaga, Spain: Atenea-Universidad de Málaga) pp. 187-206; and Concepción Núñez Rey, *Carmen de Burgos Colombine, en la Edad de Plata de la literatura española* (Madrid: Fundación José Manuel Lara, 2005).

11. Véase: Gloria Espigado Tocino, "La mujer en la utopía de Charles Fourier," in *Discursos, realidades, utopías. La construcción del sujeto femenino en los siglos XIX y XX*, María Dolores Ramos and María Teresa Vera, coords. (Barcelona, Spain: Anthropos, 2002); and María Dolores Ramos Palomo, "Herederas de la Razón Ilustrada: Feministas librepensadoras en España (1880-1902)," in *Femenino Plural, Palabra y memoria de mujeres*, (Málaga: Universidad de Málaga, 1994) pp. 85-104.

12. Karen Offen, "Definir el feminismo: un análisis histórico comparative," *Historia Social* 9: 103-136 (1991); Mary Nash, "Federica Montseny: dirigente anarquista, feminista y ministra," *Arenal, Revista de historia de las mujeres* 1(2): 259-271 (1994); and Susana Tavera, "Federica Montseny y el feminismo: unos escritos de juventud," *Arenal, Revista de historia de las mujeres* 1(2):307-329 (1994).

13. See: Shirley Mangini, 1999. *Las modernas de Madrid...op., cit.* and Concepción Fagoaga "La herencia laicista del movimiento sufragista en España," in *Las mujeres entre la historia y la sociedad contemporáne*, a Anna Aguado, ed. (Valencia, Spain: Generalitat Valenciana, 1999). For latter years: Sofía Rodríguez,"Mujeres perversas, La caricaturización femenina como expresión del poder entre la guerra civil y el franquismo," *Asparkía, Revista de Investigación Feminista* 16: 177-199 (2005).

14. See: Anne-Marie Sohn, "Las mujeres entre la madre en el hogar y la "garçonne," in, *Historia de las mujeres. Vol. 5. Siglo XX*, Georges Duby and Michelle Perrot, eds. (Madrid: Grupo Santillana de Ediciones, 2000) pp. 128-130; Miren Llona González, *Entre señorita y garçonne, Historia oral de las mujeres bilbaínas de clase media (1919-1939)* (Málaga: Atenea, 2002); and Rebeca Arce Pinedo. "De la mujer social a la mujer azul: la reconstrucción de la feminidad por las derechas españolas durante el primer tercio del siglo XX," *Ayer, Revista de Historia Contemporánea* 57: 247-272 (2005).

15. Dolors Ricart I Sampietro, "La Iglesia y el mundo femenino," *Historia 16* 145 (1988).

16. *Cf.* Mónica Moreno Seco. "Mujeres y religiosidad en la España contemporánea," in *Reflexiones en torno al género, La mujer como sujeto de discurs*, Silvia Caporale Bizzini and Nieves Montesinos Sánchez, eds. (Alicante: Publicaciones de la Universidad de Alicante, 2001) pp. 27-45.

17. Celia Viñas Olivella, *Viento Levante* (Almería, Spain: IEA, 1991 [1st ed. 1946]) p. 118.

18. Mónica Moreno Seco, *Conflicto educativo y secularización en Alicante durante la II República (1931-1936)* (Alicante, Spain: Institut de Cultura "Juan Gil Albert," 1995) pp. 28-57. See also: Mary Vincent, "Gender and Morals in Spanish Catholic Youth Culture: A Case Study of the Marian Congregations 1930-1936," *Gender & History* 13(2): 273-297 (2001).

19. According to María Pilar Salomón Chéliz, "Mujeres, religión y anticlericalismo en la España contemporánea: ¿para cuándo una historia desde la perspectiva de género? in *El Siglo XX: balance y perspectivas* (Valencia, Spain: Fundación Cañada Blanch, 2000) pp. 241-243.

20. *Vid.*, Mónica Moreno Seco, "De la caridad al compromiso: Las mujeres de Acción Católica (1958-1968)," *Historia Contemporánea* 26; pp. 239-265 (2003).

21. *Cf.*, Mercedes García Basauri, "La mujer y la Iglesia. El feminismo cristiano en España (1900-1930)," *Tiempo de Historia* 57; pp. 22-33 (1979).

22. Mercedes García Basauri, "Beneficencia y caridad en la crisis de la Restauración, La mujer social," *Tiempo de Historia* 59; pp. 28-43 (1979).

23. Opinions written in the pioneer works of Margarita. Nelken, *La Condición Social de la Mujer en España*, 1919; María Cambrils. *Feminismo Socialista*,1925; or Carmen de Burgos Seguí, *La mujer en España*, 1927, edited by Sempere; and, above all *La mujer moderna y sus derechos*, 1927.

24. Mary Nash, "Ideals of Redemption: *Socialism and Women on the Left in Spain,"* in *Socialism and Women on the Left in Interwar Europe,* Gruber H. and P. Graves (Oxford: Berghahn, 1998) p. 354.

25. *Vid.* Inmaculada Blasco, "Tenemos las armas de nuestra fe y de nuestro amor y patriotismo; `pero nos falta algo´ La Acción Católica de la Mujer y la participación política en la España del primer tercio del siglo XX," *Historia Social* 44: 3-20 (2002); and *Paradojas de la Ortodoxi, Política de masas y militancia católica femenina en España (1919-1939)* (Zaragoza: Prensas Universitarias de Zaragoza, 2003) pp. 144-163.

26. *Vid.* Mary Nash, "El mundo de las trabajadoras: identidades, cultura de género y espacios de actuación," in *Cultura social y política en el mundo del trabajo,* J. J. A. Piqueras Paniagua and V. Sanz, eds. (Valencia: Fundación Instituto Historia Social, 1999) pp. 47-67. According to Temma Kaplan, *"union leaders and its members openly disapproved of the women's 'ungovernable' behavior,"* they showed contempt for the women's unusual ways of participating in the worker's struggles *(Ciudad roja, periodo azul. Los movimientos sociales en la Barcelona de Picasso (1888-1939)* (Barcelona: Península, 2002) p. 196.

27. Aurora Morcillo Gómez, *True Catholic Womanhood, Gender ideology in Franco's Spain* (DeKalb, Illinois: Northern Illinois University Press, 2000) pp. 130-140.

28. *Cf.* María Ascensión Martínez Martín,"Las organizaciones femeninas en el País Vasco: una doble Guerra Civil," en *Las mujeres y la Guerra Civil Española. III Jornadas de estudios monográficos. Salamanca* (Madrid: Ministerio de Asuntos Sociales, 1989) p. 249. *Vid.,* Leandro Álvarez Rey, "El Carlismo en Andalucía durante la II República (1931-36)," en *Congreso sobre la República, la Guerra Civil y el Franquismo en Andalucía* (Málaga, febrero 1989).

29. VV. AA.,"La mujer tradicionalista: las Margaritas," *Las mujeres y la Guerra Civil Española. III Jornadas...op. cit.*; pp. 188-202.

30. Rosa Cobo Bedia, *Fundamentos del Patriarcado Moderno, Jean-Jacques Rousseau* (Madrid: Cátedra, 1995).

31. Helen Graham, "Mujeres y cambio social en la España de los años treinta," *Historia del Presente* 2: 9-24 (2003). See also: Danièle Bussy Genevois, "El retorno de la hija pródiga: Mujeres entre lo público y lo privado (1931-1936)," in *Otras visiones de España,* Pilar Folguera, comp. (Madrid: Editorial Pablo Iglesias, 1993) pp. 111-138.

32. Inmaculada Blasco Herranz, *Paradojas de la Ortodoxia...op. cit.*; pp. 207-248.

33. Mónica Moreno Seco, *La quiebra de la unidad...op. cit.*; p. 168.

34. Michael Seidman, "El giro cultural," *Revista de Libros* 122: 14-15 (2007).

35. Antonio Cazorla Sánchez, "Patria Mártir: Los españoles, la nación y la Guerra Civil en el discurso ideológico del primer franquismo," in *Construir España, Nacionalismo español y procesos de nacionalización,* Javier Moreno Luzón, (Madrid, 2007) pp. 289-302.

36. Rafael Cruz, *En el nombre del pueblo: república, rebelión y guerra en la España de 1936* (Madrid, 2006) Siglo XXI.

37. *Vid.* Julián Sanz Hoya, "Catolicismo y anticlericalismo en la prensa falangista de posguerra," in *El Franquismo: El Régimen y la Oposición* (Toledo, Spain: MECD-Comunidad Castilla-La Mancha, 2000) pp. 907-923; Santos Juliá, "¿Falange liberal o intelectuales fascistas?" *Claves de razón práctica* 121: 4-13 (2002).

38. Helen Graham, "Mujeres y cambio social...", *op. cit.*; p. 14. See also: Geraldine M. Scanlon, "El movimiento feminista en España, 1900-1985: Logros y dificultades," in *Participación política de las mujeres,* Judith Astelarra, comp. (Madrid: CIS, 1990) pp. 83-101; and Danièle Bussy Genevois, "El retorno de la hija pródiga...", op. cit.; p. 127.

39. Mary Nash, 2004. *Mujeres en el mundo, Historia, retos y movimientos* (Madrid: Alianza, 2004) p. 163.

40. See: Giuliana Di Febo and Marina Saba, "La condición de la mujer y el papel de la Iglesia en la Italia fascista y en la España franquista: ideologías, leyes y asociaciones femeninas," *Ordenamiento Jurídico y realidad social de las mujeres, siglos XVI-XX. Actas de las IV Jornadas de Investigación Interdisciplinari* (Madrid: Seminario de Estudios de la Mujer de la Universidad Autónoma de Madrid, 1986) pp. 439-452. About the symbolism of the spiritual reserve of Spanish women: Aurora G. Morcillo, "The Orient Within. Women's Self-empowering Acts under Francoism" (in press).

41. *Cf.* Michael Richards, *Un tiempo de silencio* (Barcelona: Crítica,1998); and Giuliana Di Febo, *La Santa de la Raza: El culto barroco en la España franquista.* Barcelona: Icaria, 1988).

42. María Teresa Vera Balanza, "Un modelo de misioneras seglares: las mujeres de Acción Católica durante el franquismo," *La mujer en Andalucía. I Encuentro Interdisciplinar de Estudios de la Mujer en Andalucía* (Granada: Feminae-Seminario de Estudios de la Mujer de la Universidad de Granada, 1990) pp. 521-532; and "Literatura religiosa y mentalidad femenina en el franquismo," *Baetica: Estudios de Arte, Geografía e Historia* 14: 362-372 (1993). We also have an "insider's" perspective: Emilio Enciso Viana, "Cincuenta años al servicio de la Iglesia, Sucinto historial de las mujeres de Acción Católica," *Ecclesia* 1432: 21-22 (1969).

43. *Cf.* Mónica Moreno Seco, *La quiebra de la unidad...op. cit.*; pp. 78-79. See also: Enrique González Duro. *El miedo en la posguerra, Franco y la España derrotada: La política del exterminio* (Madrid: Oberon, 2003) pp. 219-239.

44. There is a recent article about everyday resistance in the Franquist period by Ana Cabana Iglesia, "La Galicia Rural durante el Primer Franquismo, Resistencia o sumisión. Elementos para un debate," *de Investigadores del Franquismo* (Albacete: Universidad de Castilla la Mancha (CD-Rom), 2003).

45. *Cit.* Temma Kaplan, *Ciudad roja, periodo azul...op. cit.*; pp. 70-135 and 269. In fact, Lt. Gen. Camilo Alonso Vega, who was in charge of the Ministry of Security and was general director of the Civil Guard in 1950 predicted then that "If we set the precedent that those who take to the streets to agitate will be welcomed with police shooting, the agitation will end." (TUSSELL, Javier, *Carrero, La eminencia gris del régimen de Franco* (Madrid, Temas de Hoy) pp. 192-205.

46. *Vid.* Gemma Piérola Narvarte, "Antes morir virgen que vivir mancillada, Aspectos del discurso moral de la Iglesia sobre la población femenina navarra en el franquismo," *Revista Gerónimo de Uztáriz*, 16: 43-55 (2000); Jorge Uría et al., *La cultura popular en la España contemporánea: doce estudios* (Madrid: Biblioteca Nueva, 2003).

47. *Vid.* Mónica Moreno Seco, *La quiebra de la unidad...op. cit.*; pp. 196-203 and 266-281. See also, from the same author: "La maldición de Eva. Mujer, Iglesia y práctica religiosa en los años sesenta, La diócesis de Orihuela-Alicante," en *II Encuentro de Investigadores del Franquismo*, Tomo II (Alicante: Instituto de Cultura "Juan Gil-Albert"-Diputación Provincial de Alicante, 1995) pp. 59-65.

48. See: María Salas, *De la promoción de la mujer a la teología feminista* (Cantabria: Sal Térrea, 1993); Pilar Bellosillo, "La mujer española dentro de la Iglesia," en BORREGUERO, Concha *et alii, La mujer española: de la tradición a la modernidad* (1960-1980) (Madrid: Tecnos, 1996) pp. 109-126; or Feliciano Montero, "El giro social de la Acción Católica Española (1957-1959)" in *V Encuentro de Investigadores del Franquismo*, José Babiano *et al.*, coords. (Albacete: Universidad de Castilla la Mancha (CD-Rom), 2003).

49. *Cf.* Asociación Mujeres en la Transición Democrática, *Españolas en la Transición, De excluidas a protagonistas* (1973-1982)\ (Madrid: Biblioteca Nueva, 1999) pp. 29-35.

50. *Vid.* Revista *Vindicación Feminista* 4 (1975): Vigil, Mariló, "La pornografía y el sadismo antifemenino," pp. 18-20; or Soledad Balaguer, "Publicidad: El machismo a flor de piel," *Vindicación Feminista* 5: 54-57 (1976).

51. *Vid.* Lola Gavira, "La mujer es una clase" y Soria, Assumpta, 1977 "Posición del movimiento obrero tradicional en relación al movimiento feminista," *Vindicación Feminista* 7 (1977).

52. Mónica Moreno Seco, 2005. "Religiosas y laicas en el franquismo: entre la dictadura y la oposición," *Arenal. Revista de historia de las mujeres* 12(1): pp. 61-89 (2005); "Mujeres en la transición de la Iglesia hacia la democracia: avances y dificultades" *Historia del Presente*. 10: 25-40 (2007).

53. Beatriz Caballero Mesonero, "Algo viejo, algo nuevo y algo azul: Vallisoletanas en el Franquismo (1959-1975)," in *V Encuentro de Investigadores del Franquismo...op. cit.*

54. *Vid.* José Babiano, "Los católicos en el origen de CC.OO," *Espacio, Tiempo y Forma*, 8: 277-295 (1995); Enrique Berzal de la Rosa. "Católicos en la lucha antifranquista, Militancia sindical y política," *Historia del Presente* 10: 7-24 (2007).

55. Manuel Guerra Gómez, *El laicado masculino y femenino...op. cit.*; p. 136.

56. For the evolution of vocations: *Estadísticas de la Iglesia Católica* (Madrid: Edice, 1989) p. 154. y http://www.redescristianas.net/2007/09/20/aumenta-la-apostasia-en-espana/ (The available data mention 150 complaints only for 2007).

57. Words by Valencia's Cardinal Agustín García-Gasco on December 12, 2008 addressing the crowd in `Por la Familia Cristiana´ (http://www.elpais.com/articulo/espana/Ataques/politicas/Gobierno/acto/Familia/Cristiana/elpepuesp/20071230elpepunac_1/Tes).

14. Secularization and Its Discontents: Courts and Abortion Policy in the United States and Spain

Adrienne Fulco

Scholars who compare European and American political parties have customarily characterized the two major American political parties as distinctly non-ideological coalitions of voters who come together every four years to nominate and elect a president. Nicol C. Rae recently observed that "[i]n the comparative study of political parties in twentieth century advanced democracies, the United States has always been something of a problematic outlier owing to the absence of organized, disciplined, and ideological mass political parties."[1] Moreover, according to Rae, when compared with other advanced industrial democracies, "American national parties have traditionally been decentralized, loosely organized, and undisciplined, with party cleavages based on cultural or regional factors rather than social class divisions."[2] But today, according to researchers who have explored the problem of polarization in American politics since the 1980s, there is now "widespread agreement that the Democratic and Republican parties in the electorate have become more sharply divided on ideology and policy issues in recent decades."[3] Commentators agree that among the factors most responsible for the sharpening of distinctions between the two parties has been the infusion of white, Protestant, conservative, religiously motivated voters into the Republican Party.[4] Thus, not only have American political parties become more ideologically oriented, but they have also come to resemble more closely the European model, in which parties represent distinct religious and secular constituencies.

The political polarization that has occurred over the course of nearly two decades was crystallized in Patrick J. Buchanan's speech at the 1992 Republican National Convention. It was there, in Houston, Texas, that Buchanan famously announced to delegates, and a national audience, that "There is a religious war going on in our country for the soul of America. It is a cultural war, as critical to the kind of nation we will one day be as was the Cold War itself."[5] Praising both Ronald Reagan and presumptive nominee George H.W. Bush for their resolute leadership on moral issues, Buchanan went on to attack Bill Clinton, the Democratic nominee, for promoting an agenda that did not reflect "the Judeo-Christian values and beliefs upon which this nation was built."[6] In addition, Buchanan specifically faulted Clinton and the Democratic Party for their support of abortion rights at their own party's July nominating convention, held in New York City:

> At...[the] top [of their agenda] is unrestricted abortion on demand. When the Irish-Catholic governor of Pennsylvania, Robert Casey, asked to say a few words on behalf of the 25 million unborn children destroyed since Roe v Wade [sic], he was told there was no place for him at the podium of Bill Clinton's convention, no room at the inn.[7]

Buchanan's praise for George H.W. Bush and Reagan is especially noteworthy because both candidates shifted their positions on abortion from pro-choice to pro-life after they decided to run for president.[8]

While a full discussion of the myriad ways in which religion has shaped intra-party competition in America over the past four decades is beyond the scope of this paper, there is little doubt that the Republican Party has become the party of religion, and that religiously determined issues have come to play an increasingly important role in electoral politics. Among those issues, which include gay rights, prayer in public schools, and the teaching of evolution, the most important by far is abortion. As Geoffrey Layman puts it, "Abortion is the defining issue in contemporary cultural and moral politics...[and] the issue that has been most central to the cultural debate both within and between the parties."[9] This development has had profound consequences not only for the electoral process but also for appointments to the U.S. Supreme Court, the arena in which battles over abortion are now frequently waged.

During the 35 years since *Roe v. Wade* was decided,[10] the abortion issue has shaped American electoral politics, and although abortion remains legal in the United States, pro-life groups, often associated with the Republican Party, have worked tirelessly to overturn the landmark ruling. Pro-life advocacy groups like Focus on the Family and the National Right to Life Committee have successfully elected legislators at both the state and federal level who have passed myriad laws that restrict a woman's right to terminate a pregnancy. At the same time, these groups have joined with other Christian conservatives to help elect presidential candidates like George W. Bush, who vowed to appoint "strict constructionist" judges to the Supreme Court, understood to mean judges committed to overturning *Roe v. Wade*. Given the crucial role the Supreme Court has played in determining abortion policy in the United States, it is useful to understand how organized interest groups, which exert influence within the Republican Party, have framed the abortion question in religious terms, so that a woman's right to choose abortion today is less secure than it was even a decade ago.

Since the 1980s, abortion reform has also occurred throughout most of Western Europe, and the constitutional courts of Italy and Spain, two countries with large Catholic populations, have both rendered decisions that resulted in the partial decriminalization of abortion in the past few decades. Moreover, both the Italian[11] and Spanish[12] rulings have been viewed as legitimate, and abortion law has remained relatively—some would say surprisingly—stable in both countries despite ongoing efforts by Catholic politicians and clergy to revive the debate.[13] It should be noted that any efforts to either expand or roll back abortion reform in both Italy and Spain take place in the political and electoral arenas, which are structurally and functionally separate from the constitutional courts. This institutional arrangement, which depoliticizes the constitutional courts, is in sharp contrast to the increasingly politicized role the U.S. Supreme Court plays in the American electoral process.

An obvious question is how to assess the stability of the abortion rulings by the Italian and Spanish constitutional courts, in comparison to the American Supreme Court's decision in *Roe v. Wade*, which has been subjected to ongoing challenges for nearly four decades. A second and related question concerns the degree to which organized pro-life groups in America, almost all of which root their opposition to abortion in religious belief, have more successfully affected the legal process than similar groups in either Italy or Spain. This paper is part of a larger project that seeks to contribute to the rich and growing literature that analyzes constitutional courts in a comparative framework. In the larger project I will include a discussion of the role of the Constitutional Court in adjudicating abortion law in Italy, but here I will focus my comparison on the way in which constitutional courts function in America and Spain. My principal objectives are to examine the role of the constitutional courts and the practices of judicial review in each country, in order to understand why the abortion question remains far more polarizing and contentious in the United States, where the separation of church and state is enshrined in the Constitution, than it does in Spain, where a large Catholic population and a history of engaged religious political parties define the political landscape. I will conclude with a consideration of the ways in which the American abortion controversy, which is driven in large part by highly active and motivated partisans who are informed by their religious beliefs, has caused the Republican Party to frame questions in religious terms, including questions that come before the Supreme Court.

The U.S. Supreme Court and Abortion Policy

The U.S. Supreme Court has played a central role in defining abortion policy in America. The 1973 ruling in *Roe v. Wade*, which provoked controversy from the day it was decided, struck down a Texas statute that had criminalized abortion except in cases where the pregnant woman's life was at stake. The statute was challenged on the grounds that it violated a woman's right to privacy, a right that was recognized by the Court in a series of cases dealing with access to contraceptives.[14] Sarah Weddington, counsel for the original plaintiff in the case, argued that just as a woman's right to determine whether she would use contraceptives was protected by a fundamental right to privacy, so too was her right to determine whether she would continue, or terminate, her pregnancy. It is significant that in the United States in 1973 there were no national abortion laws, and all statutes criminalizing abortion had been proposed and approved at the state level. Although some states, like New York and California, had already begun to reform or repeal their criminal abortion statutes before Roe was decided,[15] the effect of the decision was to overturn *all* state statutes that resembled the one in Texas because the Supreme Court's rulings are not limited to the particular parties to a case. Thus, the Court's decision in *Roe* abrogated every state law that criminalized abortion or failed to conform to the Court's analysis of the broad protections to which women were now entitled. It is for this reason that the Court's ruling was characterized as sweeping and that the judges who joined the 7-2 majority were criticized for engaging in judicial activism. Analysis of the historical record now reveals that Harry Blackmun (the author of *Roe*), and the other six justices who joined his majority opinion, were unaware that the decision would trigger such a strong and sustained response from abortion opponents.[16]

Almost immediately after the *Roe* decision was announced, pro-life advocates vowed to overturn the ruling. Over the next several years, several pro-life groups were established, most of them closely affiliated with religious organizations. They developed strategies aimed at passing legislation at the state level that would test the reach of *Roe* by establishing restrictions on access to abortion such as parental consent, mandatory waiting periods, and informed consent. Additionally, these pro-life activists quickly made abortion a matter of electoral politics and publicly announced that they would work to defeat candidates at all levels of government who supported the Court's decision in *Roe*.[17] This two-pronged strategy, directed both toward litigating in the courts and also at electing pro-life candidates, was successful. Over the past four decades, pro-life candidates have been elected to both state legislatures and the U.S. Congress, and numerous statutes restricting access to abortion have been passed.[18] Although most of these anti-abortion laws were initially found to be unconstitutional by the Supreme Court, pro-life groups and conservative Christians became increasingly active in the Republican Party during the 1980s, and they now constitute one of its most important constituencies. These groups made the election of pro-life candidates a priority, and every Republican elected to the presidency since 1980 has adopted a pro-life position by promising to appoint judges to the Supreme Court whose record indicates a willingness to overturn *Roe*. Ronald Reagan, George H.W. Bush, and George W. Bush all campaigned on pro-life platforms, and each president appointed justices who have indeed voted to uphold state statutes restricting abortion. These justices include Antonin Scalia and Anthony Kennedy (Reagan appointees); Clarence Thomas (a G.H.W. Bush appointee); and John Roberts and Samuel Alito (G.W. Bush appointees).[19] The two new Bush appointees, John Roberts and Samuel Alito, were subjected to intense questioning about abortion in their nationally televised Senate confirmation hearings, but ultimately even some of the most skeptical senators, including Democrats, voted to confirm their nominations.[20]

What, then, allows a vocal minority of pro-life voters to have such a disproportionate impact on the electoral process, which in turn directly affects judicial decision-making at the level of the U.S. Supreme Court? To answer this question, it is necessary to examine both the structure of the Court and its function in the American political system. The U.S. Supreme Court is the final arbiter of constitutional disputes, and its interpretations of the Constitution are binding at all levels of government, including the state level. On the national level, however, the Court is one of three branches of government, and it is part of the system of checks and balances that defines the entire American constitutional scheme. There are no specific qualifications for judges who sit on the Supreme Court, and their selection is based solely on the preferences of the president who nominates them. Moreover, since the justices have lifetime tenure on the Court, they usually serve long beyond the term of the president who appoints them. The justices do not need to respond to public opinion, and they can be removed from the Court only through the laborious process of impeachment, which has been initiated only once in American history.[21] From a structural perspective, the appointment of U.S. Supreme Court justices is directly linked to the electoral process in general and to the politics of presidential elections in particular. Although the work of interpreting the Constitution requires neutrality and objectivity, appointments to the Court are, by definition, fundamentally political. Consequently, decision-making by the justices on the Court must be understood within the context of the highly politicized process that determines their appointments in the first place. Since abortion was among the most salient issues for an important constituency of the Republican party, it is hardly surprising that Republican presidents have appointed justices to the Supreme Court whom they considered likely to vote to uphold laws restricting access to abortion and who would, if given the opportunity, vote to overturn the *Roe* decision. In this regard, neither Antonin Scalia nor Clarence Thomas has disappointed the presidents who appointed them.

As Jeffrey Toobin recently noted, since the death of Chief Justice Rehnquist and the retirement of Justice O'Connor, in 2005, the newly constituted Court has moved "with great swiftness…[and] Roberts, Alito and their allies have already made progress on [the conservative] agenda."[22] More specifically, "the Court, for first time in its history, upheld a categorical ban on an abortion procedure [*Gonzales v. Carhart*[23]]." Justice Ginsburg issued a blistering dissenting opinion in *Carhart*, which she read aloud from the bench, in order to emphasize her deep disagreement with her colleagues. Justice Ginsburg pointed out that although the Court had invalidated a virtually identical law criminalizing "partial birth abortion" in 2000 (*Stenberg v. Carhart*),[24] the Court's reversal could be explained by the simple fact that two new justices— Roberts and Alito—had joined the Court. It is clear that Justice O'Connor's retirement, which resulted in the Alito appointment, has shifted the Court's balance in precisely the direction the President and his conservative supporters had sought. According to Toobin, President Bush has succeeded in transforming the Supreme Court, and what now matters most, when divisive or controversial questions come before the Court, "is not the quality of the arguments but the [political and ideological] identity of the justices."[25]

The U.S. Supreme Court's structural features are closely related to its extensive but vaguely defined powers of judicial review. The Court has the power to decide cases as a matter of both original and appellate jurisdiction. Although it hears relatively few cases that involve questions of original jurisdiction, which are explicitly delineated in the Constitution and involve disputes between states or cases involving ambassadors and diplomats, the Court's appellate powers are broad but only vaguely defined in Article III, §2. As is well known, the Court's power to determine the constitutionality of statutes and actions of government officials developed over time, and the Court alone selects the particular cases it will hear on appeal. Thus, it is actual litigants, who are parties to real controversies, who bring cases to the Supreme Court, which is prohibited from issuing purely advisory opinions and only decides matters of law. With respect to the Court's rulings on abortion, all of the cases were brought on appeal by individual litigants who claimed that a lower court had committed an error of law, or that the application of a particular state or federal law resulted in a constitutional violation. What is especially noteworthy in a comparative context is that the protections afforded women seeking abortions, recognized by the Supreme Court in *Roe* and all subsequent cases, originated in *litigation* challenging state laws rather than in *legislation* initiated at either the state or national level. Several legal scholars, including Supreme Court justice Ruth Bader Ginsburg, have argued that the Court's decision in *Roe* hindered the progress of the abortion reform movement that had gained momentum in the states during the late 1960s, and, as a result, the Supreme Court became the focus of anti-abortion activists.[26] Once the locus of debate over abortion shifted from the legislative to the judicial branch of government, the courts became the arbiters of the question. Because of the many opportunities to litigate abortion rights in both state and federal courts, there has been no single definitive ruling on the constitutionality of abortion law throughout the United States. Consequently, the case-by-case approach has produced a four-decade-long struggle between opponents and supporters of abortion. State legislatures seeking to limit or abolish the right to abortion have passed a succession of laws that pro-choice advocates have then been repeatedly forced to challenge in court.

Abortion opponents have succeeded in limiting the right to abortion in two ways. First, they have lobbied effectively for state legislation that places ever more burdensome restrictions on women. These restrictions have taken the form of more elaborate informed consent requirements, which often mandate information sessions about adoption and fetal development, and stricter regulation of minors' access to abortion through mandatory parental notification and consent regulations.[27] As discussed above, pro-life groups have convinced legislators at both the state and federal levels to pass laws barring a particular abortion procedure, intact dilation and extraction; one of these laws, "The Partial Birth Abortion Act," was found to be constitutional by the Court in April of 2007.[28] Second, since the 1980s, pro-life advocacy groups have exercised enormous influence within the Republican Party, especially in presidential elections. They have been able to insist that Republican presidents appoint justices to the Supreme Court who appear to be sympathetic to their cause. The pro-life groups have succeeded because the Supreme Court is as much a part of the political process as any other institution of American government. Furthermore, after the *Roe* decision, the judicial nomination process became increasingly politicized and the participation of religiously affiliated groups grew exponentially.[29] When compared to other nations' constitutional courts, the U.S. Supreme Court is a more integral part of the political process; consequently, political activists are able to influence the composition of the judiciary and its rulings, if only indirectly. The justices are therefore perceived as having ideological preferences, and although the public holds the Court in high regard and views its decisions as legitimate, reversals of unpopular rulings, particularly in the case of abortion, are always a very real possibility.

The Supreme Court's decisions, fixed in the common law tradition, are made incrementally, and there is unlimited opportunity to revisit constitutional questions whenever litigants successfully bring a case and the justices accept it for appeal. As a result, the Court's rulings on controversial issues like abortion are always subject to legal challenge, and so long as pro-life groups actively seek to eviscerate or overturn *Roe v. Wade*, the U.S.'s abortion law [singular or plural—abortion *laws*?] will continue to be more unstable than in countries like Spain, where the Constitutional Court is not subject to the demands of electoral politics.

The Constitutional Court[30] and Abortion Policy in Spain

According to legal scholar Alec Stone Sweet, all of the European constitutions written after World War II, such as Italy and Spain's, established "enforceable, substantive constraints on government. These included constraints on legislative and executive authority, in the form of human rights, the scope and content of which go far beyond the American Bill of Rights." In addition, "with very few exceptions, all such constitutions provide for 'constitutional review' by a 'constitutional court'" that has "specialized jurisdiction" and is designed to "ensure the normative superiority of constitutional law."[31] The European constitutional courts are based on the model of judicial review developed by the Austrian legal theorist Hans Kelsen. This approach is rooted in legal positivism and designed to provide an alternative to the American model, which Kelsen and subsequent legal theorists believed risked devolving into a system characterized by a "government by judges."[32] Kelsen emphasized that judicial power must be carefully circumscribed by the constitution, and he cautioned that the constitution itself should not include human rights guarantees, which, he firmly believed, invited open-ended interpretation that would undermine the legitimacy of the judges.[33] His objective was to limit the power of judicial review to the abstract protection of the entire constitutional order.[34] To achieve this goal, he proposed that constitutional courts be authorized to review the constitutionality of legislation passed by parliament *prior* to implementation and that judges be recruited from the expert ranks of professional judges and law professors. While most European countries adopted the Kelsenian model for their constitutional courts, many have deviated from his approach in one important way: they have given courts jurisdiction over constitutional rights.[35] The Spanish Constitutional Court, Tribunal Constitucional de España, follows the Kelsenian rather than the American model in several important respects, and its structure and function have had significant consequences for its review of questions pertaining to abortion. The Spanish Constitutional Court, whose authority is conferred by the Constitution and by statute, is separate from and independent of the larger judicial system, and is governed by its own rules. The Court has twelve elected members—four nominated by the Congress of Deputies, four by the Senate (by a three-fifths majority), two by the Government, and two by the Judiciary. The judges are required to have at least fifteen years of professional practice experience, and they are drawn from the ranks of magistrates, prosecutors, university professors, public officials, and lawyers. They serve for nine years, and one third of the judges are renewed or replaced at three-year intervals.[36] Unlike the very partisan appointment process for Supreme Court justices in the United States, Spanish judges are selected in a procedure that focuses on the professional qualifications of candidates who have extensive legal experience and have been recognized by the larger legal community. This system was deliberately designed to make the Court politically independent, and to insulate it from the kind of partisanship that characterizes the American model and, in the view of Europeans, would likely undermine the legitimacy of judicial review.

The Court's jurisdiction is clearly defined, and it possesses the power of both abstract and concrete review. When politicians, including the prime minister, deputies, and the president of the parliamentary bodies, among others, refer a statute directly to the Court, it undertakes an abstract review of the constitutionality of a particular text and renders a ruling. The Court also reviews legislation referred to it when ordinary courts, in the process of adjudicating a concrete case, decide to do so. Finally, the Court hears cases that are brought by individuals in a specific controversy who raise questions of fundamental rights and have exhausted all other appeals.[37] Although originally the Spanish Constitutional Court had the power to review legislation pertaining to issues of fundamental rights and liberties *before* a statute was implemented, this power was abolished in 1985 because "[i]t proved to be a very efficient means of parliamentary obstruction."[38] This power of *a priori* review, which Belen Barreiro contends leads courts to be less cautious than when they review a law that has already been implemented, is especially relevant to the evolution of abortion law in Spain.

According to Celia Valiente, abortion has been punished in Spain since medieval times, and it was criminalized in the first penal code of 1822, the provisions of which remained virtually unchanged until the reform movement of the 1980s. In 1944, the Fascist government revised the penal code to punish abortion with a prison term of six months to six years, granting exemptions only for unmarried women.[39] The one exception to the criminalization of abortion in Spain occurred in Catalonia, where in 1936 the legislature, responding to a strong women's movement associated with the politically powerful anarchists, passed a law permitting abortion for therapeutic, eugenic, or ethical reasons.[40] Only when the Socialist Party (PSOE), whose ideology was informed by secular values, came to power in 1982 did the process of reforming abortion law in Spain begin. Although the PSOE had not campaigned on abortion in the 1970s, the issue had been raised within the party. As Valiente points out, the abortion issue divided those members who supported broad liberalization from those who were committed only to more limited reform.[41] In the 1982 election, the PSOE explicitly pledged to initiate the process of abortion reform, but the party deliberately adopted an incremental approach as an electoral strategy. By abandoning its "traditional anti-clericalism" and adopting a "more cautious approach to the Catholic Church,"[42] the PSOE broadened its appeal and won the election with an absolute majority.

Within four months of coming to power, the Socialist Cabinet wrote a modest proposal that reformed the Penal Code of 1944 by "legalizing therapeutic, eugenic and ethical abortions." This constituted a first step in the process of liberalizing a woman's right to abortion in Spain.[43] Belen Barreiro argues that the reason PSOE did not call for more sweeping abortion reform, or specify an implementation plan, was because it understood that the bill would be referred to the Court and wanted "to avoid constitutional censure."[44] Given the large Socialist majority, the Congress of Deputies and the Senate approved the bill, and, as expected, the principal opposition to the proposal came from the Alianza Popular (AP), a conservative party with ties to the Catholic Church that opposed any decriminalization of abortion. Conservatives then brought the abortion bill to the Constitutional Court for *a priori* review, contending that the text was unconstitutional.[45] They grounded their argument in Article 15 of the 1978 Spanish Constitution, the relevant section of which states: "All have the right to life and to physical and moral integrity, and may under no circumstances be subjected to torture or to inhuman or degrading punishment or treatment."[46] The AP Deputies who referred the bill asked the Court to declare the whole bill unconstitutional, but they also requested that certain aspects of the bill be more clearly defined.[47] Referral of the bill to the Constitutional Court delayed the implementation process for sixteen months until April of 1985, when the judges reached a decision.

The Court's ruling stated that certain provisions of the reform bill violated Article 15 of the Constitution. The twelve members of the Court were evenly divided, thus requiring the President of the Court to cast a second, tie-breaking vote. It is worth noting that Richard Stith, who has written a detailed account of the Court's decision, points out that the votes of the justices did not split along party lines, and five separate dissenting opinions were issued.[48] Essentially, the Court determined that "therapeutic, eugenic and ethical abortions were considered constitutional but the precise wording of the bill was to be modified to assure the protection of the foetus."[49] Thus, the Court achieved a balance between a woman's right to absolute choice to terminate a pregnancy and the value of fetal rights. Declaring that the fetus itself did not possess rights but that "human life is a superior constitutional value," the Court specified the changes that would be required in order for the bill to be deemed constitutional. In particular, the Court stipulated that the health of a woman be defined as both mental and physical, and specific provisions for regulating therapeutic and eugenic abortions must be established.[50]

Within a week of the ruling, the Spanish government revised the bill according to the Court's recommendations and resubmitted it to Parliament. Agreement was quickly reached, and during the week of debate, a poll conducted by the Center for Sociological Research found that 75% of Spanish respondents favored abortion under limited conditions, including 52% of those who identified themselves as members of the conservative AP Party, most of whose members are Catholic.[51] Even the AP, which had rejected abortion reform in 1983 and initially referred the bill to the Court, accepted the Court's ruling as binding and shifted its position in order to achieve a new compromise bill. Organic Law 9, which was approved on July 5, 1985, limited abortion to cases of rape or incest, a malformed fetus, and threats to a woman's mental or physical health, and provided for strict regulation. Of particular importance are the rules governing implementation because they determine women's access to the procedure. In addition to the requirements that abortion be performed in public or approved health facilities after physician approval, the law also mandates that women give express consent, and that a physician, other than the one who approved the procedure, direct or perform the abortion.[52] A few weeks later, the Ministry of Health issued supplementary regulations, including a controversial "conscience clause" provision allowing physicians and other hospital personnel to decline to perform an abortion on the basis of their religious or moral beliefs. Additional regulatory changes have been enacted since the passage of the 1985 law that have improved access and overcome some of the original problems of implementation.[53]

While abortion has remained a contested issue in Spain since 1985, the law has remained remarkably stable. Celia Valiente argues that Catholic opposition to abortion in Spain has been more moderate than in other countries and that "[u]nlike the United States, Germany, or Ireland, the issue no longer provokes intense conflict in the policy-making process."[54] Noteworthy in this regard is the Constitutional Court's January 1991 ruling, in which the Court first dismissed a criminal case against a married couple and a friend who assisted in procuring an abortion, and then recognized a socio-economic justification for terminating the pregnancy. The court determined that the woman was suffering mentally and physically; that the family could not afford another child; and it "concluded that if the mother were forced to give birth, her right to free development of her person would be violated."[55] Although the physician in the case was convicted, the ruling encouraged supporters of abortion reform to again seek to amend the Spanish penal code in order to bring it in line with the abortion policies of other countries in the European Union.[56] But, despite the fact the Spaniards continue to support further liberalization of abortion laws, legal reform requires parliamentary action, which, in turn, requires the kind of compromise that tends to maintain the status quo.[57] Furthermore, in Spain as in other Western European countries, abortion is understood to be divisive, and "political elites will prevent the issue from gaining agenda status, as within parties there is often no consensus on the issue."[58] Because of the need to achieve reform through the political process rather than through litigation, the Constitutional Court is embroiled in a political struggle.

Conclusions

In her analysis of the 1985 Spanish Constitutional Court ruling, Belen Barreiro points out that the PSOE anticipated that the bill would be referred to the Constitutional Court for review, and that this caused the lawmakers to draft a modest reform proposal in order to avoid censure. Arguing convincingly, she observes: "A declaration of unconstitutionality by the Court would have blocked the possibility of future reform, while the constitutionality of a moderate bill would permit further liberalization in the future."[59] The very real possibility of a referral to the Court inspired the PSOE legislators to refrain from writing the more liberal bill sought by strong supporters of abortion within the party. Barreiro further maintains that the Court's ruling adopted a compromise position that included policy recommendations important to both supporters and opponents of the bill. She explains why the Court was able to achieve this outcome by noting that "[t]his position could easily be taken by an institution that did not need to respond to any particular interests…Non-majoritarian institutions have the freedom to defend shared values which, paradoxically, parties are sometimes unable to maintain."[60] It is clear that the Spanish Constitutional Court's decision, which the government and individual citizens regarded as legitimate, helped to ease the conflict around the abortion issue. Compared with the four-decade-long history of the U.S. Supreme Court's treatment of abortion issues, the Spanish result seems remarkable, particularly from an American perspective. Moreover, although there have been attempts to challenge the original ruling, abortion law in Spain has remained stable.

What accounts for the stability of the Court's abortion decision? While there are many factors to take into account when comparing two very different constitutional courts, certain distinctions do seem to be especially relevant. The first involves the selection process for judges. Of crucial importance: the method of selecting judges to sit on the Spanish Constitutional Court is divorced from both the electoral system and the ordinary partisan politics that defines and shapes the American nomination process. Unlike their American counterparts, justices on the Spanish Constitutional Court are highly respected, seasoned professionals who are not selected on the basis of their partisan affiliations, and who, therefore, are more fully insulated from the dynamics of partisan politics. As a result, when called upon, they were able to render a decision on the volatile abortion question that was moderate in tone, specific in its recommendations, and, as the poll results cited above confirm, in tune with Spanish public opinion. The second noteworthy factor is related to the degree to which the public, government, activists, and political parties regard the rulings of the Court as legitimate and impartial. Despite the fact that some activists outside of government were disappointed with the ruling, the Spanish parliamentary parties regarded the Court's decision as fully legitimate, in part because the decision acknowledged the arguments of both sides and issued recommendations that all parties could accept.

So, when the government returned to the drawing board to recast the abortion reform bill, all parties felt motivated to produce a revised version that would meet the constitutional requirements stipulated by the Court. It appears that the referral process itself facilitated such an outcome because the Court's opinion promoted moderation and consensus. In effect, the Constitutional Court's specific jurisdiction and clearly defined powers appear to allow it to play a constructive role in policy-making, even in such a contentious area as abortion. In this regard, the legitimacy of the Spanish Court is of special importance. Although the Catholic Church was adamantly opposed to abortion reform, because the Court is a competing, secular, authoritative voice, especially on constitutional matters, the Church could not prevent reform of the penal code once the matter had been referred for review. Whereas in the United States the Supreme Court's abortion decisions have often amplified conflict, partisanship, and the hardening of positions, the Spanish Constitutional Court's ruling allowed all parties to reach a compromise. Consequently, the Constitutional Court was in a position not only to facilitate moderate compromises, but also to soften the clash between secular and religious partisans.[61]

The U.S. Supreme Court occupies a similarly authoritative position, but the selection of justices in recent years has been influenced by religious activists, especially opponents of abortion, and as a result, questions of religious faith have surfaced in the confirmation hearings of most nominees, including John Roberts and Samuel Alito, the newest members of the Supreme Court. As many commentators have emphasized, for the first time in history five of the nine justices currently sitting on the U.S. Supreme Court—a majority—are Catholics whose church doctrine is demonstrably opposed to abortion. Much current research demonstrates that "there has been increasing polarization of the electorate along religious lines," especially over the last three election cycles;[62] thus, the question of abortion, so important to religious partisans, has thoroughly politicized the judicial appointment process. Each resignation from the Court prompts intense activity among interest groups, and abortion eclipses all other issues with respect to the nominees' qualifications and the public's understanding of an individual justice's voting records. Indeed, the president's power to nominate justices has become a central issue in presidential elections; a significant number of votes now appear to turn on the expectation that the Republican candidate will appoint pro-life justices and the Democrat, pro-choice ones. Thus, the partisan nature of the appointment and confirmation process means that the Supreme Court is continually at the center of a very divisive debate and, unlike its Spanish counterpart, its decisions exacerbate rather than diminish differences between those who support a woman's right to choose an abortion and those who seek to limit or eliminate access to abortion. Ironically, the question of justices' religious preferences is more pertinent today in the United States than it is in Spain, and the divisions between the two major American political parties increasingly reflect the religious and secular leanings of their supporters. In this respect, the ongoing controversy over abortion being fought out in the judicial arena is a barometer of the deepening disagreements among religiously motivated Republicans and secularist Democrats, and American political parties now appear to be more like European parties that have traditionally split along church-state lines. But whereas in Spain that traditional split has been softened by the creation of a religiously neutral zone of constitutional adjudication, in the United States that zone has been shrinking.

ENDNOTES

1. Nicol C. Rae, "Be Careful What You Wish For: The Rise of Responsible Parties in American National Politics," *Annual Review of Political Science* 10 (2007): 10, 170, http://arjournals.annualreviews.org (accessed 8/6/08).

2. Nicol C. Rae, "Be Careful What You Wish For: The Rise of Responsible Parties in American National Politics," 172.

3. Geoffrey C. Layman, Thomas M. Carsey, and Juliana Menasce Horowitz, "Party Polarization in American Politics: Characteristics, Causes, and Consequences," *Annual Review of Political Science* 9 (2006): 89, http://arjournals.annualreviews.org (accessed 8/6/08).

4. John C. Green has provided persuasive empirical support for this trend in his recent book, *The Faith Factor* (Westport, CT: Praeger Publishers, 2007).

5. Patrick J. Buchanan, Republican National Convention Speech, Houston, Texas, 1992. http://www.buchanan.org/pa-92-0817-rcn.html (accessed 8/6/08).

6. Ibid.

7. Ibid.

8. As Governor of California, Reagan signed into law the Therapeutic Abortion Act, which liberalized abortion, in June of 1967.

9. Geoffrey C. Layman, "'Culture Wars' in the American Party System: Religious and Cultural Change among Partisan Activists Since 1972," *American Politics Research*, 27, no. 1 (1999): 103. http://apr.sagepub.com (accessed 8/6/08).

10. Roe v. Wade, 410 U.S. 113 (1973).

11. The Italian Constitutional Court issued important rulings in 1971 and 1975.

12. The Spanish Constitutional Court ruled on the abortion question in 1985 and 1991.

13. Prior to the March 2008 parliamentary elections, the Spanish Conference of Bishops urged Catholic voters to "defend traditional values and elect leaders 'responsibly.'" [Tracy Wilkinson, "Catholic Church Wades into Political Fray in Spain; Bishops Remind Voters of Their Duty to Uphold Traditional Values in Elections. Socialist Party Officials Protest," *Los Angeles Times*, March 5, 2008. http://articles.latimes.com/2008/mar/05/world/fg-spain5 (accessed 8/6/08)].

14. Griswold v. Connecticut, 381 U.S. 479 (1965); Eisenstadt v. Baird, 405 U.S. 438 (1972).

15. Between 1967 and 1973, one-third of the states, beginning with Colorado, had begun to decriminalize abortion and liberalize the laws. See: J. Lewis and Jon O. Shimabukuro, "Abortion Law Development: A Brief Overview," *Almanac of Policy Issues*. http://www.policyalmanac.org/culture/archive/crs_abortion_overview.shtml (accessed 6/15/07).

16. In her recent book, *Becoming Justice Blackmun* (New York: Times Books, 2005), Linda Greenhouse provides an excellent account of both the process by which Justice Blackmun developed his arguments in *Roe* and his efforts to persuade his fellow justices to join the opinion. What is striking about her discussion is Blackmun's confidence that his constitutional analysis was correct.

17. Two illuminating accounts of the work of pro-life groups in response to Roe are Kristin Luker, *Abortion and the Politics of Motherhood* (1984) and Barbara Hinkson Craig and David M. O'Brien, *Abortion and American Politics* (1993).

18. Laws restricting abortion were passed in many states, including Ohio, Missouri, and Pennsylvania, which in turn provoked challenges from pro-choice litigants. Congress passed several laws restricting abortion, including the Hyde Amendment (1976) and the Partial Birth Abortion Ban Act (Public Law 108-105, 2003) which makes illegal a particular abortion procedure.

19. The one exception is Justice David Souter, a G.H.W. Bush appointee, who, over time, has evolved into a moderate-to-liberal leaning member of the court, and who tends to uphold abortion rights.

20. The Senate vote for Roberts was 78-22 (September 29, 2005). United States Senate, U.S. Senate Roll Call Votes 109th Congress, 1st Session, http://www.senate.gov/legislative/LIS/roll_call_lists/roll_call_vote_cfm.cfm?congress=09&session=1&vote=00245 (accessed 6/15/07).

    The Senate vote for Alito was 58-42 (January 31, 2006). United States Senate, U.S. Senate Roll Call Votes 109th Congress, 2nd Session, http://www.senate.gov/legislative/LIS/roll_call_lists/roll_call_vote_cfm.cfm?congress=109&session=2&vote=00002 (accessed 6/15/07).

21. Justice Samuel Chase was impeached in 1804 but acquitted in his Senate trial in 1805. See Bruce A. Ragsdale, *The Sedition Act Trials*, Federal Judicial Center, http://www.fjc.gov/history/sedition.nsf/autoframe?openForm&header=/history/s (6/11/07).

22. Jeffrey Toobin, "Five to Four," *The New Yorker*, June 23, 2007, 35.

23. *Gonzales v. Carhart*, http://en.wikipedia.org/wiki/Case_citation550_U.S._2007.

24. *Stenberg, Attorney General of Nebraska, et al. v. Carhart*, 530 U.S. 914 (2000).

25. Toobin, "*Five to Four*," 35-36.

26. In addition, Justice Ginsburg has argued for years that the Roe decision would have been more persuasive had it been grounded in a constitutional argument about equality, which finds explicit expression in the Constitution, rather than in the right to privacy, which is derived from other explicit constitutional guarantees. In a 1993 lecture, Justice Ginsburg reiterated her claim: "Doctrinal limbs too swiftly shaped, experience teaches, may prove unstable." See Linda Greenhouse, "Judge Ginsburg Still Voices Strong Doubts on Rationale Behind Roe v. Wade Ruling, " *New York Times*, Nov. 29, 2005. http://www.nytimes.com/2005/11/29/politics/ginsburg.html (accessed 5/19/07).

27. According to the Center for Reproductive Rights: "Forty-four states have adopted laws requiring a young woman to obtain the consent of or notify one or both parents prior to an abortion, but in nine of those states, the laws are enjoined or not enforced. Most of the statutes apply to young women under 18 and provide for a court bypass procedure should a young woman be unable to involve her parents. Most measures include exceptions for medical emergencies." Center for Reproductive Rights. "Restrictions on Young Women's Access to Abortion Services." *Domestic Factsheets.* http://www.reproductiverights.org/pub_fac_restrictions.html (accessed 5/16/07).

28. Gonzales v. Carhart, 550 U.S._(2007).

29. See Richard Davis, *Electing Justice: Fixing the Supreme Court Nomination Process* (New York: Oxford University Press, 2005).

30. Tribunal Constitucional de España.

31. Alec Stone Sweet, "Why Europe Rejected American Judicial Review: And Why It May Not Matter," *Michigan Law Review*, 101, no. 8, (2003): 2745. http://jstor.org (accessed 6/22/07).

32. Sweet, "Why Europe Rejected American Judicial Review: And Why It May Not Matter," 2766.

33. Sweet, 2768.

34. Luis López Guerra, "The Function of Constitutional Courts," (summary of paper presented at Association of American Law Schools Conference on Constitutional Law, Washington, D. C. June 5-8, 2002), Association of American Law Schools, http://www.aals.org/profdev/constitutional/lopezguerra.html (accessed 6/1/07).

35. Sweet, 2768. He argues: "Since World War II, Europe has experienced a rights revolution, a hugely important movement to codify human rights at both the national and supranational levels."

36. Olga Cabrere, "A Guide to the Spanish Legal System." *Law and Technology Resources for Legal Professionals.*http://www.llrx.com/node/1287/print#court (accessed 6/9/07).

37. Belen Barreiro, "Judicial Review and Political Empowerment: Abortion and Spain," *West European Politics.* 21, no. 4 (1998): 147-162. http://find.galegrouop.com.itx. infomark (accessed 5/19/07).

38. Belen Barreiro, "Judicial Review and Political Empowerment: Abortion and Spain." The author argues that the *a priori* review was used in Parliament by forces opposed to the Socialist "absolute majority" on a variety of issues, including abortion, when the party came to power in 1982.

39. Celia Valiente, "Gendering the Abortion Debate in Spain," in *Abortion Politics, Women's Movements and the Democratic State*, ed. Dorothy McBride Stetson (N.Y.: Oxford University Press, 2001), 229.

40. Rishona Fleishman, "The Battle Against Reproductive Rights: The Impact of the Catholic Church on Abortion Law in both International and Domestic Arenas," *Emory International Law Review*, 14 (2000): 293. http://lexis-nexis.com/universe (accessed 5/5/07).

41. Celia Valiente, "Gendering the Abortion Debate in Spain," 232.

42. Belen Barreiro, "Judicial review and political empowerment: Abortion in Spain."

43. Ibid.

44. Ibid.

45. Celia Valiente, "Gendering the Abortion Debate in Spain," 233-234.

46. Constitution of Spain ch. 2, sec. 1, art. XV. Legislationline. http://www.legislation-line.org/legislation.php?tid=160&lid=127 (accessed 6/3/07). This provision of the Constitution was originally included in order to outlaw capital punishment.

47. Barreiro, "Judicial Review and Political Empowerment."

48. Richard Stith, "New Constitutional and Penal Authority in Spanish Abortion Law," *American Journal of Comparative Law*, no. 3 (1987): 517, http://jstor.org (accessed 5/5/07).

49. Barreiro. "Judicial Review and Political Empowerment."

50. Ibid.

51. Edward Schumacher, "Spanish Parties Agree to Vote for Law Permitting Some Abortions, *New York Times*, April 20, 1985. http://query.nytimes.com/gst/fullpage.html?sec=health&res=9B01E6DE1E38F933A15757C0A963948260&scp=1&sq=edward%20schumacher%20spanish%20parties&st=cse.

52. United Nations, Population Policy Data Bank, Population Division of the Department of Economic and Social Affairs of the United Nations Secretariat. http://www.un.org/esa/population/publications/abortion/doc/spain.doc (accessed 5/18/07).

53. Celia Valiente, "Gendering the Abortion Debate in Spain," 238-41.

54. Valiente, "Gendering the Abortion Debate in Spain," 230.

55. Reed Boland, "Selected Legal Developments in Reproductive Health in 1991," *Family Planning Perspectives*, 24, no. 4 (1992): 179, http://www.jstor.org.

56. Reed Boland, "Selected Legal Developments in Reproductive Health in 1991," 180.

57. Joyce Outshoorn, "The Stability of Compromise: Abortion Politics in Western Europe," in *Abortion Politics in Cross-Cultural Perspective*, ed. Marianne Githens and Dorothy McBride Stetson (New York: Routledge, 1996), 154.

58. Ibid.

59. Belen Barreiro, "Judicial Review and Political Empowerment."

60. Ibid.

61. I am indebted to Professor Mark Silk, Director of the Program on Public Values at Trinity College, for this astute insight. I would also like to thank Professor Silk for his thoughtful comments on earlier drafts of this paper.

62. Mark Silk and John C. Green, "The GOP's Religion Problem," *Religion in the News*, 9, no. 3 (Winter 2007), http://caribou.cc.trincoll.edu/depts_csrpl/RINVol9No3/GOP'sReligionProblem.htm (accessed 8/10/08).

15. Human Rights and the Confrontation between Religious and Constitutional Authority: A Case Study of Israel's Supreme Court

Frances Raday

The Confrontation, Seen through the Lens of Constitutionalism

This chapter focuses on the confrontation between religious and constitutional authority, as it affects the rights to freedom of conscience, freedom of religion, and gender and ethnic equality. It will analyze the Supreme Court's reviews of decisions made by religious authorities. As background, I will first discuss the way in which constitutional norms should, as a matter of constitutional principle, deal with clashes between the right to culture or religion, on one hand, and the right to equality and freedom of conscience and religion, on the other.[1] I will then seek to measure the Court's jurisprudence within this conceptual framework. In order to determine which principles should govern the role of constitutional law in regulating the interaction between religious values and equality, I shall examine the theoretical arguments supporting deference to cultural or religious values over universal values. Those arguments, I shall contend, must not prevail. There are various situations in which constitutionalism must cope with claims for deference to religious authority. The boundaries of a religious culture will not necessarily be coextensive with the constitutional realm. Within the constitutional realm, there may be a dominant religious culture and minority subcultures, or there may be a mosaic of subcultures. Furthermore, even in a religiously homogeneous society, the imposition of religious norms may vary at the levels of family, workplace and church/mosque/synagogue. There may be a different appreciation of the applicability of the norms in each of these institutional frameworks.

Jack Levy has taken autonomy claims by minority communities and organized them into a useful typology. Levy describes various claims for external rules limiting the freedom of non-members and for internal rules limiting the freedom of members—rules intended to protect an endangered culture or cultural practice.[2] However, as I shall show, the claim to pluralistic freedom of religion is not self-legitimizing; rather, it is dependent in a constitutional framework upon the very concepts of equality and liberty that religious regimes deny women, homosexuals, and heretics. Hence, were the rules of Levy's typology used to defeat equality claims *they would use the value of liberty to defeat liberty and of equality to defeat equality.* Levy's typology is applicable *mutatis mutandis* to demands by the leaders of majoritarian religions that would make religious values dominant; demands, in other words, which seek to bind individuals to religious norms that violate their human rights under the state constitution. The difference, in cases where the religion is majoritarian, is that the justification of cultural vulnerability does not apply. Hence, any limits that should be imposed on minority community autonomy in order to protect the human rights of those injured by community norms are applicable with increased force to the majoritarian religions. In Israel, Judaism is the majoritarian religion, however it is sometimes argued that in its traditionalist form—ultra-Orthodox Judaism—it is threatened by the secular ethos of the State and hence should be protected against extinction.

Multiple theories of justice have been advanced in support of deference to cultural or religious values. I will examine three: the "multiculturalist" approach, which contends that preserving a community's autonomy is so important that it overrides equality claims; the "consensus" approach, which states that if cultural or religious values have the sanction of political consensus in a democratic system then this is enough to legitimate their hegemony; and the "consent or waiver" approach, which claims that when individuals consent to cultural or religious values, that consent must be respected.

Multiculturalism

Communitarians claim that adherence to the traditions of a particular culture is necessary to give value, coherence, and a sense of meaning to our lives, and this claim is used to justify traditionalist cultural or religious hegemony over universalist principles of equality. Alasdair MacIntyre argues that the ethics of tradition, rooted in a particular social order, are the key to sound reasoning about justice.[3] Communitarianism of this kind is closely allied with anthropological concepts of enculturation and cultural relativism—the idea that moral consciousness is unconsciously acquired in the process of growing up in a specific cultural environment.[4] From this conception of how human morality evolves, some have concluded that there is no objective social justice, and that therefore each cultural system has its own internal validity which should be tolerated.[5] The culture is identified by its existing patterns and standards; recognition of the culture's intrinsic value seems to go together with a desire to preserve these standards.[6] Normative communitarianism is thus oriented toward the preservation of cultural traditions. When the communitarian norms are based on religion, traditionalism often means deference to written sources formulated between the sixth century B.C. (the Old Testament), the first century A.D. (the New Testament), and the seventh century A.D. (the Qur'an).

This communitarian argument, however, is logically flawed. If cultural relativism is taken to its logical conclusion, it undermines not only the value of human rights but also the value of communitarianism itself, since communitarianism is also the product of a particular cultural pattern of thinking.[7] Indeed, taken to extremes, cultural relativism is another name for moral nihilism; if cultural relativism were to be taken as the foundation of a legal system, it would be impossible to justify any moral criticism of the system's norms.[8] At this level, multiculturalism could not advance any attempt to engineer legal policy in a positive legal system. Alternately, we could regard cultural relativism merely as a tool that helps us distinguish ethnocentric from universal standards, so that we would be able to refrain from insisting that ethnocentric values be mandatory on a global scale. This form of multiculturalism would not, I contend, override human rights as they exist today—as universally shared ideals, recognized by most of the nations of the world which have ratified the human rights treaties.[9]

Second, let us look at how the preservation of tradition affects, in particular, the right to equality. If the preservation of tradition is an aspect of communitarianism, as some of its proponents suggest, then the claim that communitarianism overrides universal principles (such as the right to equality) must stand or fall alongside the claim that traditionalism itself overrides universal principles. But there is a whole battery of reasons why traditionalism cannot legitimately be said to override the principle of equality. Traditional patterns cannot form the dominant foundation for contemporary meaningfulness, except in a static society. It may be that the ethical norms of a society are themselves a factor in determining the dynamism of the society, and it is not inconceivable that a society that believes in traditionalism as an ethical imperative might "choose" to be static. However, where and when a society changes as a result of environmental or socio-economic developments not dictated by that society's ethical traditions, a rigid application of traditional norms will produce dissonance.[10] Communitarians do not tell us how we can continue to apply the community's traditional values to a changed society without producing dissonance. A perfect example would be clinging to traditionalist patriarchal norms (such as excluding women from the public sphere) in a world where women, in fact, work outside the home and are often responsible for their own, and their children's, economic survival; in a world, in fact, where they are no longer "protected" and "supported" within the hierarchy of an extended traditional family. As a matter of political ethics, if traditionalism is allowed to trump egalitarianism, it will be an effective way of continuing to silence any voices that were not instrumental in determining the traditions. As Susan Okin shows, the Aristotelian-Christian traditions cited by MacIntyre in defense of communitarian theory are not women's traditions.[11] Women were excluded not only from the active process of formulating those traditions but also from inclusion, as full human subjects, in the very theories of justice developed within those traditions.[12] The same can be said for Judaism and Islam. Women's voices are silenced where traditionalist values are imposed.

Consensus

What, besides communitarianism, could justify the domination of religious/traditionalist patterns of social organization in the legal system? Might a broad social consensus become a legitimizing factor?

Michael Walzer has argued that justice is relative to social meanings; a given society is just, for instance, if its substantive life is lived in accordance with the "shared understandings" of its members.[13] This view legitimizes the adoption of particularist principles of justice over universalist ones. The process of reaching shared understandings is seen as dynamic, based on a dialectic of affirmation by the ruling group and dissention by others. Walzer's theory of justice has been criticized as it applies to situations of "pervasive domination."[14] Okin points out that in societies with a caste or gender hierarchy, it is not just or realistic to seek either shared understandings or a dialectic of dissent.[15] Where there is pervasive inequality, the oppressed are unlikely to acquire either the tools or the opportunity to make themselves heard. Under such circumstances, one cannot assume that the oppressed have a shared understanding of justice. Rather, there might be two irreconcilable accounts of what is just. A "shared understandings" theory only could be applied to this situation if the dissenters were given an equal opportunity to express their worldview and challenge the status quo. The principle and practice of equality are, hence, a prerequisite for the application of the shared understandings theory and the claim for gender equality must be immune to oppression by the dominant shared understanding if the system is to operate in a just fashion.

If the community, per its religious convictions and cultural practices, condones the unequal treatment of groups within it, at what level should "shared understanding" be ascertained? If there are slaves, Dalits (treated as untouchables), women, or homosexuals within the community, and they are excluded or treated unequally, such subgroups cannot be said to agree with the community's shared understanding, even if these groups do not formulate dissent. The silencing of subgroups should preempt—that is, prevent—wholesale deference to the autonomy of a community; such deference cannot coexist with concern for the autonomy of oppressed subgroups.[16] This is true of the subgroup of women in traditionalist cultures and monotheistic religions. Their sharing of the community understanding, where that understanding is based on a patriarchal tradition, cannot be taken for granted, even if they do not express dissent. In the words of Simone de Beauvoir: "Now what peculiarly signifies the situation of women is that she—a free and autonomous being like all other humans—nevertheless finds herself living in a world where men compel her to assume the status of the Other. How can independence be recovered in a state of dependency? What circumstances limit women's liberty and how can they be overcome?"[17] More recently, in the words of Okin: "When the family is founded in law and custom on allegedly natural male dominance and female dependence and subordination, when religions inculcate the same hierarchy and enhance it with the mystical and sacred symbol of a male god, and when the educational system establishes as truth and reason the same intellectual bulwarks of patriarchy, the opportunity for competing visions of sexual difference or the questioning of gender is seriously limited."[18]

Nevertheless, multiculturalist and consensus philosophers present the clash between the religious and liberal agendas on human rights as symmetrical. On this basis, both Charles Taylor and Paul Horowitz critique the impact of the liberal state on religious subgroups.[19] Arguing for a more supportive and accommodating approach toward religious belief and practices, they claim that liberalism is not value-neutral—it is a "fighting creed": "At the very least, liberalism's focus on the autonomous individual and on the maximization of individual concepts of the good tends to give it in practice an emphasis on freedom over tradition, will over obligation, and individual over community."[20] The impression given is of symmetry between religious and liberal values.[21]

There are good grounds for rejecting the symmetry thesis. For instance, there is no symmetry between religious and liberal human rights values. Inverting Taylor's and Horowitz's critique of liberalism, you find the values of tradition over freedom, obligation over will, and community over individual. While liberal values leave space for the religious individual and, to a considerable extent, the religious community, religious values do not recognize the entitlement of the liberal individual or community. There is no symmetry between the normative dominance of liberal values (freedom, will, individual) and the normative dominance of religious values (tradition, obligation, community) because the latter does not even acknowledge the private space of the dissident, the heretic, or the silenced voice within its jurisdiction. These values are primarily tools for the perpetuation of existing power hierarchies. The claim for symmetry is, therefore, based on tolerance of inequality and lack of liberty for those disenfranchised within the religious community. This is a flawed basis for communitarian theory.

Consent

Even if we reject the arguments that multiculturalism and consensus justify the imposition of inegalitarian cultural or religious norms, this does not invalidate direct individual consent to those norms. The autonomy of the individual is the ultimate source of legitimacy. If someone genuinely chooses to accept certain cultural practices or religious norms, his or her choice should be respected. This right to choose is an essential part of the freedom of religion and of the right to individual autonomy.[22] The need to recognize individual autonomy is a practical as well as a theoretical matter because, in situations of genuine consent, there will be no complaint by a sub-group against the religious authorities of the community. Hence, there will usually be no opportunity for the constitutional authority to intervene. However, recognition of individual consent to religious authority and its concomitant disadvantage is problematic. Being subjected to religious authority inherently reduces one's capacity for public dissent. Thus, consent is suspect, and it is incumbent upon the state to increase the possibility of genuine consent, and to verify the existence of genuine consent, by a variety of methods. I shall now mention some of them.

There are situations when inegalitarian norms are so oppressive that they undermine, at the outset, the oppressed group's capacity to genuinely dissent. In such a situation, no consent can be considered genuine. Truly oppressive practices can properly be classified as repugnant, and consent will not validate them.[23] In such extreme cases, mandatory legal techniques should be employed to protect individuals from their sub-equal status.[24] Thus, the invalidation of consent may be applied in cases of extreme oppression—examples of which include slavery, coerced marriage, and mutilation (including female genital mutilation), as well as polygamy, when it is part of a coercive patriarchal family system.[25]

However, absent repugnant practices, consent to inequality is not automatically invalid; but it will still be suspect. In the context of pervasive oppression or discrimination, consent cannot be assumed from silence. And even express consent is not necessarily evidence of genuine consent. Rather, all consent must be suspect, since pervasive oppression seriously diminishes the possibility of dissent and hence the probability of genuine consent. Individuals in a religious/cultural community who consent to the perpetuation of their inequality often have little real choice in the matter. Often, because of their socio-economic status, they have few (if any) alternatives to accepting the group's dictates. When individuals are compelled by socio-economic necessity to accept an inferior status, their consent cannot be freely given. Ascertaining whether such consent is genuine presents a difficult challenge for normative systems. Nevertheless, some measures can negotiate this precarious divide and enhance individual autonomy, thus helping individuals give or withhold genuine consent. For instance, compulsory education laws should require that all children be exposed to information regarding fundamental human rights, including the right to gender equality.[26] Socio-economic alternatives to consent must also be made available.

The state should also scrutinize, *ex posteriori*, individual consent to unequal treatment, and should be able to void it when consent is not genuine. If the inequality is not repugnant, then the state cannot intervene to void consent unless requested to do so. However, since consent to inequality is suspect, the state should be highly responsive to requests to void consent. In legal terms, this would mean that consent to inequality should be considered voidable.[27] Since the possibility of legitimizing inequality rests primarily on consent, the voidability of consent is an effective way of ensuring, *ex post facto*, that members of oppressive religious communities are not being forced to consent to having their human rights violated. Consent to a patriarchal marriage regime, for instance, will usually be made when a woman is young and dependent on her own traditionalist family; such consent should be voidable at any later stage, if and when the woman finds the terms of her traditionalist marriage unacceptable.

The Claim to Equal Religious Personhood within the Church/ Mosque/Synagogue

Recent years have seen increased demand by those who are marginal within religious communities, particularly women and homosexuals, for proper acceptance within their communities. They are claiming equal religious personhood. This claim, too, may be brought on the constitutional level; examples include demands for non-discrimination standards in churches, same-sex marriages and equality, as we shall see in a full discussion below, the constitutional saga of the Women of the Wall. The Women of the Wall stood up for their right to participate in Orthodox ritual in an equal, egalitarian way; the Women sought their right to do so in the public space, and petitioned the Supreme Court to enforce that right.

There can be no denying that traditionalist cultural and religious ways of life have been an important source of social cohesion and individual solace for many people. There is also no doubt that, in the foreseeable future, these traditions are not going to disappear. Hence, on both an ideological and a pragmatic basis, efforts to achieve equality for women and homosexuals should work, as far as possible, both within the constraints of the traditionalist or religious culture as well as outside them.[28] Nussbaum proposes a universally applicable model for dealing with the religious dilemma: "The state and its agents may impose a substantial burden on religion only when it can show a compelling interest. But... protection of the central capabilities of citizens should always be understood to ground a compelling state interest."[29] This required protection of central capabilities extends to those functions particularly crucial to humans as dignified free beings who shape their own lives in co-operation and reciprocity with others. Nussbaum's list of central human functional capabilities includes many of the rights and freedoms denied women by traditionalist cultures and religious norms: e.g., the right to hold property or seek employment on an equal basis; the right to participate effectively in political processes; the right to move freely from place to place; the right to have one's bodily boundaries recognized and respected; the right to be safe from sexual abuse; the right to have, in Nussbaum's formulation, the social bases of self-respect and non-humiliation; and to be treated as a dignified being whose worth is equal to that of others, which, she adds, "entails, at a minimum, protections against discrimination on the basis of race, sex, sexual orientation, religion, caste, ethnicity, or national origin."[30] For legal or constitutional purposes, this all translates fairly easily into the language of human rights protected under the UN treaties; indeed, as a constitutional matter, the way to give substance to the Nussbaum/Sen capabilities approach is to guarantee them through rights, whether political and civil, or economic and social. Nussbaum herself acknowledges the close connection between the two and the importance of rights per se.[31]

I agree with Nussbaum's emphasis on the need for sensitivity to cultural and religious differences, but I would also contend that the role of constitutional law is to express and endorse the bottom line of her argument: "[w]e should refuse to give deference to religion when its practices harm people in the areas covered by the major capabilities."[32] There is a difference in emphasis between this approach and Susan Moller Okin's position that "...no argument [should] be made on the basis of self-respect or freedom that the female members of the culture have a clear interest in its preservation. Indeed they might be better off if the culture into which they were born were either to become extinct (so its members would become integrated into the less sexist surrounding culture) or, preferably, to be encouraged to alter itself so as to reinforce the equality of women."[33] In my view, there is an argument to be made—on the basis of freedom—that some female members of a traditionalist culture may have an interest in that culture's preservation. That is the reason why, as Okin adds, the preferable course is to encourage cultures and religions to reform so that they accord equal rights to women members. It is only when cultures and religions fail to do this—when they do not offer equal personhood for women—that the State can offer a right of exit to those who want it.

As the case of the WOW clearly shows, there is a growing body of feminist thought *within religions* that demands equality through the dismantling and reformation of religious hierarchies. However, there has been little attempt, practical or theoretical, to translate this dissent into constitutional rights. Such claims have been made in regard to traditionalist cultures. In the United States and Canada, for example, tribal women have demanded equal cultural personhood: they wished to retain their tribal membership when marrying persons outside the tribe. A similar claim was made by the Women of the Wall when they demanded the right to pray in the public space—a space customarily reserved for men. In all of these examples, the women's claims were absolutely valid: the women were attempting to improve their terms of membership and bring their communities into line with modern standards of gender equality. However, there is also an apparent anomaly in this claim: it is based on both the right to membership on the one hand, and a rejection of the terms of membership as offered, on the other hand.

When women seek equal personhood within traditionalist cultural or religious communities, theirs is a holistic and far-reaching claim, and the State, in responding to this claim, risks infringing on community autonomy. Women's claim for equality may transform the *modus vivendi* of the group in a way that conflicts with the wishes of the majority of its members, both male and female. Thus, States should be more reluctant to intervene in religious or cultural groups and, for the most part, should not invalidate the community rule per se. Individual women's dissent does not necessarily justify intervention by the State, or prohibition of a traditional community's internal norms and practices.

Nevertheless, there are ways in which the State can and should intervene. If religious discrimination infringes upon a woman's human dignity, or if it involves violence, or results in economic injury—then intervention is justified. Furthermore, even in cases of functional or ceremonial discrimination, there will be situations in which the State should take a constitutional stance—for instance, when the claim for equality is consonant with some authoritative internal interpretation of the group norms or, alternately, when a critical mass of women within the group supports the claim for equality. When these conditions are met, States should act decisively in denying State support, facilities, or subsidies for the group's discriminatory activities.[34]

But this is a difficult issue, as is any issue where we must consider judicial intervention, and the effectiveness of such intervention, in constitutional issues of women's equality and religion. Gender rights will inevitably clash with cultural or religious norms, and although the normative hegemony of gender equality has been established at the international level,[35] thereby establishing State obligations at the constitutional level, this principle is only patchily applied. The application depends on political will. Some constitutional courts have attempted to implement gender equality in the face of religious resistance, but such efforts have usually been ephemeral or feckless when the government has not supported them. It is apparent that the courts cannot be given the sole burden of securing human rights for women. Both international obligation and constitutional theory require the intervention of government.[36]

Israel's Supreme Court—Judicial Review of Decisions by Religious Authorities

In order to understand the Supreme Court's decisions on religious matters, it is essential to understand the political and constitutional context within which its decisions are made. The State of Israel was founded after the Holocaust with the purpose of providing self-determination for the Jewish people—a category that can be defined in religious terms.[37] [38] Israel's Declaration of Independence included a promise to ensure complete social and political equality to all its inhabitants regardless of religion, race, or sex; it inherited the Ottoman Millet system, which granted exclusive jurisdiction over personal law to the religious courts of the three communities—Jewish, Muslim, and Christian. Thus, the regime of State and religion is *promotionalist* and pluralistic. By granting jurisdiction over personal law to the religious courts, the State empowered the courts to handle all issues of license and prohibition in marriage and divorce, as these matters are expressly excluded from the scope of the Women's Equal Rights Law 1951; other matters of family law are subject, under the 1951 Law, to the principle of equality for women, whether they fall under the jurisdiction of the rabbinical court or not. On matters of property, maintenance, inheritance, and custody, the civil courts have jurisdiction, unless one of the parties has already referred those issues to a religious court in the context of divorce proceedings—

in which case they are subject to a well-developed civil regime of family law.

The right to equality does not appear in Israel's Basic Laws on human rights. The reason is opposition from the religious lobby. There have been attempts to legislate a constitutional right to equality, but the religious parties in the Knesset have always demanded that if the right is included, it must not be inapplicable to the laws of personal status, license, and prohibition in marriage and divorce. Thus, we are faced with the choice between a qualified principle of equality, on one hand, and a constitution with no mention of equality at all. And so the two Basic Laws on Human Dignity and Liberty and on Freedom of Occupation, legislated in 1992, do not include equality as an express value.

I will say a little about equality and human dignity. Although it did not include the right to equality per se, The Basic Law: Human Dignity and Liberty, which was enacted in 1992, nevertheless made it possible for the courts to interpret human dignity as encompassing the right to equality. Indeed, I would say that the right to human dignity not only gave an opening for the inclusion of equality, but also *necessitated* its inclusion: at the end of the 20th century, it was quite impossible to conceive of human dignity without personal equality. Indeed, many of the Supreme Court justices believed that the concept of human dignity incorporated the value of equality. Whatever the interpretation given to human dignity, however, the Basic Law: Human Dignity and Liberty, entrenches all legislation that existed before it was passed—including legislation that grants jurisdiction to the religious courts over personal law. Hence, even though equality is included by law under the broader rubric of human dignity, the *promotionist* framework, in which religious autonomy is given to the different communities in Israel, remains in place despite the passing of the Basic Law on Human Dignity and Liberty.

Four groups are affected by this *promotionist* status quo: women, Arabs, the secular, and Jews who are not recognized by the Orthodox authorities. These groups do not immediately strike us as the classic stigmatized groups—i.e., groups that have been discriminated against. These are not groups that international laws seek to protect against discrimination. Normally, when people talk about minorities, they don't think about sub-sects in Judaism and they do not think about the secular. However, Israeli reality, under the Israeli legal system, is such that these two groups have indeed become disadvantaged.

Women

All three monotheisms—Jewish, Muslim, and Christian—function through patriarchal institutions that impose patriarchal norms. According to Israeli law, membership in a community is determined by birth or legal conversion;

therefore, secular women fall within the jurisdiction of the religious court of their community—as do religious women. The result is the imposition of a patriarchal regime on all Israeli women, both religious and secular. This arrangement—which gives religious courts jurisdiction over personal status law—also effectively excludes women from judicial decision making on matters of marriage and divorce, as there are no women rabbis, khadis, or priests in the various religious courts.

Since Israel was created, women have turned to the Supreme Court for redress against this religious patriarchy. Of the petitions brought to the High Court, many were brought against rabbinical court decisions and occasionally sha'ari court decisions on marriage and divorce. Many secular young couples are attempting to escape the religious regime by arranging private marriage ceremonies; many have petitioned the Court to have the State recognize these marriages. These various petitions have had an interesting life in the High Court.

The High Court has consistently rejected petitions against the rabbinical courts, which often refuse to "force" a husband to grant a *get* (Jewish divorce).[39] Without a *get*, a woman cannot remarry, and any children she has from an adulterous union will be *mamzerim* (bastards) who will be permanently prohibited from marrying in a Jewish ceremony. A *get* can only be given by the husband, through free consent, and only the rabbinical court, under Jewish Law, has the authority to either "compel" or "oblige" the husband to consent. If the rabbinical court compels a divorce and the husband continues to refuse to grant a *get*, he may be imprisoned until he relents. The Court has rejected women's petitions to the rabbinical court to use its authority to give either form of relief—a compulsion order or an obligation to divorce.[40] The Court has also refused to invalidate an agreement made by a wife (and authorized by the rabbinical court) to waive her financial rights in return for a *get*.[41]

The High Court has consistently refused to intervene in rabbinical court decisions regarding the *get*. The only shift that can be detected over time is a shift in rhetoric. In the 1950s and 1960s, the High Court's decisions were laced with learned *halachic* (Jewish Law) analysis justifying the rabbis' conclusions.[42] However, in a recent case,[43] the High Court was critical of the Jewish Law's norms, recognizing a woman's plight when her husband refuses to release her from a failed and sometimes violent marriage and the rabbinical courts won't force her husband to grant a divorce. Justice Cheshin remarked that "Under Jewish law even a slave is freed after seven years. It is horrifying that a woman is not." Nevertheless, despite his justified indignation and powerful rhetoric, Justice Cheshin, like the other judges on the case, did not find a way to intervene. Why?

The answer is the rabbinical courts' history of having exclusive jurisdiction in statute law.

In a different case, a petition was aimed against a rabbinical court's refusal to oblige a wife to agree to receive a *get* from her husband. The Court refused to intervene.[44] That decision, however, does not prove that the Court treats men and women equally when it comes to obtaining consent to a *get*. On the contrary, it illustrates that the *halachic* requirement still favors men: in this case, the man had already remarried without his first wife's consent; he had done so with the rabbis' permission; he wasn't charged with criminal bigamy; and the rabbinical court decision, which was upheld by the High Court, was that his inheritance had to be divided between the two wives. This asymmetry has itself been the subject of a petition: a woman asked the Court to cancel a rabbinical license allowing her husband to remarry without her agreeing to give him a divorce. The woman petitioner had claimed discrimination on gender grounds, since women are not entitled to a similar rabbinical license. She also based her claim on religious grounds, since only with Jews, and not non-Jews, is it legally possible for a husband to obtain such a license and, with it, exemption from the offense of bigamy.[45] Justice Agranat justified the unequal treatment of Jewish and non-Jewish men on the grounds that their religions are different. As for the unequal treatment of men and women, he recognized the injustice to women and expressed his regret at the failure to find an equitable solution for women's remarriage. However, acknowledging this asymmetry—this injustice—did not lead him to label this a case of unjustifiable discrimination. He did not regard the injustice as grounds for non-recognition of the license, but merely suggested that rabbinical power should be used sparingly. He went so far as to say that married women are spared a worse fate because their husbands are granted a rabbinical license to remarry. By providing men with an escape route from marriage, this spares women who refuse to agree to a divorce from the prospect of imprisonment for not releasing their husbands from the marriage when men refuse to obey a rabbinical mandate to divorce.

In cases where the rabbinical courts attempted to alleviate the suffering of spouses who were waiting for a delayed *get*, the High Court, acting strangely and self-righteously, intervened to overturn their decisions. Thus, in one case, the Supreme Court refused to sanction the decision of a rabbinical court leveling punitive maintenance payments against a husband who was unreasonably withholding a *get*.[46] In another case, the *Lev Case*,[47] the rabbinical court imposed a restraining order on a wife who refused to give her husband a *get*, preventing her from leaving the country until she released him. Although the order was given under a recently bestowed statutory power, the High Court invalidated it on the grounds that it disproportionately violated the wife's freedom of movement. Based on the facts of this particular case, the High Court's decision seems to favor women; but in fact, on the macro-level, it disadvantages them because of the lack of symmetry between husbands and wives: negation of the rabbinical courts' power to prevent a recalcitrant spouse from leaving the country will, in most cases, result in the disempowerment of women.

Let us look, for the moment, beyond the questions of license and prohibition in marriage and divorce. Applying the residual right to equality in family life under the 1951 Women's Equal Rights Law, the Supreme Court has, in a number of cases, applied the principle of equality. In the early years of the State, immediately following the enactment of the Law, the Court cancelled Jewish Law rules in cases where both parties had not expressly chosen to be governed by those rules. This created inequalities for women in the sphere of married women's property, domicile rights, and guardianship rights.[48] In the 1994 *Bavli Case*,[49] the High Court of Justice ruled that the rabbinical courts must abide by the principle of equality in the division of matrimonial property. Justice Barak held that the *halachic* principle of separation of matrimonial property could not satisfy this requirement, since it resulted in women receiving a negligible share of the property following a divorce. The Court's decision was in alignment with the Women's Equal Rights Law, which excluded from the purview of the equality principle only the matter of license or prohibition in marriage and divorce, and not related matters such as property, maintenance and custody. The decision provoked violent opposition from religious groups and is not applied, in practice, by the rabbinical courts.

Let us look at what happens when Muslims petition against the sha'ari court's decisions. In two cases that did not involve license and prohibition in marriage and divorce, the High Court demonstrated considerable deference to the sha'ari courts. In the 1955 Bria case,[50] a widowed mother of three, who had remarried, fought to keep custody of her children. Her dead husband's sister had applied to the sha'ari court for custody, and the widow petitioned the High Court of Justice to invalidate the application. She made her claim on the basis of Muslim law, under which a mother who remarries ceases to be the natural guardian of her children. But the High Court refused to grant her petition. There was disagreement among the justices as to whether the provisions of the Muslim law discriminated against women. One of the three justices found discrimination. A second remained silent on the issue. And the third saw no discrimination, "since the question was which of two women was to be given guardianship of the child." All three justices agreed that the Muslim law was indeed relevant to the case. Only under one condition—if it was proven that the

Muslim courts had "intentionally ignored" the provisions of the Women's Equal Rights Law in judging the good of the child—would the High Court interfere. The Court dismissed the claim that a skillful *q'adi* (Muslim judge) could find ways to disguise the fact that his decision was based on religious law and not on the Women's Equal Rights Law. In a more recent decision, the High Court of Justice required the sha'ari court to take a psychologist's opinion into account in determining the good of the child.

The patriarchal character of these religious systems is evident not only in the substantive rules, but also in the institutional makeup and procedures of the religious courts. In the religious courts of the three communities, judges are all male. The rules of evidence in rabbinical and sha'ari courts discriminate against women. Some small inroads have been made: In a Supreme Court decision, it was held that women must be allowed to appear as "pleaders"—advocates— before the rabbinical courts. This ruling has been put into effect in the rabbinical courts.[51]

There is also a struggle over the place of women in the public sphere. The impact of religious values on public life was addressed in 1988, in the Shakdiel and Poraz cases.[52] The issue in Shakdiel was the decision—made by the Minister for Religious Affairs and a Ministerial Committee set up under the Jewish Religious Services Law of 1971—to not appoint Leah Shakdiel as an elected member of a local religious services council, a decision made on the grounds that she was a woman. The issue in Poraz was the Tel Aviv Municipal Council's decision not to appoint women to the electoral board for the Tel Aviv municipal rabbi. Opposition to these appointments was based on claims that, under Jewish Law, women may not elect or be elected to public office. The women petitioned for their right to participate, and their petitions were accepted by the Court, which recognized women's right to equality as a "fundamental principle" of the Israeli legal system.

Both appointments were to bodies established by legislation. Those bodies, although dealing with religious affairs, were clearly statutory civil institutions. Undeniably, these cases establish that women are entitled to equal participation in State administrative bodies, even those bodies that deal with religious services. However, one should not automatically assume that the two High Court decisions will affect the constitutional balance between equality and religion. Both decisions affirmed the principle of women's equality (which they deemed a fundamental principle) and struck a blow against male hegemony. In Shakdiel, Justice Elon held that the principle of equality is to be "balanced against other legitimate interests of individuals or the public." Hence, he argued, "had there been a prohibition in the halakha against women serving on religious councils . . .

a compromise would have to be found between the two approaches. Although the municipal council is a civil statutory body and is hence subject to civil law, it deals with halakhic affairs . . . and thus it would be desirable to seek ways to bridge the opposing interests."[53] In Poraz, Justice Barak held that the Court's duty was to balance "the general principle of equality, on one hand, and particularistic interest in the appointment of an electoral board, which should be able to carry out its functions properly, on the other." He held that the balancing process was "horizontal, not vertical . . . we do not have a situation here of a clash, in which one of the principles predominates over the other. Equality is an important principle but it is a relative principle."[54] Justice Barak went on to say that, even in this horizontal balancing process, equality is of paramount importance, and infringement will only be permitted under one condition—that there is no other way to implement the particular purpose behind a specific law. However, he then stated that the principle of equality was determinative in this case only because there was, as a matter of fact, no real religious barrier to the proper functioning of a municipal rabbi if women sat on the electoral board.[55]

In the above decisions, the Court recognized *halakha* as relevant to determining the right of women to participate in public bodies. This clearly indicates a willingness, on the part of the Court, to tolerate the encroachment of inegalitarian *halakhic* values on areas of public life, since the bodies in question were, as the Court itself stressed in both cases, public bodies set up under the civil law. The Supreme Court could have advanced the cause of equality by deciding that, unless the legislature expressly stated otherwise, it did not intend to condone the unequal treatment of women in this sphere, and defended that principle—equality—in the face of *halakha* and opposition from rabbis.

Jews Who Are Not Recognized by the Orthodox Authorities

During the British Mandate, the Orthodox rabbinate was designated as the representative authority for the Jewish community, and this designation was continued by the State of Israel. Despite lobbying by the Conservative and Reform movements, the Orthodox rabbinate has not recognized those movements, nor does it recognize their authority when it comes to conferring personal status through marriage or conversion or the right to an equal share of public resources. The two movements have demanded recognition, however, and these demands have largely been channeled through the courts.

With regard to conferring personal status, the Supreme Court has not allowed the Conservative and Reform movements constitutive powers within Israel. The Court has refused to recognize non-Orthodox rabbis' competency when it comes to performing marriage ceremonies.[56] The Court has refused to recognize conversions performed by non-Orthodox rabbis in Israel. However, the Court has shifted towards recognizing the competence of the Reform and Conservative rabbis who carry out marriages and conversions abroad.[57]

The clash between the Orthodox monopoly over the public space (on one hand) and the right to freedom of worship (on the other) was enacted in the constitutional saga of the Women of the Wall, which was the subject of four decisions by the High Court of Justice (I have acted as counsel in the hearings). WOW prays in a group, wearing prayer shawls and reading aloud from the Torah Scroll—a manner customary for men but not for women. This is a subject of controversy among Orthodox Jewish authorities. When WOW attempted to pray in this manner at the Western Wall Plaza, which is a central symbolic site for religious and historical Jewish identity as well as a national space, there was violent reaction by other Orthodox worshippers and the secular authorities responded by forbidding the WOW from praying at the Wall. (The police and the Administrator of the Wall, who is an ultra-Orthodox rabbi, intervened to prevent the WOW's active prayer at the Wall, claiming this was necessary to prevent a breach of the peace and desecration of the Wall.)

In response, the WOW petitioned the Supreme Court sitting as High Court of Justice. Their petition was based on their constitutional right to freedom of worship, their right of access to the Wall and, less emphatically, their right to equality as women.[58] Although the Supreme Court rejected the WOW's petition, the majority opinions of Justices Meir Shamgar and Shlomo Levin recognized in principle the WOW's right of access and freedom of worship. Justice Shamgar, who was then the President of the Court, held that the most severe *halakhic* ruling should not govern who is allowed to pray at the Wall; rather, all who wish to pray there in good faith should be allowed to. Shamgar recommended that the government find a solution that would "allow the petitioners to enjoy freedom of access to the *Kotel* (Western Wall), while minimizing the offense to the sensitivities of other worshippers." He based his recommendation on the need to respect human dignity, and the need for mutual tolerance between groups and opinions. He did not mention the disempowerment of women, or the need to respect their constitutional right to participate equally in the public arena. He was silent on the issue of equality, even though he noted, ever-so-tentatively, one of the primary manifestations of that inequality: the objection to hearing women's voices:

"The singing of the petitioners aroused fury, even though it was singing in prayer; and anyway is there any prohibition of singing by the *Kotel*? After all, there is dancing and singing there not infrequently and it is unthinkable that the singing in dignified fashion of pilgrims, whether Israeli or foreign, soldiers or citizens, whether male or female, should be prevented. In view of this, it may be, and I emphasize 'may be,' that the opponents are confusing their opposition to the identity of the singers with their opposition to the fact of the singing, and this should not be."

Justice Levin based his decision, in which he recognized the WOW's right to pray in their own manner at the Wall, on his view of the site as both religiously and also nationally and historically significant for all the different groups and individuals who come there in good faith for the purpose of prayer, or for any other legitimate purpose.

Although the struggle for women's equality—and in particular, for the right to participate in the full ceremonial worship of Judaism—is at the core of the conflict, the majority judgments all but ignored the issue. Their recognition of the WOW's right to pray was based on the women's right to freedom of worship—not on equality. The majority, in this case, upheld the need to protect pluralism but did not address the issue of religious patriarchy. It was only in the minority opinion, written by Justice Menahem Elon, who was then the incumbent of the "religious seat" on the Supreme Court, that the issue of equality for women was discussed. However, Elon raised the issue only to conclude that it was impossible to examine it in the context of a site of such central importance to Judaism.

In response to the Supreme Court's recommendation, the government set up a series of committees. Their deliberations failed to provide a solution, however, and so the WOW turned once more to the Supreme Court. In Hoffman II, Justice Eliahu Mazza wrote the Court's opinion and Justices Dorit Beinish and Tova Strasberg-Cohen concurred. The Court held that the majority in Hoffman I had recognized the WOW's right to pray in their manner at the Wall. It thus concluded that the recommendations of the various governmental committees, in seeking alternative sites, had all been in contravention of the directions of the Court. Indeed, the Court held—on the basis of its own impressions from a tour of the sites—that none of the alternative sites could serve, even partially, to implement the WOW's right to pray in the Western Wall Plaza. The Court directed the government to implement the WOW's prayer rights at the Wall within six months.

This courageous and pioneering decision marked a significant step towards the implementation of the WOW's previously abstract right. It clarified that the Hoffman I decision fully recognized the WOW's right to pray, in their own manner, in the Western Wall Plaza. It also transformed the Shamgar recommendation into something more emphatic—a judicial directive; and it concretized the government's obligation to implement the right as something fixed in time and place. However, the Court refrained from actively intervening: it stopped short of establishing the prayer arrangements at the *Kotel*. This somewhat evasive conclusion can probably be attributed to the Court's defensiveness in the face of ongoing allegations—by politicians, religious elements, and some academics—that the Court is too activist, particularly in matters of State and religion.

In Israel, reactions to the Hoffman II decision were aggressive. The religious parties immediately presented a bill to convert the area in front of the Western Wall into a religious shrine exclusively for Orthodox religious practice. The bill would have imposed a penalty of seven years' imprisonment on any person violating the current (Orthodox) custom of prayer at the Wall. The bill was supported by a number of Knesset members from secular parties. Popular reaction to the Hoffman II decision was also hostile. The religious right's response was predictably vicious. However, even academics, intellectuals, and journalists generally committed to a liberal point of view were overtly hostile to the WOW. In newspaper articles and public discussion, they claimed that their actions were a "provocation." This claim is not as surprising as it may seem; it is consonant with the general opinion of Israel's secular majority that the Jewish religion is what the Orthodox establishment says it is. The secular liberal community has no interest in women's struggle to open up Orthodoxy and make it more egalitarian. It sees that struggle as irrelevant to human rights concerns.

The Attorney General asked the President of the Supreme Court to grant a further hearing of the case and to overrule Hoffman II. This was a surprising legal move, since the decision had been unanimous. The Attorney General's action was clearly political, demonstrating the government's reluctance to implement the WOW's human rights in accordance with the Court's directive. The President of the Court, Aharon Barak, granted the request and appointed an expanded panel of nine justices to reconsider the issue.

In Hoffman III, the Court was divided, and gave an ambivalent decision. The majority judgment[59] held that the WOW's right to pray in their own manner at the Western Wall Plaza had been recognized, but it was not absolute. Furthermore, the best way to implement it in a manner that would not offend other worshippers would be to provide the WOW with an alternative place to pray, properly adapted for that purpose, at Robinson's Arch, an archaeological site that lies south of the Western Wall Plaza but out of direct eye contact with it, and has a separate approach and entrance. Robinson's Arch is not an area that has traditionally attracted Jewish worshippers, although it sometimes draws Reform and Conservative Jews who—unlike the WOW—cannot participate in the separate prayer areas for men and women at the Western Wall Plaza. The majority decision provided that, should the government fail to convert Robinson's Arch into a proper prayer area within 12 months, the WOW would have the right to pray in their manner in the Western Wall Plaza. This rather strange, conditional judgment gained majority support in the nine-member Court through tactical alliances. The two religious members of the Court,[60] although opposed to any recognition of the WOW's rights of prayer in the Western Wall Plaza, endorsed the Robinson's Arch option. The other four members of the Court wrote a minority opinion[61] advocating full and immediate implementation of the WOW's right to pray in their way in the Western Wall Plaza forthwith.

The WOW case is heavy with symbolism. The violent opposition to the WOW, condoned by both the public and officialdom, symbolizes the silencing of women through the ages; it speaks to the traditionalism and patriarchalism at the heart of Jewish nationhood. The petitions represented a universalist, pluralist, and feminist ethic, and their fate is of great significance not only for religious women and men but also for the secular world and constitutional values. Had the petitions succeeded, it would have signified the victory of pluralism and tolerance over fundamentalism. Instead, the ambivalent outcome of the case illustrates the Court's weakness—its inability to uphold constitutional human rights in the face of violent religious opposition and in the absence of governmental support.

The Secular

The secular are also disadvantaged by the imposition of religious values on public life. Secular Israelis have brought two types of petitions before the High Court: those which address the place of religion and secularism in public life; and those that challenge the religious monopoly over various aspects of private or family life.

The secular petitioners have had little success when their demand for secularism in public life has clashed with religious sensitivities. Thus, when secular citizens petitioned to open a main thoroughfare through an ultra-Orthodox neighborhood on the Sabbath, the High Court sided with the religious, privileging their sensitivities over the seculars' freedom of movement.[62] The Court rejected a challenge to a law that prohibited the import of non-kosher meat on the grounds that there was no injury to human dignity in such a measure.[63] A challenge was made to a law that allows the deferment of army service for youths studying in institutes of religious study (*yeshivot*). The High Court, while admitting that this exemption violates the principle of equality, nevertheless declined to intervene, on the grounds that the exemption serves a positive social purpose: it encourages ultra-Orthodox youth to enter the labor market.[64]

In cases where religious values have a coercive impact on family life or private life, the Court has been more willing to intervene to protect secular freedoms. Thus, the Court recognized the right of secular families to inscribe the tombstones of deceased family members in languages other than Hebrew—and with the Gregorian date—in graveyards managed by religious burial companies (which had objected to non-Hebrew inscriptions[65]). In a series of decisions regarding secular marriages outside of Israel between Israeli Jews, the Court recognized the validity of the marriages for the purpose of registration.[66] It also held that the marriage could be dissolved by a court and did not require a *get*,[67] and that the mutual obligations of the parties would be determined on the basis of their partnership as a contractual undertaking.[68] The cases did not directly address the issue of secular rights and freedoms. Rather, the Court relied on two other factors—the interest of the family and freedom of expression—as reasons for intervening. To some, these cases represented a revolution in personal law in Israel, creating an alternative civil marriage institution.[69] But this is going too far. At present, the marriages that the Court has recognized are ones that have been performed outside Israel, and the Court has not overturned its prior decisions which invalidated marriage ceremonies conducted privately, in Israel, between Jews who are eligible to marry under Jewish Law.[70] More problematic is that the rabbinical courts will get to determine whether a *get* will be needed to dissolve a civil marriage.

Arabs

For Israeli-Palestinians in Israel, the most central issues of cultural and religious autonomy have to do with language, education, and religion. Arabic is one of the two official languages of Israel; informally, it is the second official language.[71] The significance of this is that in Israel, there is an obligation to publish all official state documents in Arabic as well as Hebrew, and, additionally, individuals have the right of access to state institutions in Arabic. Ilan Saban called this right remarkable and radical, as it a) requires an investment of considerable resources and b) gives considerable symbolic recognition to the Israeli-Palestinian collective culture.[72] However, Saban also points out that a dissonance has developed between, on one hand, the legal and socio-political status of the Arabic language, and, on the other hand, the fact that Hebrew is, in practice, the sole language used in state institutions (aside from those in Arab localities). In a recent decision, the High Court of Justice held that Israel is obligated to respect Arabic as the language of the Israeli-Palestinian minority: "Israel is a Jewish and democratic State and, as such, it is obligated to respect the minority within it: the person, his culture and the person's language."[73] The Court held that all official signs must be in Arabic as well as Hebrew, whether they are in Arab or non-Arab localities.

The education system, public and private, is divided by language: there is Arabic-speaking education and there is Hebrew-speaking education. Public education is State-funded and private education is almost completely subsidized.[74] Israeli-Palestinians may register their children in Hebrew-speaking education, if they choose.[75] Thus, in terms of the right to choose education in the minority's own language, the rights of Israeli-Palestinians are fully protected, but not exclusionary. In terms of the cultural content of education, the State Education Law of 1953 emphasized love of Jewish culture and values and memory of the Holocaust.[76] There is no doubt that the curriculum and the matriculation requirements, which are determined by the Ministry of Education, have emphasized Hebrew education, Jewish history, and literature, and have not been adapted to meet the educational demands of a national collective Arabic culture. However, a February 2000 amendment to the State Education Law, while restating the declared purposes of public education in Israel and its general aims—"to love humankind. . .to instill the values of Israel as a Jewish and democratic State and to respect human rights and freedoms. . .peace and tolerance"[77] —also includes an important new clause: "to know the language, culture, history, heritage and unique tradition of the Arab population and of other population groups in Israel, and to recognize the equal rights of all the citizens of Israel."[78]

Freedom of religion is fully protected for Jews, Muslims, and Christians, and there is, as noted above, *promotionalism* for the three monotheistic religions in a religiously pluralistic way. The pluralism of religious freedom is recognized in the employment regulations: although the national rest day and festivals are Jewish, employers are obliged by law to grant days off to workers on their religion's rest days and festivals. The personal law of Israeli citizens is determined according to the religious community they were born into. This arrangement is the heritage of the Millet system, which was introduced under the Ottoman rule, maintained under the British Mandate, and continued by Israel after it attained independence. Matters of personal status in marriage and divorce are determined in accordance with religious laws by the religious courts of different communities. The Jewish, Muslim, and Druze religious courts are regulated by statute and the judges' salaries are paid by the State. The problem for all communities is less that of freedom *of* religion than freedom *from* religion. There is no alternative to civil marriage and divorce for the secular populations of these communities.

At the normative level, there seems to be little problem regarding the religious freedom granted to Judaism, Islam and Christianity. There is, however, a dissonance between the legal and socio-political status of the rights: the division of budget privileges. In the Adalah II case, Adalah, an NGO that champions Israeli-Palestinian minority rights, claimed that Muslim burial grounds were being financed from the State budget at a lower level than Jewish burial grounds. The High Court accepted the petition and ordered the State to provide equal budgets to the different religious groups in proportion to their population size. Justice Zamir held: "There is a need to determine priorities in the distribution of budgets. However, these priorities must be based on material considerations which conform to the principle of equality and not invalid considerations, such as religion or nationality."[79]

The Israeli Supreme Court has been severely criticized for over-activism. Most recently, in a review of Aharon Barak's book, *The Judge in a Democracy*, Richard Posner attacked the Court's jurisprudential doctrine, which he claimed was undermining democracy by exercising assumed constitutional powers. Whatever the case—and I do not accept this critique—it is belied by the jurisprudence of the Court in the sphere of confrontation between religious and constitutional authority. In this sphere, the Court has shown deference to religious norms and sensitivities.

ENDNOTES

1. For a fuller exploration of certain aspects of the hierarchy of values, see Frances Raday, "Religion, Multiculturalism and Equality-The Israeli Case," *Israel Yearbook on Human Rights* 25 (1995): 193.

2. See Jack T. Levy, "Classifying Cultural Rights," in *Ethnicity and Group Rights*, eds. Ian Shapiro and Will Kymlicka (New York University Press, 1997): 39.

3. Alasdair MacIntyre, *After Virtue: A Study in Moral Theory* (University of Notre Dame Press, 1981).

4. Melville J. Herskovits, *Cultural Anthropology* (Knopf, 1955): 326-29.

5. Clyde Kluckhohn, "Ethical Relativity: Sic et Non," 52 *J. Phil.* 663 (1995); "Morality differs in every society and is a convenient tenet for socially approved habits." Ruth Benedict, "Anthropology and the Abnormal," in *The Philosophy of Society*, eds. Rodger Beehler and Alan Drengson (Methuen, 1978): 279, 286.

6. Alasdair MacIntyre, *Whose Justice? Which Rationality?* (University of Notre Dame Press, 1988).

7. See Alison Dundes Renteln, *International Human Rights—Universalism versus Relativism* (Sage, 1990): 61-78.

8. Kluckhohn, "Ethical Relativity: Sic et Non," 41.

9. Evidence that gender equality is a universally shared ideal is to be found in the fact that 170 states have ratified CEDAW; while it is true that Islamic States and Israel have many reservations on religious grounds—primarily to Article 16, which provides for equality in family law—these reservations are dubious under the principles of international law.

10. In his discussion of the changing meaning of child sacrifices, Peter Winch writes: "... it would be no more open to anyone to propose the rejection of the Second Law of Thermodynamics in physics. My point is not just that no one would listen to such a proposal but that no one would understand what was being proposed. What made child sacrifice what it was, was the role it played in the life of the society in which it was practiced; there is a logical absurdity in supposing that the very same practice could be instituted in our own very different society." (Peter Winch, "Nature and Convention," in Beehler and Drengson, supra note 41: 15-16).

11. See Susan Okin, *Justice, Gender and the Family* (Basic Books, 1989): 41-62.

12. Ibid.

13. Michael Walzer, *Spheres of Justice: A Defense of Pluralism and Equality* (Basic Books: 1983): 312-13.

14. Ibid.

15. Okin, 62-73.

16. In John Cook's words: "[Cultural relativism] amounts to the view that the code of any culture really does create moral obligations for its members, that we really are obligated by the code of our culture - whatever it may be. In other words, Herskovits's interpretation turns relativism into an endorsement of tyranny." John Cook, "Cultural Relativism as an Ethnocentric Notion," in Beehler & Drengson, supra note 41, at 289, 296.

17. Simone de Beauvoir, *The Second Sex*, H M. Parshley trans. and ed. (Knopf, 1989) (1952): 688-89.

18. Okin, *supra* note 12, at 66.

19. Charles Taylor, *Philosophical Arguments* (Harvard Univ. Press: 1995): 249; Paul Horowitz, "The Sources and Limits of Freedom of Religion in a Liberal Democracy: Section 2(a) and Beyond," 54 *U. Toronto Fac. L. Rev.* 1, 14 (1996).

20. Horowitz, supra note, 55; Taylor, supra note, 55.

21. Logically, in the case of an irresolvable clash of values, the outcome of symmetry would be stalemate and not, as suggested by Taylor and Horowitz, justification for accommodation and support for religious values that otherwise clash with human rights.

22. See Nitya Duclos, "Lessons of Difference: Feminist Theory on Cultural Diversity," 38 *Buff. L. Rev.* (1990): 325.

23. See Sebastian Poulter, "Ethnic Minority Customs, English Law and Human Rights," 36 *Int'l & Comp. L.Q.* (1987): 587. Indeed, even those writers who regard autonomous choices to forfeit autonomy as irrevocable impose a strict test of

voluntariness on consent to such severe forms of self-harm. See Joel Feinberg, *Harm to Self: The Moral Limits of the Criminal Law* (Oxford Univ. Press: 1986): 71-87, 118-19.

24. Thus, for instance, in the case of polygamy, wives should be released of all marital obligations but their rights to maintenance, property, and child custody should be protected.

25. But see Martha C. Nussbaum, *Women and Human Development: The Capabilities Approach* (Cambridge Univ. Press: 2000): 229-30. Joel Feinberg, in reviewing the writings of John Stuart Mill on the issue of polygamy, concentrates on the impact of the voluntary decision of the woman to marry on her future autonomy, stating: "...but it would be an autonomously chosen life in any case, and to interfere with its choice would be to infringe the chooser's autonomy at the time he makes the choice." Feinberg, supra note 60, 78.

26. Compare Wisconsin v. Yoder, 406 U.S. 205 (1972) with Re State in Interest of Lack, 283 P. 2d 887 (1955).

27. See F. H. 22/82, *Beit Yules v. Raviv*, 43(l) P.D. 441, 460-64 (in Hebrew). Consent to inequality may be held contrary to public policy.

28. That women rebel against patriarchal standards that disadvantage them in traditionalist societies is an empirical fact. Martha Nussbaum has documented the widespread dissent among women in traditionalist cultures or religious communities in her outstanding work on women and culture. With regard to the view that women's (inferior) status in traditionalist cultures should not be examined on the basis of universalist norms, which undermine cultural diversity, she analyzed "anti-universalist conversations" and, despite answering many of them effectively, concluded: "Each of these objections has some merit. Many universal conceptions of the human being have been insular in an arrogant way and neglectful of differences among cultures and ways of life." For this reason, she attempts to reconcile the clash between liberal values and cultural or religious norms without relying on the priority of the right to equality. Accordingly, she adopts Amartya Sen's "capabilities approach" to provide "political principles that can underlie national constitutions" in a way specific to the requirements of the citizens of each nation. Nussbaum's sensitivity to cultural diversity is extremely important.

29. Ibid., 202.

30. Ibid., 79.

31. Ibid., 96-101.

32. Ibid., 192.

33. Okin, *supra* note 12, at 22-23.

34. Although, once again, states should be circumspect in intervening to invalidate functional or ceremonial discrimination.

35. In international treaties and in decisions of international treaty bodies and tribunals.

36. This conclusion is based on research into comparative constitutional and international legal regulation of the clash between religion and culture and women's right to equality: Raday, "Culture, Religion and Gender," I.Con, *International Journal of Constitutional Law* Vol 1 No 4 (2003): 663.

37. This is not the only available definition: Jewishness may be considered cultural, historic, ethnic or merely circumstantial depending on the perception of the observer.

38. My article in Fordham.

39. Bagats 1371/96 *Rafaeli v. Rafaeli 51(1) P.D. (1996),* 198.

40. *Noni v. Noni 40(3) P.D. (1982),* 744.

41. *Rachel Avraham v. Grand Rabbinical Court 2001(2)P.D. (2000), 1488; Hacri v. Hacri 20(2) P.D. (1966), 685.*

42. Rozenshweig.

43. *Rafaeli.*

44. *Sabag v. Sabag 53(4) P.D. (1997): 49.*

45. Boronovski v. Chief Rabbinate, (1971) 28(1) P.D. 7.

46. The Court preferred to preserve the "real" purpose of maintenance payments rather than countenance extending their function to discourage abuse of the power to withhold a divorce: *Mira Solomon* v. *Moshe Solomon,* 38[4] P.D. 365.

47. Bagatz 3914/92 *Lev v. Rabbinical Court,* 48(2) P.D. (1992), 491.

48. Frances Raday, "Equality of Women under Israeli Law?" 27 *Jerusalem Quarterly* (1983): 81-108.

49. *Bavli v. Rabbinical Court of Appeals,* 48(2) P.D. (1994), 221.

50. *Halima Bria* v. *Qadi of the Shari'a Muslim Court et al.,* [1955] 9 P.D. 1193.

51. *HCJ 6300/93 Center for Training of Rabbinical Pleaders vs. The Minister of Religion PD 48(4) 441*: 449.

52. H.C. 153/87 *Shakdiel* v. *Minister for Religious Affairs et al.,* 42[2] P.D. 221(1988); Bagatz 953/87 *Poraz* v. *Lahat, Mayor of Tel Aviv et al.* 42[2] P.D. 309 (1988).

53. *Shakdiel,* 242-243.

54. *Poraz,* 336.

55. Justice Barak relied on the prior decision of Justice Elon: "Justice Elon showed in the *Shakdiel* decision that there is no *halakhic* prohibition of participation by women in elections of functionaries to public office. It can be assumed that there are certain rabbis who think as he does and hence will be candidates for municipal rabbi." (At 337).

56. בג"ץ 47/82 קרן התנועה ליהדות מתקדמת בישראל נ' שר הדתות, פ"ד מג (2) 661.

57. Bagatz 2579/99, Rodriguez-Toshbeim v. Min of the Interior.

58. They claimed that the Administrator, in acting, had exceeded the limits of his statutory powers, as determined in the Regulations under the Holy Places Law. Upon submitting their petition, the Minister of Religious Affairs promptly amended the Regulations under the Law in order to expressly "prohibit the conducting of any religious ceremony which is not according to the custom of the place and which offends the sensitivities of the worshipping public..."

59. Justice Michael Cheshin, supported by Justice Barak and Justice Or.

60. Justice England and Justice Terkal.

61. Justices Mazza, Beinish, Strasberg-Cohen and Shlomo Levin.

62. Horev (Bar Ilan).

63. Mitterell II.

64. Bagatz 6427/02 *The Movement for Quality Government in Israel v. The Knesset.* (not published).

65. Bagatz 294/91, *Chevra Kadisha* (burial society) *"Community of Jerusalem" v. Kestenbaum*, 46(2) P.D. (1991), 464; Bagatz 6024/97, *Shavit v. Chevra Kadisha of Rishon le Zion*, 53(3) P.D. (1997), 600.

66. Bagats 143/62, *Punk-Schlesinger v. Minister of the interior,* 17 P.D. (1962), 225.

67. Bagats 2232/03, *Plonit v. Rabbinical court of Tel-Aviv- Jaffa* (not published).

68. *Plonit v. Ploni, 58(2) P.D.* (1999), 213.

69. The Marker 29.5.07.

70. Bagats 130/66, *Segev v. Rabbinical Court, 21(2) P.D.* (1966), 505.

71. See David Kretzmer, "The Legal Status of the Arabs in Israel," (1990): 51.

72. See Ilan Saban, "The Collective Rights of the Arab-Palestinian Minority in Israel: Do They or Do They Not Exist and the Extent of the Taboo," *26 Iyunei Mishpat 241* (2002): 244-45 (author's trans.) (on file with author), which argues that international discourse has changed over the past decade and now includes collective rights, like cultural autonomy. Saban also cites, in particular, the General Assembly Declaration on Minorities of 1992. However, he does not claim that a right to autonomous self-government has been developed; rather, he concentrates on minorities' collective rights to language, culture, education, religion, etc.

73. C.A. 12/99, Jamel v. Sabek, 53(2) P.D. 128 (author's trans.) (on file with author).

74. See Saban, "The Collective Rights of the Arab-Palestinian Minority in Israel," 45.

75. See H.C. 4091/96, *Abu Shamis v. City of Tel Aviv* (1997) (not published) (author's trans.) (on file with author).

76. See State Education Law, 1953. For background information on Israel's education laws, see *State of Israel Ministry of Education, Facts and Figures* (July, 2001), available at www.education.gov.il.

77. State Education Law, 1953, as amended on Feb. 2000 (author's trans.) (on file with author).

78. Ibid. art 2(11).

79. See H.C. 1113/99, Adalah Legal Center v. Ministry of Religion, 54(2) P.D. 164 (author's trans.) (on file with author) [hereinafter Adalah II].

16. A Cynical Look at "The Secularism Debate" in Turkey

Mine Eder

Religion and Islam have long been powerful political instruments for most of the center-right parties in Turkey. Parties on the left—and the People's Republican Party, in particular—have used secularism, and strict separation of Islam and the state, as the fundamental platform to get votes. This paper will argue that behind the secularism debate that has continued for two decades in Turkey[1] lies the utter failure of both sides to address and solve the classic issues of political economy: rising unemployment and poverty, declining incomes in the countryside,[2] and the failure of the state to provide basic public services such as education and health care. While issues such as headscarves, the status of religious schools, and alcohol consumption occupy the country's social and political agenda, the most crucial issues have been left out of the public discussion. The fact that issues such as poverty, inequality, and social/economic exclusion require basic structural policy and priority changes can also explain why both sides might prefer quick appeals to their constituencies through debates on secularism. This paper suggests that a host of factors—depoliticization of the economic issues since the 1980s against a backdrop of premature economic liberalization in Turkey; the "obsession with identity politics" rather than economic issues as a global trend, particularly since 9/11; and the absence of a genuinely social democratic platform in the country, despite lip service from both the Islamists and the so-called leftists—can be blamed for the crucial absence of such political economy issues from Turkey's political agenda.

Some have characterized the landslide victory of the Development and Justice Party (AKP) in the November 2002 elections as the rise of "Islamist Calvinists." Others have identified this electoral victory, in which the AKP received 34%

of the popular vote but ended up claiming 66% of the parliamentary seats (initially 363 seats in a 550-seat parliament), as the ultimate response of a long marginalized "small Anatolian capital" finally managing to get its voice heard.[3] Still others underscored the role of the 2000-2001 financial crisis in Turkey— which was the biggest crisis to date, causing approximately 1 million jobs to be lost—and called the electoral victory the "revenge of the dispossessed."[4] Despite these various interpretations of the rise of an explicitly Islamist party (at least in its origins) into power in Turkey, much of the debate has centered on the "political tsunami"[5] that the rise of the AKP created, rather than its economic causes and implications.[6] The following questions were constantly raised in the media: Is the AKP a threat to the secular foundations of the regime? Is the AKP a "takkiye"[7] party claiming to be like "Christian Democrats" or moderate Islamists or "democratic conservatives," while really harboring a radical fundamentalist agenda? Is this all part of a long-term Gramscian strategy to install Islamist values and practices? Is the AKP's goal to "install" a radical Islamist regime? The secular planks of the state bureaucracy, the presidency, the higher courts, the Higher Education Council (YOK), and the People's Republican Party (CHP) all voiced similar questions, fears, and concerns.

This dichotomous image—with the secular republic at the center, represented by the military and the bureaucracy, facing an increasingly hostile Islamist and parochial periphery[8]—was also a metaphor long used in defining the Turkish political landscape.[9] What this widely accepted dichotomous image of Turkish politics misses, however, is the visible continuity in economic policy and practices, particularly since the start of the neo-liberal transformation in the 1980s. This is not to reject the idea that a new, pro-Islamist bourgeoisie is now emerging in Turkey, anxiously converting its newly acquired economic power into political power. Money has indeed been changing hands as a result of the rapid neoliberalization process of the economy. This paper considers the notion that the rise of the AKP can be seen through the lens of the rise of new Anatolian bourgeoisie clashing with and gradually replacing with the "old," republican, staunchly secular bourgeoisie. While this interpretation is certainly plausible, it tends to overlook the continuity of some of the fundamental aspects of Turkey's political economy. These are: the extensive premature neoliberalization of the country's economy; sustained unemployment and poverty; a growing "black" or informal economy and economic uncertainty; and the increasing macroeconomic vulnerability of the economy due to current account deficits and mounting domestic and international debt.

The first part of this chapter evaluates the overall economic performance of the AKP government and argues that economically, the AKP represents a continuation rather than a rupture. In fact, building on the recovery from the

Figure 16-1

Central Government Consolidated Budget Debt Stock (Billion $)

	1999	October 2002 (after crisis)	2004	2005	2006
Domestic debt	42.4	86.2	167.3	182.4	178.9
Foreign debt	34.6	54.8	68.5	63.9	66.6
Total	78	141	235	246.3	245.5
Source: Undersecretariat of Treasury. www.treasury.gov.tr					

2000-2001 financial crisis, the AKP maintained very close ties with the IMF and carefully followed its benchmarks. The aim of this section is not to single out the AKP as solely responsible for the fundamental weakness of Turkey's economy, but rather to underscore that the AKP was really no different from its secular counterparts in its close pursuit of neo-liberal policies, and, likewise, in its failure to address some of the lingering structural economic problems in the country. The second part of this essay analyzes the terms of the secularism debate, reflecting on the complete disconnect between the existing parties, be they secularist or pro-Islamist, with the basic problems embedded in the country's political economy. The third section focuses on the explanations for why the secularism debate has become so prevalent in Turkey's political discourse at the expense of major political economy issues such as poverty, inequality, and unemployment.

Plus Ça Change...?

The May 2007 IMF report on Turkey describes the country's macroeconomic vulnerabilities as follows:[10]

> Turkey is more vulnerable than most emerging markets. Staff analysis suggests three factors, current account deficit, real currency overvaluation and past credit growth can largely explain why financial markets in some countries were more affected than others during May-June [2006] turbulence ... Other less favorable fundamentals, low reserve cover, high public debt, uncertain inflation outlook and high degree of dollarization and political risks also leave Turkey susceptible to abrupt changes in investor sentiment. . .

One of the fundamental criticisms of the AKP government has been that despite Turkey's relative macroeconomic stability,[11] both its foreign and domestic debt have steadily increased (See Figures 16-1 and 16-2).

In the aftermath of the November 2002 elections, the AKP government's commitment to the IMF program[12] reflected two things: the importance the government had placed on the 6.5% surplus for the public sector in its primary budget as a ratio to the gross domestic product,[13] and a contractionary monetary policy to stem inflation and resolve this debt.[14] As was the case with all prior governments, the availability of external borrowing opportunities and the glut of liquidity in the global economy have eliminated any incentives to actually reduce this debt rather than simply resolve it. As a result, the economy's vulnerability to an external shock has also become very visible during the AKP era, particularly when compared to other emerging markets (See Figure 16-3).

While the declining inflation numbers (from 54% in 2001 to 9.6% in 2006) and the steady economic growth in the post-2001 period were presumably the successes of the AKP government, three aspects of this disinflation and growth were highly problematic (See Figure 16-4).

First, despite the decline in inflation, the rates of interest remained very slow to adjust. In fact, the real rate of interest on the government debt instruments remained above 10%—well above the world average—which created very heavy fiscal pressures. The persistence of high interest rates was also responsible for attracting heavy flows of short-term speculative finance capital between 2003 and 2006. This also had a significant influence in the foreign exchange markets, leading to a 40% appreciation in dollar terms.[15] The associated import boom and the rise of internal domestic demand also began to create the current account balance problems—all of which paralleled the series of developments prior to the 2000/2001 financial crisis. Thus, the economic growth was very much triggered by the speculative flows into the markets, which is already highly problematic.

It is also important to note that the overvalued Turkish lira creates the illusion of falling ratio of net public sector debt to GNP. Total public debt as a ratio of GNP has presumably declined from 91% in 2001 to 63.5% in 2005—which is largely due to foreign debt measured in new Turkish liras. When calculated in real terms, public foreign debt has increased by more than 50% (Figure 16-2 at right). Another illusion was the success in exports. The increasing export numbers also conceal the concomitant rise in the import component in Turkish exports as well as the arbitrage benefits of importing with dollars and selling in euros. This rise could not solve either the increasingly import-dependent nature of the industries nor the gradual elimination of industrial input goods-producing state economic enterprises through rigorous privatization. The final illusion is about the flow of foreign direct investment into Turkey, which has visibly increased during the AKP period. The party succeeded in luring the so-called Islamic capital: the investors from the Arab world and the rest of the Middle East. What

Figure 16-2
Comparative Budget Debt Stock During AKP Period, Before the Crisis and After the Crisis

	2004 1999=100	October 2004 Oct. 2002=100	2006 1999=100	October 2006 Oct. 2002=100
Domestic debt	395.0	194.3	421.9	207.3
Foreign debt	192.7	124.8	192.5	121.3
Total debt	302.4	167.3	319.5	173.9
Source: Undersecretariat of Treasury. www.treasury.gov.tr				

Figure 16-3
Comparative Indicators on Turkey's External Debt (2005) (%)

	Emerging Markets	Turkey
External debt/National income	26.3	51.7
External debt/Exports (goods & services)	67.4	178
External debt repayment/exports (g&s)	13.8	34.4
Short term debt/reserves	23.3	69
Debt generating foreign capital flows/GNP	37.5	62.4
Annual rate of debt increase 1989-2006	5.1	9.9
Annual rate of debt increase 1998-2006	3.8	10.1
Source: 2007 Annual Report by Independent Social Scientists. www.bagimsizsosyalbilimciler.org.		

is often overlooked, however, is that the bulk of the FDI is from the privatization receipts plus real estate and land purchases by the foreigners. It is well known that neither of these items is a sustainable source of foreign exchange.

Secondly, and perhaps more important, most of this economic growth during the AKP period was jobless growth.[16] Despite the rise in GDP and exports, the unemployment rate has plateaued at 10%. The most dramatic and perhaps the most visible loss of employment has been in agriculture and the rural sector. Agricultural employment has been reduced by 2.9 million workers since 2001.[17] The percentage of people employed in agriculture in the total employed population in Turkey has declined from 36.1% in 2000, to 27.3% in 2006.[18] This dramatic decline has not been balanced by a rise in non-agricultural work; an expansion of aggregate labor supply by more than 4 million people since 2001 has also added to unemployment pressures.

The precipitous decline in agricultural employment also underscores two fundamental problems that have been unaddressed, and indeed have worsened, during the AKP government. One is the overall decline in agricultural production. The second is the associated rural and urban poverty. The removal of most of the agricultural subsidies as a part of the overall restructuring of agriculture in the aftermath of the 2000-2001 financial crisis accounts for some of the rising rural decline.[19] According to the restructuring plan carried out under the auspices of the World Bank, most of the input and product subsidies were drastically reduced, and the scope and capacities of the state cooperatives, which have long functioned as state guarantees on unsold agricultural goods and staples, have been reduced. The subsidies and state incentives, the World Bank argued, were trade-distorting, creating unfair competition in the global agricultural markets. The reduction in trade barriers in the imports of agricultural goods as a part of the overall agricultural trade liberalization program was also a part of this restructuring. Though long championed by the U.S. and countries with numerous agribusinesses on the World Trade Organization (WTO) platform, Turkey and most of the developing countries have long resisted such pressures. The financial crisis, however, gave the World Bank significant leverage to push for liberalization and opening of the domestic market. As a result, Turkey has become a net importer of agricultural goods (2003-2006) for the first time in its history.[20]

Most important, the direct income subsidy support program (DIS), which was presumably designed to provide financial assistance to farmers in this transition period, ended up being a complete policy failure. Even the World Bank itself acknowledged that providing assistance on the basis of land ownership in a country where land ownership is still rather ambiguous was a serious impediment to the implementation of the program. If anything, DIS contributed to the income gap in agriculture by completely de-linking subsidies from production and linking them to the already unequal income level.[21]

Secondly, despite the AKP's election promises, poverty levels in the country remained persistently high throughout the AKP period as well. At first glance, Turkey, with its relatively low levels of food poverty (approximately 2%) and its arguably strong social networks, might not appear to have a significant poverty problem. This impression, however, is quite misleading when one considers the risk-of-poverty rate, which is defined as 60% of the median of the net income of all households. In 2003, 26% of the population was below this line. More

Figure 16-4
Key Macroeconomic Indicators

	2000	2001	2002	2003	2004	2005	2006
GNP growth rate	6.3	-9.5	7.9	5.9	9.9	7.6	6.0
Inflation CPI	54.9	54.4	44.9	25.3	10.6	8.2	9.6
Real wage growth (%)	2.1	-20.1	1.1	5.1	3.9	-0.1	1.3
Unemployment rate (%)	6.5	8.4	10.3	10.5	10.2	10.2	9.9
Budget balance/GNP (%)	-10.9	-16.2	-14.2	-11.2	-7.1	-2.0	-0.8
Non-interest primary budget balance/GNP (%)	5.7	6.8	4.3	5.2	6.1	7.4	8.6
Foreign trade balance (billion $)	-23.8	-7.1	-11.4	-18.2	-30.6	-39.8	-40.1
Exports (fob billion $)	30.7	34.3	40.1	51.1	66.9	76.7	91.9
Imports (fob billion $)	54.5	41.4	51.5	69.3	97.5	116.5	132.0
Current account balance (billion $)	-9.8	3.4	-1.5	-8.1	-15.6	-22.6	-31.6
Current account balance/ GNP (%)	-4.9	2.3	-0.8	-2.8	-5.3	-6.4	-7.9

Source: TR Central bank www.tcmb.gov.tr and Undersecretariat of Treasury   www.treasury.gov.tr

striking are the high numbers among the working population; "risk of poverty rate" among those who are employed is 23%, which means that approximately one out of four employed persons in the country is among the "working poor." This number is threefold the EU25 average.[22] Declining real wages also contributed to growing poverty (See Figure 16-4). Furthermore, the image of social networks working as buffer zones to alleviate poverty has also increasingly disappeared in recent years, as new urban migrants have been unable to find steady employment and/or bring their families from the countryside.[23] Another major problem is the growing informalization of the economy. The statistics underscore that more than 50% of the country's existing labor force work informally, i.e., without any social protection and/or access to social security. The disparity between the number of self-declared industrial workers in national household surveys and the industry labor statistics also suggests that there is a substantial amount of subcontracting and informalization of industrial work as well. More important, a 2005 joint SISI/World Bank report indicated that more than 30% of the population lacks any access to health care, including access to a green card designed for the poor.[24]

This is not to suggest that many of the reasons behind the persistent poverty levels, such as the financial crisis of 2000-2001,[25] were all the AKP's making. These are fundamental problems in Turkey's political economy that were brewing long before the AKP's rise to power.[26] However, the AKP's utter failure to address the root causes of such economic issues represents a continuity rather than a rupture in Turkish politics. In short, as Yeldan[27] summarizes:

> Contrary to traditional stabilization packages that aimed at increasing the interest rates to constrain the domestic demand, the new orthodoxy aimed at maintaining high interest rates for the purpose of attracting speculative foreign capital from the international financial markets. The end results in the Turkish context were the shrinkage of the public sector in the speculative-led growth environment; deteriorating health and education infrastructure which necessitate increased public funds urgently; and the consequent failure to provide basic social services to the middle classes and the poor.

One could also add that the AKP government has also contributed to the "privatization" of social services by underscoring the need for philanthropic activities, encouraging micro-credits as well as NGO involvement. The debate on welfare state reform law in Turkey (which was vetoed by the president in 2006) also showed that the AKP, in line with neo-liberal expectations, favored a private sector approach, a "work-fare" rather than a full-fledged functioning welfare state when it comes to social issues.[28]

Finally, the AKP has also not addressed the issue of narrowing the socio-economic gender gap in the country. Literacy rates for females are still lower than males'; the same is true for school attendance ratios. More important, only 16% of the nonagricultural workers in the country are women, far below the other developing countries. Among the female adult population (i.e., over 15), only 25% of women are economically active, far below the average of 49%, for instance, in the case of France. Even though the political mobilization of women by the AKP at the grassroots levels has indeed occurred (with the "women party branches" becoming very active on the ground, at the macro level), no significant improvement in the socio-economic status of women has been observed during the AKP period. Women are very active in the informal sectors of the economy such as domestic help, house cleaning, etc. which often go unnoticed. The informal and contingent nature of these economic activities, however, does not reduce the vulnerability of these women.

A Review of the Secularism Debate in Turkey: The Withering of the Political Economy?

Despite the severity of the social and economic problems discussed above, an overview of the political debates during the AKP government's tenure, particularly between the AKP, on the one hand, and, on the other hand, the main opposition party People's Republican Party (CHP), the office of President, Ahmet Necdet Sezer, as well as the military, reveals that such issues emerged very rarely in public discussions. Rather, most of the debates have revolved around recasting, redefining, and "defending" secularism in the country. As is well known, one of the main issues of contention became the headscarf. The headscarf issue has been an ongoing source of tension since long before the AKP government. In fact, Turkish governments have sporadically implemented headscarf bans in public offices since the 1960s. It was the rise of Necmettin Erbakan's party (the Welfare Party) in the aftermath of the December 1995 elections, and the coalition government with the True Path Party, which began to increase the political tensions over secularism and the headscarf. The aftermath of the 1997 postmodern coup, where Erbakan was "asked" to resign from his post, underscored the sensibilities of the Turkish army and its self-acclaimed mission of guarding the secularist foundations of the republic. It was also after the 1997 coup that the headscarf ban came to be implemented more rigidly: women wearing headscarves were banned from state employment, holding elected posts in the parliament, and, most important, attending universities.

One of the severest political crises in the country occurred when one of the female MPs from the eventually closed Virtue Party, Merve Kavakql, attempted to attend the swearing in ceremony at the general assembly on May 2, 1999, with her headscarf. The incident has drawn significant media attention and controversy from all circles. The Islamists framed the entire issue in terms of individual rights and liberties and the political representation of women wearing headscarves. The secularists, then represented by Bulent Ecevit's Democratic Left Party (DSP), the party with the largest number of seats in the parliament in the 1999 national elections, voiced concerns that the presence of headscarfed women in the parliament posed both a symbolic and real threat to the secular foundations of the republic.

Though lifting the headscarf ban was one of the AKP's electoral promises prior to 2002 elections, the AKP actually kept a lower profile when it came to the headscarf issue. Even though the injustice of not having access to higher education on the basis of headscarf was voiced quite frequently, the AKP government was careful not to confront the Higher Education Council (YOK) head on. YOK is an institutional creature of the post-coup, 1982 constitution, designed to coordinate (and/or "control," according to some) universities in Turkey; it is also a staunch defender of secularism and the headscarf ban.

Nevertheless, the AKP's entire time in government was consumed by the secularism debate, culminating with the most recent presidential election crisis, which triggered the dissolution of the parliament and the July 22, 2007 elections. The prospect of having Abdullah Gul, otherwise a soft-spoken, well-regarded Minister of Foreign Affairs, as a president with a wife who wears a headscarf (and who, incidentally, has taken the Turkish state to the European Court of Justice on the headscarf issue and lost), was enough to not only mobilize millions of people to demonstrate and hold protest rallies, it also triggered a so-called e-coup, where the Turkish army put a memorandum on the Internet on April 28, 2007. In the memorandum, the military "urged" the Constitutional Court to suppress Gul's presidential bid by declaring the parliamentary vote unconstitutional on the grounds that an insufficient number of MPs (two-thirds of the parliament, or 367) were present in the general assembly. Though no such majority had been required in the prior presidential elections of Turgut Ozal and Suleyman Demirel, the decision of the main opposition party (CHP) to take the voting to the Constitutional Court was largely interpreted as a foxy political move and a shrewd bit of legal maneuvering. The consequent court decision to declare the vote unconstitutional—which made choosing a president impossible—paved the way for new parliamentary elections.

The controversy over Gul's presidential bid, however, was not the first time that the AKP government had tested the political waters and tried to "normalize" its socially conservative agenda. One such controversy, for instance, occured over the revisions of the penal code in September 2005, when the government pushed to criminalize adultery. (It quickly withdrew its bid upon protests from Turkish women groups and the EU.) Once again, the secularists were alarmed that their lifestyle would be threatened. Significant controversies also emerged over proposals such as lighter sentencing and penalties for men who agree to marry women they have raped, with different penalties for men if the woman raped is a virgin, a married woman, or a widow. These proposals scandalized women groups, who were effective in removing such proposals from the floor.

The AKP's attempt to fulfill another campaign promise—the vow to treat *all* high school graduates, including the high school graduates of imam-Hatip Okullar,[29] equally in university entrance examination—also captured the political agenda. The graduates of these schools began to enter non-religious professions through universities, and became very successful at sought-after schools. In 1999, however, the Higher Education Council changed the university entry rules of such professional schools and made such transitions more difficult. In May 2004, the Ministry of Education tried to overturn this regulation; it drafted a law that would have allowed, among other things, the students from "professional" schools to compete for university entrance with those from other high schools. The law passed from the house on May 23, 2004, amidst severe opposition from the CHP, and it was vetoed by the president. On June 1, the Prime Minister decided to shelve the law until a future date.[30]

Another major controversy and political crisis accompanied the revisions of primary and high school books. The attempt to introduce "Islamic creationism" as a legitimate "alternative" to evolutionism in schoolbooks is an old issue in Turkey. Creationism was introduced into the biology books in 1985: a paragraph offered an alternative to evolutionism. (At the time, the post-coup government thought that fostering religiosity might be an effective way of countering the rise of leftism and eventual Kurdish separatism.) The attempt to assert its beliefs and marginalize Darwinism prompted a significant outcry from academics and the scientific establishment. The mysterious appearance of a lavish "Atlas of Creation" in the high school libraries in November 2006, as a part of a broader campaign to introduce "life by intelligent design,"[31] also showed that the Creationist movement in Turkey was very well-funded.[32] The movement also got an enormous boost from the Minister of Education, Huseyin Celik, who argued the following in a TV interview: "If it's wrong to say Darwin's theory should not be in the books because it is in line with atheist propaganda, we can't disregard intelligent design because it coincides with beliefs of monotheistic religions about creation."[33]

There were also various incidents, particularly at the local level, that alarmed the secularists. The attempt to create special red light districts on the outskirts of urban centers in order to "cleanse" the cities of alcohol and sex; the prayer requirements implemented by some school directors; and the attempt to establish gender-segregated public transport systems were among the many such controversies.

Finally, two major political scandals revealed the darker side of this controversy. One occurred in 2005: the disbarring a prosecutor from Van for attempting to investigate the bomb blasts in the Kurdish town of Semdinli, in Hakkari, one of the poorest cities in Turkey. The prosecutor was about to discover some clandestine links between the Turkish army and the Army's Second in Command, Yasar Buyukanit, when he himself was accused of having clandestine ties to a religious community and was swiftly removed from office. The second incident was the assassination of the head of the Danistay, a high administrative court, in May 2006. Several months prior to the assassination, Danistay had blocked the promotion of a nursery teacher on the claims that she was wearing a headscarf not during the work hours but after work. This patently extreme sentence drew a reaction from the Islamist press, with *Vakit*, one of the most outspoken and radical Islamist newspapers, printing the photographs of the Danistay decision makers. When it turned out that there were actual links between the young Islamist lawyer and some retired army officers, however, the secularists' outrage became muted, as this incident might have been a set-up aimed at discrediting the AKP government. As Tugal[34] points out, "Neither the secularists nor the Islamists could provide conclusive evidence for their claims. But the drama revealed the hitherto covert conflict between the military and the police. The concentration of the hard-line secularists in the Army, and of religious conservatives in the ranks of the police, threatens low-level conspiratorial wars within the security forces as well as against the civilian population." Hrant Dink, famous Armenian journalist, underscored, on January 2007 in Turkey, some of the malicious aspects of the so-called deep state.[35]

The proliferation of issues related to secularism—and the escalation of each and every issue into a small or major political crisis,[36] or even a regime question[37]— demonstrates how the secularism controversy has monopolized the public debate. The escalation of such controversies into a political crisis, and the ease with which both the AKP government and main opposition party CHP were willing to use such disputes to appeal to their own constituencies and transform such disputes into all-out cultural wars,[38] also meant, however, that some of the highly problematic economic policies and strategies of the AKP government, and the fundamental problems embedded in Turkey's political economy, went almost unnoticed. It was as if these economic issues were left to the technocrats and, as such, were behind the realm of the public debate. The economic illusions described above, such as rising GDP, rising exports, and FDI flows, also made it rather difficult to directly criticize AKP's meticulous pursuit of IMF policies.

Why haven't political economy issues been a part of the public debate in Turkey? Why do parties on both ends of the secularism debate essentially continue to tout this issue as a "cultural war" and focus on values, norms, and social controversies rather than discussing the structural economic issues?

Absence of Social Democratic Alternatives and Lack of Economic Voting

One of the main reasons why the political debate in Turkey has centered around secularism rather than political economy issues has been the absence of a social democratic tradition.[39] Some scholars have even claimed that the AKP, thanks largely to the utter failure of other secular parties to address these fundamental economic issues, has actually been able to fill precisely this vast political vacuum.[40] The AKP appeared to be a clean alternative to the 1990s, during which, as Keyder[41] puts it, "[The] Turkish economy lurched throughout the decade from one financial blow-out to another—in 1994, 1999, 2001 via trail of bankruptcies, debt, graft, inflation and fiscal crises that required continuous credit infusions by the IMF." The mainstream parties, whether Kemalist, secularists or center-right, proved incapable of voicing or soothing the grievances of neo-liberalization.

The AKP's appeal as a social democratic alternative can also be attributed to the failure of the CHP to transform itself[42] into a European-style, social democratic party that focuses on economic and political rights. The steady decline of the party's popularity since the 1990s culminated in the 1999 election, when the party received only 9% of the popular vote, below the 10% threshold necessary to gain seats in the parliament—and thus remained out of the parliament. Keyman and Onis,[43] in explaining this decline, point to three main causes: the damage of the 1980 military coup on social democracy, as the society became increasingly de-politicized; the split in the center-left axis between DSP and CHP; and, most important, the failure of the party to address social and economic issues and distribution crises which lead to increased detachment of the party from the society. This failure stemmed from the party's organic link between Turkey's state-centric national development and modernization project. As Keyman and Onis explain:[44]

> The post-1980 period, in fact, gave rise to a serious crisis of state-centrism; the legitimacy once enjoyed has been withdrawn in the society at large, its democracy deficit has steadily increased, the national developmentalism has been seriously challenged and replaced with neoliberal economic rationality. Its secular national identity has been criticized and attacked by the resurgence of Islam. Its homogenous vision of society has been challenged in ethnic terms by the Kurdish question. Its top-down mode of governing has been exposed to calls for democratization from civil society organizations and civil initiatives and its uni-dimensional, security-based foreign policy has become

inadequate for coping effectively with the increasingly complex and multi-dimensional international challenges.

Failing to shed its state-centric image and its reputation as the ultimate defender of the modem Republic, the CHP could only develop an opposition strategy based on real and/or perceived threats to the secular regime. Developing a society-centered alternative economic agenda, with an emphasis on social justice and distribution, proved rather difficult thanks to the state-centrism and top-down modernization paradigm that CHP has long operated in.

Meanwhile, decline of a classical social democratic tradition or its dilution á la "third way," has also been a global trend since the 1980s. Thus, Turkey's political experience parallels that of the rest of the world. It is also important to point out, however, that left and center-left parties, at least in terms of the ideological self-placement of voters, have historically not received more than 30% of votes.[45] Even at its highest—during which the then new, young leader of CHP, Bulent Ecevit, launched the "left-of center" slogan in CHP—left parties received, at most, 35% of the vote. Thus, one can argue that developing a political platform based on secularism, rather than social democracy, and focusing on social justice and equitable growth, was the more politically convenient strategy for CHP.

More important, however, the conspicuous absence of political economy issues from the political debate can also be explained by the relative weakness of economic variables in the party preferences in Turkey. Central to the economic voting argument is uncertainty about the candidates—are they sincere? Will they keep their pledges?—and the parties make past economic performance the best guide for assessing the future political prospects. Carkoglu[46] develops an aggregate vote function that relates variations in electoral support for incumbents in 21 elections during the 1950-1995 period to macroeconomic conditions—namely, the consumer price index; real per capita GNP; and unemployment. He finds[47] that "rising unemployment and inflation rates lead to declining electoral support for incumbents whereas higher per capita GNP growth rates lead to higher levels of support." Baslevent, Kirmanoglu, and Senatalar[48] also point out that in the 2002 national elections, voters clearly punished the incumbent parties for the financial crisis.[49] Time after time, in every national survey, voters systematically point out that economic problems such as unemployment are more salient than the headscarf issue.[50]

However, non-economic factors—namely, cultural and ideological factors—appear to play a more important role than socio-economic ones. Kalaycioglu[51] posits a model of party preference to explain voting behavior in Turkey. Using economic self-satisfaction as a criterion, he finds that voting behavior is motivated more by cultural and ideological factors. Esmer,[52] in his own analysis of voting behavior, also concludes that the most important determinant of party choice is left-right ideology, and that indicators of economic well-being are not good predictors. Carkoglu and Eder[53] also find that ethnicity and religiosity are far better predictors of party preference than economic indicators of vulnerability and informality.

In short, opinion data on the Turkish public suggest that even though voters think that pocketbook issues are the most important issues in Turkey, they do not necessarily vote based on economic performance. These findings explain why the parties would want to use the secularism issue and play up the "cultural wars" in order to get more votes. From a perspective of pure political rationality, there is hardly anything surprising about why the parties would want to differentiate themselves based on where they stand on the secularism issue.

9/11 Factors: Changing International Context and Defining Turkey as a "Moderate Islamic Model"

The changing international environment, particularly in the aftermath of 9/11, was a crucial reason why the secularism debate became so salient in Turkey's political landscape. Huntington's now notorious "clash of civilization" thesis, which underscored a cultural war on the international arena, made the rise of a pro-Islamist party in Turkey all the more interesting. The growing association of Islam (or some elements of Islam) with terrorism, and the Bush administration's tendency to read international politics through such cultural lines, in effect following Huntington's thesis, began to transform Turkey's image almost overnight. Turkey was now becoming a model for the rest of the Islamic world, particularly the Middle East; it was becoming proof that Islam and democracy are compatible. Turkey was the country with the moderate, good face of Islam.[54]

This largely essentialist reading of Turkey conveniently played into the AKP's hands. The AKP used the language of "civilizational reconciliation" and presented itself to the world as the bastion of democracy in Turkey with an Islamist face. One can even argue that the decision to start membership negotiations with Turkey in December 2002 can be partly attributed to the EU's eagerness to shed its growing image as an exclusively Christian club. The growing obsession with identity politics, plus concerns over Muslim migrants, contributed to the urgency of keeping Turkey "included."

Meanwhile, as Tugal[55] perceptively points out, the AKP became a symbol of thoroughgoing Americanization in Turkey. The AKP not only supported Washington and the neo-liberal economic model, it also adopted the U.S. religious model, presenting itself as a new conservative democratic party.

Indeed, in foreign policy issues—and notwithstanding its failure to pass the parliamentary resolution to allow the American troops to pass through Turkey in the Iraq war—the AKP has supported the U.S. line assiduously. The most recent example was the decision to send troops to Lebanon despite significant public resistance. The AKP also appears to be willing to play a leading role in the U.S.'s, Greater Middle East Initiative, which the AKP has marketed as a way for Turkey to play a more leading role in the Middle East.

However: perhaps one of the main side-effects of the AKP's image of moderate Islamism in Turkey—and of the CHP's staunchly orthodox opposition—has been that discussions of democracy are intertwined with the issue of secularism. Democracy debates in the country became increasingly defined through religious freedoms (or lack thereof); through the overblown role of the military presence in Turkish politics; and through secularists' undemocratic responses, as was the case in the April 2007 e-coup. Clearly, these are very important debates, and they cannot be ignored. What this narrow definition of democracy misses, however, is the utter absence of a "public sphere"[56] that can subject the governments to democratic control. Despite the burgeoning civil society, which has more and more civil society groups voicing their concerns, there is very little scrutiny of public affairs by the citizens.

Nowhere is this absence of accountability more evident than in the realm of economic policies. It's as if economic issues and concerns have withered away from the political realm. The language of the globalization, "necessities of the market place," and the constraints of the IMF have all been assumed away. The neo-liberal project of strictly separating economic matters from politics has now been completed. As Turkey approaches it next election on July 22, 2007, the economic promises, programs, and manifestos of all the parties, left or right, Islamist or secular, all look very much alike. Even if they did not, there is very little public pressure on the elected officials to give an account of what they do or why they adopt the economic policies that they adopt.

The intense political debate on secularism—some of the rhetoric based on perceived rather than real threats—and the associated hijacking of democracy debates in the country, have left little room indeed for a discussion of political economy issues. Issues such as persistent unemployment, rising rural poverty, declining agriculture with no corresponding industrial growth, the declining infrastructure in education and health—all fundamental threats to a functioning democracy—remain virtually out of political deliberation. With its highly centralized, non-accountable economic decision making, its lack of internal party democracy, the absolute control of the party leadership, and its ultimate "my way or the highway" governing style, the AKP is really no different from any of the secular, center-left, or center-right parties, and Tayyip Erdogan is no different from other secular, center-left, or center-right leaders. As such, despite its rhetoric of EU membership, its initial attempt to recognize the Kurdish problem followed by immediate retreat, and its emphasis on religious freedoms, the AKP has not really addressed the fundamental pillars of Turkey's democratic deficit.

Can the political economy issues ever be brought back in? Can the secularism debate ever stop overshadowing some of the fundamental economic debates that are urgently needed in the country? Given the ideological and cultural polarization in the country, the absence of a genuine social democratic tradition, the relative absence of economic voting and the international lure of the so-called Turkish model of "moderate Islam," which has gradually narrowed the democracy debates in the country to different shades of secularism, such prospects are highly unlikely, casting serious doubts on the likelihood of a genuine deliberative democracy in the country.

ENDNOTES

1. Turkey's secularism debate has recently blown into a full-fledged war with the rise of the pro-Islamist Justice and Development Party, AKP.

2. I.e., the near collapse of agriculture.

3. www.esiweb.com.

4. M. Munir, "Turkey - Revenge of the dispossessed - The Islamist AKP rode to victory in Turkey's elections on a wave of popular discontent. The newcomers to power," *Euromoney* (November 2002), pp. 70-77.

5. (as some scholars called it).

6. Soli Özel, "After the Tsunami," *Journal of Democracy*, Vol. 14 Issue 2 (April 2003), p. 80, 15p; for earlier discussions see Ziya Öniş, "The Political Economy of Islamic Resurgence in Turkey: The Rise of the Welfare Party in Perspective," *Third World Quarterly*, Vol. 18, No. 4 (Sep. 1997), pp. 743-766.; Haldun Gulalp, "Globalization and Political Islam: The Social Bases of Turkey's Welfare Party," *International Journal of Middle East Studies*, Vol. 33, No. 3 (Aug. 2001), pp. 433-448.

7. *Takkiye*: a well-known Islamic practice of dissimulation.

8. ...mainly composed of the peasantry, small farmers, and artisans.

9. Şerif Mardin, "Center-Periphery Relations: A Key to Turkish Politics?," *Daedalus*, Vol. 102, No. 1, Post-Traditional Societies (Winter 1973), pp. 169-190.

10. IMF (2007), "Turkey: Fifth Review and Inflation Consultation Under the Stand-By Arrangement, Request for Waiver of Nonobservance and Applicability of Performance Criteria, Modification of Performance Criteria, and Rephasing of Purchases—Staff Report; Staff Supplement; Press Release on the Executive Board Discussion; and Statement by the Executive Director for Turkey" *IMF Country Report*

No. 07/161, accessible through: http://www.imf.org/external/pubs/ft/scr/2007/cr07161.pdf

11. (which, in all fairness, can be considered a significant success in and of itself following the aftermath of the 2000-2001 financial crisis).

12. ...as outlined in the 19" Stand-by agreement of January 8, 2002.

13. i.e., balance on non-interest expenditures and aggregate public revenues.

14. Marcie J. Patton, "The Economic Policies of Turkey's AKP Government: Rabbits from a Hat?" *Middle East Journal*, Vol. 60, Issue 3, (Summer 2006), pp. 513-536.

15. E. Yeldan, (2007), "Patterns of Adjustment under the Age of Finance:The Case of Turkey as a Peripheral Agent of New-Imperialism", p:1-24, accessible through: http://www.bagimsizsosyalbilimciler.org/Yazilar_Uye/YeldanDec06.pdf

16. Ibid. 14.

17. Ibid. 16.

18. www.treasury.gov.tr.

19. Agricultural liberalization was not detailed in the IMF programs but was linked to World Bank funding and reform agenda. The two were, of course, linked as the reducing subsidies were a part of fiscal discipline (a part of stabilization) as well as long-term structural adjustment, i.e., liberalization and commercialization of agriculture.

20. This transition has been far from smooth. For instance, tensions between the IMF's requirement of fiscal discipline and the government's inability to provide high base price behind the political roil between the government and the hazelnut producers in 2006. In July 2006, AKP faced its first mass protest with 80,000 hazelnut producers in the Black Sea Region blocking the Samsun highway to protest the government cuts in agricultural subsidies.

21. Ironically, since income subsidy was based on hectares of land, the more land one has, the larger the subsidy a farmer could get. It is also interesting to note that despite its own problems with CAP (Common Agricultural Policy) and EU's own failure to eliminate product subsidies, EU, by and large, has been very supportive of the World Bank induced agricultural restructuring in Turkey (See EU's Progress reports on Turkey).

22. http://tuik.gov.tr/Start.do (TUIK 2005); F. Adaman and C. Keyder, "Poverty and Social Exclusion In the Slum Areas of Large Cities in Turkey," accessible through http://ec.europa.eu/employment_social/spsi/docs/social_inclusion/2006/study_turkey_en.pdf (2006)

23. Ayse Bugra and Çaglar Keyder, New Poverty and the Changing Welfare Regime of Turkey, Report prepared for the United Nations Development Programme = Yeni yoksulluk ve Türkiye'nin degisen refah rejimi (Ankara: UNDP, 2003); Ç. Keyder, "Globalization and Social Exclusion in İstanbul," *International Journal of Urban and Regional Research*, Vol. 29 (2005).

24. SIS/World Bank (2005). *Turkey: Joint poverty assessment report*, SIS and Human Development Sector Unit: Europe and Central Asia Region of the World Bank; Ayse Bugra, "Poverty and Citizenship: An Overview of the Social-Policy Environment in Republican Turkey," *International Journal of Middle East Studies*, Vol. 39, No. 1 (Feb. 2007), pp. 33-52.

25. (which led to an unprecedented rise in urban unemployment and insufficient job growth (despite steady economic growth), which is a global trend in the world economy. The restructuring of agriculture in Turkey since the 1990s created significant rural impoverishment, as well as the utter failure/insufficiency of the welfare state to provide basic services such as decent health care and education).

26. Mine Eder, "Implementing the Economic Criteria of EU Membership: How Difficult is it for Turkey?" *Turkish Studies*, Vol. 4 Issue 1, (Spring 2003) pp. 219-244.; F. Adaman, "Country Study: Turkey," *Report on Social Inclusion in the 10 New Member States*, http://europa.eu.int/comm/employment_social/emplweb/publications/index_en.cfm (2003); Ayşe Buğra and Calgar Keyder, "The Turkish Welfare Regime in Transformation," *Journal of European Social Policy*, Vol. 16 Issue 3, (Aug. 2006), pp. 211-228.

27. Yeldan, 2007: 14.

28. Keyder and Bugra, 2006; Ayse Bugra, "Poverty and Citizenship: An Overview of the Social-Policy Environment in Republican Turkey," *International Journal of Middle East Studies* 39(1): 33-52 (2007) Historical Period: 1923-80s; A. Buğra and S. Adar, "Social Policy Change in Countries without Mature Welfare States: The Case of Turkey," *New Perspectives on Turkey*, n. 38 (2008).

29. Originally, these schools were set up to train Muslim functionaries, but over time their graduates vastly out numbered the need for imams.

30. William Hale, "Christian Democracy and the AKP: Parallels and Contrasts," *Turkish Studies* 6(2): 293-310 (2005) Historical Period: 1948-2002.

31. (which has direct ties and parallels with the creationist movement in the U.S.).

32. The book went so far as to link Darwinian evolution to the roots of terrorism.

33. *Reuters*, November 22, 2006.

34. Cihan Tual, "NATO's Islamists: Hegemony and Americanization in Turkey," *New Left Review*, Issue 44, (Mar./Apr. 2007) pp. 5-34.

35. This term, widely used in Turkey, refers to some of the highly nationalist clandestine elements within the state known for their self-appointed mission of "defending" unity of the republic.

36. (as was the case in presidential elections).

37. …which happened throughout the AKP government's tenure.

38. See Toprak in this volume.

39. …which, given the speed of globalization and increasing social vulnerabilities in the economy, is rather paradoxical.

40. Fuat E. Keyman and Ziya Önis, "Globalization and Social Democracy in the European Periphery: Paradoxes of the Turkish Experience," *Globalizations*, Vol. 4 Issue 2, (June 2007), pp. 211-228.

41. Çaglar Keyder, "The Turkish Bell Jar," *New Left Review*, Issue 28, (Jul./Aug. 2004), pp. 65-84.

42. (particularly since the start of Turkey's neo-liberal experience in the 1980s).

43. Keyman and Onis, 2007: 215.

44. Keyman and Onis, 2007: 15.

45. Ersin Kalaycioglu, "The Eclipse of the Left and the Rise of the Right," Conference Papers - Midwestern Political Science Association, 2006 Annual Meeting, pp. 1-23, 10 charts, 2 graphs.

46. Ali Çarkoglu, "Macro Economic Determinants of Electoral Support for Incumbents in Turkey, 1950-1995," *New Perspectives on Turkey* (17): 75-96 (1997) Historical Period: 1950-95.

47. Carkoglu, 1997: 90.

48. Cem Başlevent, Hasan Kirmanoğlu and Burhan Şenatalar, "Empirical Investigation of Party Preferences and Economic Voting in Turkey," *European Journal of Political Research*, Vol. 44 Issue 4, (June 2005), pp. 547-562.

49. It is also important to note that Baslevent et al. (2005) also underscore that while Turkish voters punish incumbents with poor economic performance, they do not necessarily reward them during times of good economic performance.

50. A. Çarkoğlu and B. Toprak, *Türkiye'de Din, Toplum ve Siyaset (Religion, society and politics in Turkey)*, (Istanbul: Turkish Economic and Social Studies Foundation (TESEV): (2000)); A. Çarkoğlu and B. Toprak, *Değişen Türkiye'de Din, Toplum ve Siyaset* (Istanbul: TESEV Yayiniari: (2006)).

51. E. Kalaycıoğlu, "The shaping of party preferences in Turkey: Coping with the post-Cold War era," *New Perspectives on Turkey* 20: 47–76 (1999).

52. Sabri Sayari and Yilmaz Esmer, ed. L. Rienner, *Politics, Parties, and Elections in Turkey*, 237p. Historical Period: 1946-2000 (AN: H001660566.01).

53. Çarkoğlu and Eder "Informality and economic vulnerability in Turkey" (article under revision) (2006).

54. Tugal, 2007; Meliha Benli Altunisik, "The Turkish Model and Democratization in the Middle East," *Arab Studies Quarterly*, Vol. 27 Issue 1/2, (Winter/Spring 2005), pp. 45-63; Metin Heper and Sule Toktas, "Islam, Modernity, and Democracy in Contemporary Turkey: The Case of Recep Tayyip Erdogan," *Muslim World*, Vol. 93 Issue 2, (Apr. 2003) p. 157.

55, Tugal, 2007.

56. (to use a Habermasian term).

CONTRIBUTORS

Kada Akacem
Professor of Economics at the University of Algiers; President of the Scientific Council of the Faculty of Economic Sciences.

Asher Arian
Distinguished Professor of Comparative Politics, City University of New York Graduate School; Scientific Director of the Guttman Center of Applied Social Research, Israel Democracy Institute, Jerusalem.

Boutheina Cheriet
Professor in Comparative Education and Research Methodology, University of Algiers; Former Deputy Minister in Charge of the Family & Women's Affairs, Democratic and Popular Republic of Algeria.

Mine Eder
Professor, Department of Political Science and International Relations at Bogazici University, Istanbul, Turkey.

Giulio Ercolessi
Prominent journalist and commentator and co-founder of the website italialaica.it; former Secretary-General of the Italian Radical Party.

Camille Froidevaux-Metterie
Maître de conférences en science politique (Associate Professor of Political Science) at Universite Paris II Pantheon-Assas.

Adrienne Fulco
Associate Professor and Director of the Public Policy and Law Program at Trinity College, Hartford, Connecticut.

Ariela Keysar
Associate Research Professor in Public Policy and Law and the Associate Director of the Institute for the Study of Secularism in Society and Culture at Trinity College.

Barry A. Kosmin
Research Professor in Public Policy and Law and founding Director of the Institute for the Study of Secularism in Society and Culture at Trinity College.

Hassan Krayem
Policy Specialist and Governance Programme Manager, UNDP, Lebanon; Lecturer in the Political Studies and Public Administration Department, American University of Beirut.

Lina Molokotos-Liederman
Research Affiliate, Project 'Education and Religion in Europe,' Groupe de Sociologie des Religions et de la Laïcité (GSRL/CNRS), Paris, France; Laboratoire de Recherche Sociale et Politique Appliquée (RESOP), University of Geneva, Switzerland.

Frances Raday
Professor of Law: Elias Lieberman Chair in Labor Law, Hebrew University of Jerusalem; Director of the Concord Research Institute for Integration of International Law in Israel, at Colman College of Management and Academic Studies; Chair of the Israeli Association of Feminist and Gender Studies.

Sofía Rodríguez López
Research Fellow, History, Geography and Art History Department, Universidad de Almería, Spain; specialist in 20th Century Women's Movements in Spain.

Silvia Sansonetti
Researcher at the University of Rome 'La Sapienza'; Scientific Director of the 'Observatory on Secularization' project sponsored by the Critica Liberale Foundation and CGIL.

Manar Shorbagy
Senior Consultant, The Arab Center for Development and Future Studies; teacher in the Political Science Department, The American University in Cairo.

Binnaz Toprak
Professor and Chair of the Department of Political Science and International Relations, Bogazici University, Istanbul, Turkey.

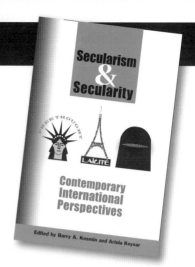